G000147327

Managing Integration

The European Union's Responsibilities Towards Immigrants

Editors: Rita Süssmuth & Werner Weidenfeld

MIGRATION POLICY INSTITUTE

BertelsmannStiftung

Library of Congress Cataloging-in-Publication Data

Managing integration : the European Union's responsibilities towards immigrants / Rita Süssmuth and Werner Weidenfeld, editors.
  p. cm.
"Bertelsmann Stiftung"
Includes bibliographical references.
ISBN 0-9742819-2-1
  1. European Union countries—Emigration and immigration—Government policy. 2. European Union countries—Emigration and immigration—Government policy—Case studies. 3. Immigrants—Government policy—European Union countries. 4. Immigrants—Government policy—European Union countries—Case studies. I. Süssmuth, Rita. II. Weidenfeld, Werner. III. Bertelsmann Stiftung (Gütersloh, Germany) IV. Migration Policy Institute.
  JV7590.M33 2005
  323.3'2912'094--dc22
                              2005052210

© 2005 Bertelsmann Stiftung

The Bertelsmann Foundation gratefully acknowledges the contributions of the Migration Policy Institute in having undertaken responsibility for editing and distributing this edition of "Managing Integration: The European Union's Responsibilities Towards Immigrants" in the United States of America and other countries.

Design: Patricia Hord.Graphik Design, phgd.com

TABLE OF CONTENTS

THE EUROPEAN UNION'S ROLE IN IMMIGRATION AND INTEGRATION POLICY

António Vitorino

Migration in general is quite an old and worldwide phenomenon. In the last decade, immigration has become a very relevant phenomenon in all European societies. The consequences that follow on an economic, political, social, and demographic level cannot be overlooked. As set out in 2000 in the Lisbon Strategy: "The Union has set a new strategic goal for the next decade: to become the most competitive and dynamic knowledge-based economy in the world capable of sustainable economic growth with more and better jobs and greater social cohesion, . . . a Union where the economic and social aspects of the ageing of population become more evident . . . and where the labour market for immigrants and refugees represents a crucial component of the integration process. People are Europe's main asset and should be the focal point of the Union's policies." Moreover, because it concerns the core values of freedom, security, and justice, the European Commission, as guardian of the treaties, could not abstain from closely following that evolution, while at the same time beginning to take some important steps toward setting a framework for regula-

tion and cooperation among the Member States.

The European Union presents itself to the world as a place of opportunities. In order to be consistent with this image and with the principles for which it stands, the European Union cannot close its doors to all those who want to share in this community and who aspire to a different but better life. As stated in the Presidency Conclusions of the Tampere European Council-a landmark that sets out the main Justice and Home Affairs (JHA) guidelines for the five-year period now ending: "The European Union has already put in place for its citizens the major ingredients of a shared area of prosperity and peace. This freedom should not, however, be regarded as the exclusive preserve of the Union's own citizens. Its very existence acts as a draw to many others worldwide who cannot enjoy the freedom Union citizens take for granted. It would be in contradiction with Europe's traditions to deny such freedom to those whose circumstances lead them justifiably to seek access to our territory. This in turn requires the Union to develop common policies on asylum and immigration, while taking into account the need for a consistent control of external borders to stop illegal immigration and combat those who organise it and commit related international crimes."

It seems clear that the flow of international migration by itself justifies the need for a well-defined policy in this area. An open-door policy would be completely unrealistic and ominous for both the Member States and the countries of origin of the immigrant communities. Since all EU Member States are affected by this increasing flow, the need to develop a common immigration policy at the EU level is wisely put forward as a JHA priority. At the same time, it is imperative to keep in mind that this aspect of policy is intimately connected to other policy areas-such as asylum policy, the fight against organized crime, illegal immigration, external border controls, or cooperation with third countries-in what can be referred to as an interdependent process.

The European Commission has adopted a three-track approach in this area by promoting the admission of immigrant communities needed by the European Union, by observing its humanitarian obligations as a subscriber to international conventions, and by combating illegal immigration of those who do not fall under the two previous categories. This policy is considered to be not only a consequence of but also a realistic approach to the end of border controls between most of the Member States and to the existence of a common external border.

There are several circles of influential actors (the European Union, govern-

ments, nongovernmental organizations, social partners, and civil society) operating at different levels (local, regional, federal, national) to set up an adequate policy-not to mention the role played by intertwined policies that any coherent and efficient immigration policy would call for. Another important aspect of interaction lies in the concepts of micromanagement and subsidiarity, both particularly important from an integration policy perspective. Although the European Union can set out clear-cut guidelines in the area of integration, it cannot properly meet all the different demands that real integration imposes. The so-called urban factor will have a major role too.

Integration policy should be a crucial part of any immigration policy strategy. Since any proper assessment of immigration should not only focus on the costs to the host societies but also take into account the great advantages that come as a consequence of immigration, it would be unreasonable and even intolerable to deny certain rights to immigrant communities or to neglect to set up a proper frame of obligations similar to the one already existent for EU citizens. The concept of civic citizenship here implied is vital to build up a feeling of belonging, to strengthen the involvement of the immigrant communities in the daily life of civil society, and to legitimize the whole process of integration.

This concept should embrace a strong practical facet, since the European Union cannot claim to be a political bulwark of shared democratic values and nondiscrimination if it leaves the status of thousands of residents in the

European territory unregulated. The European Union is a community of citizens. Accordingly, the Charter of Fundamental Rights has become a reference document for the extension of civic citizenship to third country residents. Its importance is also underlined by the 2004 approval of a directive on the status of third country nationals' long-term residency in the European Union, with respect to employment, education, social protection, freedom of association and movement, and other areas. In this regard, it is of paramount importance to see that the EU Constitution receives quick approval.

Despite the lack of an official (common) definition of integration, consensus should be based on a balance between the rights entrusted to immigrants (Article 63 of the Treaty establishing the European Community)- which ensures their economic, sociocultural, and political participation in civil society-and the identity of the society that welcomes them, as well as a respect for the host society's values and basic rules. Therefore, it seems quite obvious that this effort of integration implies the need for strong mutual respect.

The novelty and shock arising from the coexistence of different cultures in one society-which lies at the root of misunderstandings and discriminatory behaviors-must be overcome. Some areas require more careful scrutiny and follow-up, such as the labor market, education and language training, housing, social and health services, cultural environment, and citizenship and nationality. Recalling the subsidiarity principle and the urban factor, this task is the responsibility of each Member State working at different administrative layers and in close connection with immigrants' countries of origin. Being closer to the problems at hand, national authorities are far better prepared to analyze and identify target areas of integration and to pursue more concrete action.

As far as the legal framework is concerned, four areas have been set as priorities: family reunification, long-term resident status, admission for employment, and admission and status of students and people coming to the European Union for other nonremunerated purposes. There have been important developments with regard to the first two areas in the last year, and a few words should be addressed to these developments.

Since family reunification has been one of the main sources of immigration to the European Union, the Council of Ministers' directive on family reunification is seen as a major step towards the creation and strengthening of sociocultural stability, allowing for better and easier integration of third country nationals in the Member State, while at the same time promoting economic and social cohesion. The directive was enacted in September 2003 and emphasizes the objectives defined at the 1999 EU summit in Tampere and reaffirmed by the Laeken European Council in 2001. The right to family reunification is subject to laws relating to public order and public security. Member States may choose to impose other conditions within the limits set by the aforementioned directive.

The directive on the status of third country nationals who are long-term residents, enacted in November 2003, aims at trimming the legislation and differing national practices relating to the legal requirements and rights entrusted to third country nationals who are long-term legal residents. It also aims to implement the conditions enumerated under point 4 of Article 63 of the Treaty establishing the European Community. The directive in question is conceived as a true instrument of integration in the host society, since the persons it covers will be able to enjoy full protection against expulsion and treatment similar to the protections provided to EU citizens in the economic and social domain. It sets up a frame-work of conditions for the concession and removal of long-term resident status and related rights. The subsidiarity principle calls for EU action in this area, but it only sets up a minimum common standard. All further action is left to the discretion of the Member States.

So far, performance on the tasks assigned to the European Commission and in particular to JHA in these past five years is positive, but there is a clear need to carry on with the work with similar willingness and dedication. The ultimate goal is to create and maintain an open and secure European Union.

THE INTEGRATION CHALLENGE: LIVING TOGETHER IN A EUROPE OF DIVERSITY

RITA SÜSSMUTH AND WERNER WEIDENFELD

Migration is a worldwide phenomenon. Europe has received a significant share of this migration. Currently, nearly all countries in Europe act simultaneously as sending, receiving, and transit countries of migration. Estimates by the Organisation for Economic Co-operation and Development (OECD) for the end of the twentieth century place the documented migrant population in the European Economic Area (EEA)—excluding naturalized or undocumented migrants, or those awaiting asylum procedure—at more than 20 million foreigners or 5.3% of the population. Other estimates, for example by the International Organization for Migration (IOM), state that migrant stocks are even higher, at around 56 million foreigners or 7.7% of the entire European continent's population. These migration movements have a variety of causes and factors. On the supply side of migration, issues such as poverty, social inequality, political instability, broad access to information, and geographical mobility have increased migration pressure. On the demand side of migration, economic and demographic developments have channeled migration flows to some countries, increasing migration pressure.[1]

There is a growing understanding in the international community that no country can manage migration through unilateral policies alone. But for the last decades, political decision makers on all levels demonstrated only limited readiness to view immigration as a part of the social and economic reality. This tendency has been accompanied by disagreement on the necessity of immigration, how to structure immigration flows, and the extent societal integration should be facilitated.

If one compares the immigration policies of European countries during the last three decades with those of countries such as Canada, Australia, and the United States, it becomes apparent that European migration policies have been characterized by reactive, shortsighted measures with an emphasis on control. Migration policy in Europe has only recently begun changing from being primarily defensive to more proactive and focusing on a more comprehensive and coherent approach.

One of the enlarged European Union's biggest tests in the years to come will be how it manages immigration and integration. If European Member States rise to this challenge, they will be able to harness the benefits that immigration can trigger. If they fail to do so, immigration could harm Member States' long-term economic and social prospects or create social division.

Europe can neither construct impermeable borders that prevent immigration nor can it integrate all immigrants wishing to come to Europe. A central issue in the enlarged European Union is how to successfully organize plural, open societies with growing multicultural and multinational elements. Europe no longer faces the question of whether to do this, but rather the question of how this can best be done. At the Tampere Summit, Member States made progress on this issue.

THE COMMON EUROPEAN ASSESSMENT

Six key developments will force the European Union to take up greater responsibilities in the area of immigration and integration in the future:

1. Immigration is a growing and permanent part of Europe's future.
2. All Member States of the European Union are affected by the flow of international migration.
3. During the 1990s migration became the largest component of population change in most Member States. Migratory pressure is likely to remain high in the foreseeable future, given the rapid expansion of young adult populations in many

developing countries, economic and social differences, and political instability.
4. As ten new Member States joined the European Union in 2004, some migratory flows that were viewed as immigration prior to EU expansion will now be understood as internal mobility in the expanded European Union.
5. Beyond the need for internal reforms, demographic developments in all European countries necessitate the implementation of new measures to attract highly skilled immigrants as well as qualified labor migrants in select branches of the economy where temporary labor shortages emerge.
6. The freedom of movement and the removal of many internal borders in the European Union make immigration a key common issue; flawed integration policies in one country have a pronounced effect on the European Union as a whole.

European integration policy has changed in most EU Member States. The main difference has been the introduction of language courses and courses that familiarize migrants with the host country's constitution and culture. Since the terror attacks on 11 September 2001, not only has security been tightened, but debates on the peaceful coexistence of people from different cultures have intensified. These debates have focused on migrants from Islamic countries and have encompassed such issues as the relationship of the state and religion, the freedom to wear a headscarf or other religious symbols in public schools, and religion in school curricula.

These developments have led to growing recognition that Europe not only needs immigration but that it must also manage migration by acting collectively at the European level.

We now face the challenge of moving from good ideas and intentions to implementing policies that shape European politics. The task of the European Union and its Member States is to formulate a comprehensive migration and integration policy and to establish sustainable cooperation in the controversial area of integration. It is important not to deny or ignore people's fears relating to migration. These fears are often based on real problems and conflicts that have resulted from shortsighted migration management and misguided policies. A central part of migration policy in the expanded European Union will be to create a comprehensive framework for migration and integration in the European Union. Even though each Member State has a unique approach to managing migration and fostering integration according to its history, culture, and economic development, Europe must develop a common, coherent framework for immigration and integration policy with clear guiding principles and objectives.

Europe needs a common integration policy that can enjoy the support of its people and the support of a parliamentary majority; that addresses current integration deficits; that is attractive to high-skilled migrants; that creates synergy by networking the effects of scattered or uncoordinated integration efforts in the Member States; and that ensures transparency and builds trust between native and immigrant societies in Europe.

DEFINING INTEGRATION

In order to create effective integration policies in Europe, two issues must be clarified among its Member States: Which persons or groups should be the focus of integration policies? In what ways and to what degree should integration be pursued (language skills, economic integration, social integration, cultural integration, political participation, etc.)?

These two questions must be answered together, forming a comprehensive context for integration. The answers to these questions will also depend on the length of an immigrant's stay in Europe. A general principle that should always apply is that all immigrants must be integrated, regardless of the motivation for immigration or duration of stay. However, the integration of long-term or permanent immigrants should be more comprehensive than that of temporary immigrants. For temporary immigrants, policies should focus on labor market integration as well as language skills; in the case of long-term immigrants, policies should focus on societal, cultural, and political integration, language skills, and integration into the labor market.

Social integration can have various aims. On the one hand, it can strive to create a *melting pot* model of social cohabitation, whereby cultural traditions of immigrants fuse with those of the host country. On the other hand, it can strive to create a *salad bowl* model of social cohabitation, whereby different cultures and traditions peacefully coexist, without dissipating or fusing together. Individual Member States as well as the European Union as a whole are based on pluralistic social structures that respect cultural diversity. This contradicts social models that promote complete homogenization or assimilation of immigrants. Pluralistic societies have the duty to grant immigrants the freedom of self-organization and to remain open to cultural diversity.

Integration must, therefore, not be characterized by forced assimilation, but must offer both sides—immigrants and the population of the host country alike—the opportunity to be receptive to each other. This is not at odds with the expectation that immigrants respect and abide by the basic values of the host country. Integration is the process of becoming an accepted part of a foreign society and of accepting that society, based on the principles of equality, human rights, diversity, and inclusion. The most important factor of integration is acceptance, and this means maintaining a positive perception and appreciation of diversity. Integration is a long-term process with short-term targets. It is a two-way process based on rights and obligations of both the immigrant and the host society.

Integration is a key issue in molding communities according to the values and norms of European democracy. Integration does not mean that migrants culturally assimilate into the dominant culture of a host society, shedding their identity; rather, integration consists of recognizing and respecting a host country's constitution and laws. Integration means more than having shelter and protection in a host country. Issues such as legal certainty (visa status), compliance with national laws, peaceful coexistence, and access to education, employment, social security, and civil rights are central aspects of integration. Having the ability to communicate and access to employment are necessities not only for immigrants but also for citizens of a host society. Integration is a complex process that is by no means free of conflict and that requires great effort from both immigrants and citizens of the host society. Without acceptance, tolerance, and a positive climate for integration, the complex process of integration cannot be effective.

The successful integration of immigrants ensures, on the one hand, that immigrants are able to participate in the economic, social, cultural, religious, political, and civic life of their host society, and, on the other hand, that immigrants respect the fundamental norms and values of the host society and actively take part in the integration process.

Integration requires a multidimensional definition, which must also be based on a balanced policy mix of horizontal and vertical integration. Horizontally, comprehensive integration policies should incorporate economic, social, cultural, religious, political, and civic integration. Vertically, policies should include not only local and regional measures, which directly manage integration, but also broader instruments at the national level and the European level. Integration policies should focus on helping immigrants strengthen their ties to destination countries, rather than on temporary or rotational immigration.

Building a European Framework

European migration and integration policies need to be secured in a long-term, coherent framework, and at the same time they should be responsive and tailored to the diverse needs of Member States. The success of such policies will depend on deepening partnerships between a wide range of political and civic actors, as well as on a proper allocation of resources. In addition to governmental actors at the local, national, and European levels, numerous nongovernmental actors, such as churches, trade unions, political parties, migrant organizations, and the media, strongly influence the integration process. Thus, forward-looking integration policies need to involve not only governments and state authorities at all levels (federal, state, local), but also civil society; above all, however, these policies must involve immigrants.

A coherent top-down and bottom-up integration policy must take into account the different perspectives of immigrants—understanding immigrants as individuals and as institutional partners representing their communities—and the society of the host country. It must clearly define the rights and obligations of both groups. A European framework that considers the multidimensional nature of integration policy will complement national regulations without rendering them invalid; clearly lay down the basic rules for peaceful coexistence between different cultures, both inside and outside the borders of the European Union; and provide means to compare, measure, and evaluate integration policies. Such a framework could be a central element of the ambitious integration policies called for in Tampere.

A European framework should address the following elements:

Family

The legal, economic, and social protection of family members of legal residents is explicitly stated for the first time in Article 33 of the Charter of Fundamental Rights of the European Union. The family also has a central role to play in the integration of immigrants as it represents a fixed point of reference for them in the host country. The question of family reunification, therefore, not only relates to steering migration, but is also closely linked to integration policy. Today, people entering the European Union within the framework of family reunification already represent a considerable percentage of total immigration. It is therefore necessary to differentiate between the importance of family reunification for integration policy purposes and reunification as a means of immigration. In order that family reunification does not dominate other channels of immigration, only the core family (parents and their children) of immigrants legally residing in an EU Member State should have the right of reunification. As far as children are concerned, younger children generally have better chances of successful integration. The maximum age of family reunification should be uniform throughout the European Union.

Family members should also be granted broad access to the host society following family reunification. Besides access to education and training opportunities, family members must also be allowed the right to pursue employment or self-employment. Immigrant families should not be subject to any discrimination with respect to the purchase of residential property.

EDUCATION AND THE LABOR MARKET

Immigrants need to become familiar with the social order of the host country in order to live and work independently. Integration courses are an appropriate and reasonable instrument for doing this. These courses should equip immigrants with basic language skills and with knowledge of the constitutional and legal system of the host country. Integration courses should be obligatory. Refusal to attend should have consequences, while participation should be positively reinforced. A challenge for the host country is to make integration courses and systems of schooling and training accessible to immigrants, while keeping standards in these institutions high.

Integration into the labor market is of equal importance. It is therefore essential that immigrants receive a work permit soon after entering the country. To offer incentives in this field, firms that provide legal foreign workers with training aimed at labor market integration, for instance, should be eligible for special assistance. Advisory and assistance programs for foreign workers who wish to set up a business on their own must also be expanded. At the same time, it is necessary to strike a balance between employment initiatives for the labor force as a whole and programs aimed at the rapid integration of legal foreign workers into the labor market. EU citi-

zens should have guaranteed preference for job openings for six weeks before nonresidents can be considered. Job openings would be published on the EURES network, the European electronic employment services system.

It is also necessary to foster the mobility not just of EU citizens, but also of immigrants. Permanent residents within the European Union should likewise be granted freedom of movement for purposes of work. International students who graduate from a university in the European Union should be granted a work permit on completion of their courses. Improving the acceptance of foreign degrees is also necessary in order to make European universities and the European labor market more attractive to international students.

SOCIAL SECURITY

One sensitive issue is that of integrating immigrants into the social security systems of host countries. In principle, there are two possibilities: delayed integration and immediate integration. Linking insurance and social benefits to the national citizenship of an EU country would mean a restriction on the individual rights of immigrants. Article 12 of the Treaty establishing the European Community, prohibiting discrimination, must be incorporated into EU regulations concerning the integration of immigrants into social security systems of host countries. Most immigrants pay taxes and social security contributions in their host countries and are able to claim benefits in return. Therefore, the aim of EU policies in this area should be to integrate immigrants into the social security systems of host countries immediately. For immigrants, this means that besides benefiting from the associated rights, they also assume obligations in the host country. Equal access to social security systems is important for integration and identity formation.

CITIZENSHIP AND POLITICAL PARTICIPATION

Permanent residents residing in any EU Member State must be granted a right to naturalization after a minimum stay. This period of time must be harmonized in all EU Member States. Dual citizenship should be possible. A special residence status, civic citizenship, for third country nationals with long-term residency, supplemented by a separate residence status for family members joining them under family reunification, should be created. The period of time after which this status would be granted should be uniform throughout the European Union. The concept of civic citizenship as outlined in the Presidency Conclusions of the Tampere and Thessaloniki European Councils must become an irreplaceable instrument for integration in this context. It offers an attractive package of rights to persons who reside in a Member State for a period of five years or longer. Civic citizenship does not offer a separate set of rights for third country nationals, but rather a common baseline of rights and obligations shared by all residents in the European Union irrespective of their nationality.

Integration also means political participation, which in turn constitutes a significant element of identification with the host country. Granting immigrants the right to political participation at the local level means that they can become involved in political processes in their immediate environment by voting and by assuming office. Therefore, after a specified waiting period, which should be the same in all Member States, third country nationals should be granted both the right to vote and to serve in elected office at the local level. This should constitute a central element within the concept of civic citizenship and is based on the EU Charter of Fundamental Rights. The concept of civic citizenship can thus become an important and powerful tool for integration, as it clearly defines rights and duties of both immigrants and the host society and is an alternative solution to integration without necessitating naturalization. This concept must be further developed to more precisely state the rights and duties of immigrants and host countries.

RELIGION AND CULTURE

The European Union respects the diversity of culture, religion, and language. The Member States must therefore enforce these freedoms. Strengthening these rights means empowering immigrants and, likewise, minorities. For example, introducing the teaching of Islam as part of religious curricula or teaching antiracism in schools, as called for in the EU directive, would reinforce these freedoms. Additionally, greater support should be given to intercultural institutions that allow immigrants and the native population to interact. While promoting tolerance and understanding from an early age cannot completely prevent conflicts of culture and values in society, it can help to deal with these conflicts constructively and peacefully.

TRANSPARENCY AND EFFECTIVENESS: THE OPEN METHOD OF COORDINATION (OMC)

Besides the aforementioned core elements, concrete goals and policy objectives are required at the EU level, which can be translated into national, regional, and local policies. One of the best instruments to this end-the OMC-was introduced by the European Commission. The OMC's strength is that it initiates a cross-national learning process, based on common indicators, benchmarking, and monitoring. Its advantage lies in the free exchange of policy ideas and best practices on integration measures by the Member States. Consistent data on commonly agreed indicators that measure integration would enhance this exchange. In principle these indicators can be divided into three categories: legal and political, economic and social, and cultural.

The OMC is an important means for the European Union to create competitive integration policies. Competition, when used as a tool, can promote national and regional integration policies in an objective and transparent way. Through competition, Member States are able to objectively compare their policies. Moreover, competitive integration will trigger a healthy sense of innovation and motivation between Member States, encouraging them to raise their standards of integration at a national level. The European Union needs a competitive integration policy if it is to attract economically prosperous immigrants.

TOWARDS A HOLISTIC EUROPEAN INTEGRATION POLICY

Integration is a long-term process. Although it is unclear how current policies will affect long-term integration, integration through competitive policies between Member States will help determine best practice. Integration, therefore, means taking seriously social concerns in the development of pluralistic societies. Consequently, Europeans must openly debate foreseeable developments and long-term perspectives of immigration and integration. A public dialogue on integration can thus be seen as promoting cultural progress, forming the foundation for peaceful coexistence in a diverse Europe. Furthermore, the current blockades in some Member States that are not able to come to policy-oriented conclusions with regard to immigration and integration demonstrate that the era of national thinking and practice has reached an end. Immigration and integration need to be seen and defined as a common European task. Therefore, the European Union needs a holistic approach to integration, based on social, economic, and cultural aspects, as well as on citizenship and political rights, embedded in long-term strategies, yet with enough flexibility for regional and local authorities to develop tailor-made programs for immigrants. Such an approach will empower immigrants and host societies alike to tackle the challenges of living together in a diverse Europe.

ENDNOTES

1   Rinus Penninx, *Integration Policies for Europe's Immigrants: Performance, Conditions, and Challenges*, Independent Council of Experts on Migration and Integration Expert Paper (2004), 5.

PART I

THE CONCEPTUAL AND POLITICAL APPROACH TOWARDS INTEGRATION: FROM AN INTERNATIONAL TO A EUROPEAN CODE OF CONDUCT

The Challenge of Integration: A Global Perspective

Bimal Ghosh

The term "integration" is widely, but somewhat vaguely, used in the context of migration management. Race riots, anti-immigrant violence, and continuing tension between immigrants and the host society are often seen as a failure of the country's integration strategy. In Europe, as elsewhere, limits to the host society's capacity to integrate foreigners are also frequently used as an important justification for restricting immigration.

In broad terms, integration refers to arrangements that enable immigrants (and their children and grandchildren, or second- and third-generation migrants) to actively participate in a host society through equality of opportunity and absence of discrimination on grounds of ethnicity or national origin. There is, however, no standard definition or universal strategy of integration. This is for the simple reason that countries adopt integration strategies in keeping with the societal models they set for themselves in relation to foreigners.

The integration strategies that accompany these societal models can be divided into three broad categories:[1] multiculturalism, assimilation, and segregation. Countries wedded to the model of multiculturalism (e.g., Australia, Canada, and the United States) seek to base their national identity on, and

derive their strength and dynamism from, different cultures of immigrant groups that are formally recognized and permanently accommodated. The strategy of assimilation (as traditionally followed in France, for example), on the other hand, is based on the republican model of society under which foreigners adhere to the customs, characteristics, and cultural mores of the host country under a common constitution and political rules. In a general way, these differences can be discerned in the attitudes of Europe and the United States towards integration. Most European nations seek to maintain their deep-seated culture, whereas the United States constantly transforms itself by willingly embracing new cultures while maintaining certain common ideals or values.

As opposed to multiculturalism and assimilation, a third approach is attuned to the societal model of ethnic and cultural homogeneity of the host nation. The strategy that these countries (e.g., Japan, the Gulf States, and various Central and Eastern European countries under the communist regime) seek to follow is one of segregation—or least possible integration—of foreigners.

Each of the three broad approaches mentioned earlier can of course have a litany of variations. The strategy of assimilation, for example, could be pushed further towards acculturation, under which foreigners take on the customs, values, and attitudes of the host society and identify themselves with it. Here, the emphasis is on a one-way process of cultural adjustment, with the burden of adjustment falling on the immigrants. Likewise, the multicultural model can take different forms, depending on the degrees of cultural diversity the host society is prepared to accept and the methods it uses for the purpose. Does the host society perceive itself as a salad bowl or as a veritable melting pot? Is it wedded to shallow multiculturalism, limited to its mere tolerance of different cultures and attitudes? Or is it deep enough to actively encourage and assist the immigrant groups to preserve their traits and mores, leading to cultural enrichment of the host society as a whole?

A country's integration strategy, like its societal model, closely interacts with its immigration and citizenship policies. For example, a country wedded to multiculturalism is normally more open (albeit within the limits of existing social tolerance) to immigrants and their subsequent inclusion as citizens. A country that relies on assimilation perceives citizenship as the ultimate test and reward of the foreigner's integration into the host society. In contrast, a country that steadfastly adheres to its cultural or racial homogeneity is cautious about admitting foreigners and tends to impose all kinds of restrictions on those admitted; it also encourages return and is reluctant to extend citizenship to foreigners.

A country's societal model or self-perception also influences the type of operational instruments it applies to achieve its integration objective. A multicultural society may be more inclined to follow a targeted or special approach to help migrants overcome the difficulties they face in participating in its economic and social life. Positive or preferential action in favor of the disadvantaged migrant groups, including provision of facilities for migrants to maintain some core aspects of their culture, may well be part of the approach. By contrast, a society that relies on assimilation would be reluctant to recognize the rights of migrants as a minority group or to adhere to migrant-targeted special programs on the grounds that this would separate or even stigmatize them. For such a society the preference would be to adhere to a general approach to support all disadvantaged groups, national or non-national.

To say that a country's integration strategy is shaped by is own societal model does not mean, however, that the model itself is forever an immutable one. Rather, it acts as a dynamic social construct, which may evolve and change over time, influenced by the contextual circumstances and each nation's own experience of them. Take the case of France, for example. In recent years, as the inflows of immigrants of diverse religions and cultures, especially Muslims, have increased, the country is finding it hard to rigidly apply its traditional assimilation strategy and is accepting a degree of pluralism or multiculturalism in its policy and operational approach. Concurrently, countries wedded to multiculturalism, such as the United States and Canada, are now curtailing some of their immigrant-oriented special cultural and social policies. They are doing this in order to strengthen national cohesiveness and avoid segregation, well aware that "separate can never be equal." The two approaches are thus moving towards a degree of convergence.

Some slow but significant changes can be discerned even in the segregationist approach. Faced with pressing labor market needs and demographic decline, even countries like Japan are gradually relaxing their traditional exclusionary strategies and restrictive immigration policies. On the other hand, there are clear signs that countries adhering to assimilation or multiculturalism are becoming increasingly more restrictive in their immigration and naturalization policies.

What, then, is the best or most successful integration strategy? Since, as argued previously, integration strategy is closely linked to a nation's societal model, cross-national analysis or the measurement of success of different integration strategies becomes highly problematic. Nor is it realistic to prescribe a single integration strategy for all countries or for all types of migrants. The needs and conditions of temporary and seasonal migrants or border commuters, for example, are clearly different from those surrounding long-term migrants or foreign-born settlers.

It is nonetheless possible to lay down, especially for the latter types of migrants, certain basic principles and arrangements that enable them to better

participate in and contribute to the host society, its economy, and its culture, thus enhancing the all-around benefits of migration.

Separated from the familiar surroundings and social networks of home, most long-term migrants have reason to feel insecure in the new environment of the host country. They need to have guarantees of security and human dignity, with access to certain basic human rights. The host society, for its part, is entitled to expect that the migrants would have an understanding of and respect for the laws and traditions of the host society. This also implies a two-way process of attitudinal and cultural adjustment between nationals and foreigners. A real challenge here is to strike a balance between migrants' equal partnership in the larger society and the possibility of their continuing membership in their own communities. Ethics, economics of enlightened self-interest, and democratic inclusiveness all combine to argue for such an approach.

Legal and institutional arrangements, although critically important, are not enough to create the conditions mentioned previously.[2] Also needed is a conducive climate based on mutual understanding, open-mindedness, and tolerance on both sides. How to put all these elements into a coherent and practical strategy calls for further analytical and investigative research, including careful distillation of existing empirical data.

Endnotes

1   Four traditional models are used to conceptualize the nation-state's attitude towards integration of noncitizens: first, the imperial model (e.g., the British and the Austro-Hungarian models), based on the integration of peoples of multiethnic empires under the hegemony of a dominant group; second, the ethnic model (e.g., the German model), based on common ethnicity, descent, language, and culture; third, the republican model (e.g., the French model), based on a constitution and political rules, with newcomers adhering to them; and fourth, multiculturalism, based on recognition of different cultures, with a common ideal.

2   Experience shows that caution is needed against rigid application of normative principles, however seemingly sound. For example, the French experience with public housing in the 1960s showed that rigid enforcement of the principle of equality was counterproductive as it exacerbated marginalization and segregation of immigrants.

Integration: Perception and Reality

Michael Bommes and Holger Kolb

Regional Issues

Immigration after the Eastern Enlargement of the European Union

Stereotype

A considerable number of articles and reports in the media forecast a mass immigration into the European Union after the EU eastern enlargement of May 2004. A noteworthy example of this type of forecast was offered in the German newspaper *Welt am Sonntag*. The fears and stereotypes typically associated with immigration resulting from eastern enlargement were underlined in an article in this newspaper that ran under the provocative headline "Germany Expects More Than 6 Million Immigrants."[1] Since eastern enlargement is a singular event, a secure prognosis of the probable quantity of migration flows from Central and Eastern European countries (CEEC) into Western Europe is of course highly speculative. Estimations from the different scientific disciplines, however, provide clues concerning the size and speed of potential East-West migration flows. If we compare different scientific approaches, a quite surprising common result becomes evident. Despite the great variety of assumptions and models used in the different social sciences in

order to guess future East-West migration flows, the results differ only slightly.[2] The most prominent forecasts are summarized here and are compared with common stereotypes on future migration and its expected effects.

Reality

A study of the Hamburg Institute of International Economics (HWWA) extrapolates data from EU southern enlargement and indicates a gross migration potential from the first wave of acceding countries—Slovenia, the Czech Republic, Hungary, the Slovak Republic, Poland, Estonia, Lithuania, and Latvia—of 0.2% to 0.4% of the total CEEC population per year. Taking into account the significant return migration, the total net migration from the CEEC is estimated to reach 0.1% of the total population per year. The total net migration from the CEEC is calculated at about 1 to 1.5 million people during the first fifteen years of labor mobility.[3]

The German Institute of Economic Research (DIW) uses an econometric approach to estimate the migration potential. The institute expects a yearly net migration of 220,000 in the first years of labor mobility. This net migration rate will be reduced to an annual rate of 95,000 per year at the end of the decade. The total net immigration from the CEEC to Germany is estimated to be 2 million immigrants through 2030.[4]

Other scholars follow a completely different approach. The geographers Heinz Fassmann and Christiane Hintermann rely on opinion polls and surveys in the Visegrad countries of Poland, Hungary, the Czech Republic, and the Slovak Republic. Based on one-issue surveys, the authors estimate a yearly net migration of 150,000 to Germany and 75,000 to Austria.[5]

Only the study of the Ifo Institute for Economic Research in Munich differs from this implicit consensus in the scientific community. Using econometric simulation models and building on data from migration movements during the former EU southern enlargement, the study estimates a net migration of 4 to 5 million people from the ten Central and Eastern European countries. For Germany this study would imply an annual net immigration of 250,000 to 300,000 people.[6] However, the Ifo Institute study does not take into consideration the temporal aspect of the enlargement process: that the most populous states, Bulgaria and Romania, are

not among the first group of the eastern states that will join the European Union.

Widespread stereotypes assuming mass immigration after the implementation of full labor mobility in the preaccession countries are not confirmed by the majority of scientific studies dealing with this topic. The realistic forecasts anticipate a rather moderate yearly immigration of approximately 150,000 persons to Germany and 75,000 persons to Austria. Taking into account the expectable decline of the European labor force potential (in Germany 200,000 persons per year),[7] fears of mass migration or "emigration of whole nations" seem highly exaggerated and are not substantiated by serious research. It should be stressed that the results of this research conform with the experiences of the southern enlargement. There were demands for an extended period of restricted labor mobility for the new Member States of southern Europe, which were caused by the fear of southern European workers swamping the labor markets of the other members once these countries became EU members. However, as an effect of the resulting economic growth and political stability, emigration from these countries

IMMIGRATION TO GERMANY AFTER EU EASTERN ENLARGEMENT: STEREOTYPES AND SCIENTIFIC FORECASTS

	Total	Yearly
Stereotype	4-6 million	Up to 400,000
HWWA	1-1.5 million	60,000-160,000
DIW	2 million	95,000-200,000
Fassmann/Hintermann	710,000	150,000
Ifo Institute	4-5 million	250,000-300,000

shrank. Contrary to previous assumptions, the number of southern European labor migrants in Europe fell following EU southern enlargement.[8] But this type of fear also ignores the rather positive consequences linked with the influx of mainly young[9] and qualified persons from the CEEC.[10]

IMMIGRATION FROM NORTH AFRICA

Stereotype
Due to geographical proximity, immigration from the CEEC will be especially relevant for Germany and Austria. The functional equivalent for the southern EU Member States of Italy, Portugal, and Spain is immigration from the northern African states. In these countries immigration from North Africa is similarly perceived as a major threat to national labor markets and social security systems. The violent attacks against labor migrants from Morocco in the Spanish region of Almeria were seen as a striking example of the consequences that can result from these fears.[11] In many southern European countries the transformation "from classical emigration to modern immigration countries"[12] is a fiercely debated issue.

Reality
Southern European countries, however, have regularly used special procedures for legalizing illegal foreigners within their borders in order to benefit from the human capital represented by these immigrants. The Italian government passed a bill in 1986 (Law 943/86) aimed at sanctioning the stay of illegal immigrants originating mainly from North Africa and Albania. The Spanish government concluded an agreement with Morocco to recruit up to 300,000

Moroccans for the Spanish labor market.[13] Italy passed a new quota-based immigration act with an annual maximum of 63,000 visas.[14] Portugal carried out mass legalization drives in 1992 and 1996. In the segmented labor markets of southern Europe, labor migrants compete with indigenous workers only in narrow occupational sectors and only with small parts of the domestic labor supply. Labor migration in the southern EU Member States therefore functions in a complementary rather than a substitutive manner.[15] The "late immigration countries" in southern Europe, meanwhile, have begun to deal with immigration in a more unemotional and pragmatic way. Immigration in these latecomer immigration countries will be a necessary supplement in light of dramatic population aging in these countries: the birthrates in southern EU countries—Italy 1.22, Spain 1.15, Greece 1.31, Portugal 1.44—are well below the stock figure of 2.1.[16]

POLICY ISSUES

INTEGRATION OF MEDIUM- AND LOW-SKILLED IMMIGRANTS

Stereotype
Discourses on migration in many contexts are dominated by the presumption that most migrants belong to the low-skilled workforce of their country of origin. It is assumed that this causes substitution processes for the indigenous workforce, including pressure on wages and social security standards.

Reality
General migration research and recent empirical studies on the EU eastern

enlargement show that the process of migration itself presupposes a basic stock of social qualifications and human capital in order to collect the necessary data and information on the destination area and to start the migration process itself. In their study on migration from the CEEC, Fassmann and Hintermann show that it is mainly highly qualified persons who entertain the idea of migrating to Western Europe. Twelve percent of the potential migrants in the study have a university degree, 36.3% a general qualification of university entrance, and 31.3% a vocational school education.[17] The majority of these migrants do not belong to the pool of the unskilled labor force in their country of origin.

A similar dichotomy between social perception and reality appears in the case of asylum seekers. It is a widespread stereotype that the overwhelming majority of asylum seekers are low skilled and unlikely to be integrated in the domestic labor market. This stereotype is disproved by most scientific reports, which confirm the general conclusion reached by migration research examining the characteristics of the majority of asylum seekers—namely, that they are usually well educated and rather highly qualified.[18] However, in countries like Germany, the incorporation of this human resource potential into the labor market is blocked by the current alien act, which in most cases does not allow for the granting of work permits to asylum seekers.

INTEGRATION OF MIGRANTS WHO ARRIVED THROUGH FAMILY REUNIFICATION

Stereotype

Family reunification as a central framework of current immigration processes is one of the most emotionally mobilizing topics in migration discourses. Viewed comparatively, family reunification in Germany is handled in a rather restrictive fashion. This immigration channel, however, is perceived as a major gateway for uncontrolled immigration. The new immigration law generally allows children under the age of eighteen access to the territory if they immigrate together with the other members of the family unit. Any child immigrating individually in order to join the family unit gains entry only if he or she is under the age of twelve. The Christian Democrats proposed lowering the maximum age further to ten years, arguing that this would avoid uncontrolled migration through family reunification.

Reality

By examining one of the prominent models of immigration legislation, it becomes evident that family reunification should not be regarded as a gateway for uncontrolled immigration but rather as a successful means to compete for skilled migrants. Studies on US immigration have shown that admission of relatives to the United States on the basis of family reunification results in an above average human resource potential.[19] US immigration policy acknowledges the positive effects of family reunification.

Contrary to the rather restrictive policies in Europe, US immigration law even allows for the immigration of more distantly related family members.[20] If family reunification is implied, this is taken as an argument in favor of granting a green card offering both permanent residence and a work permit in the United States. Two-thirds of all green cards are issued for family migrants, and only 11% are given to independent and employment-based immigrants.[21] The political model for an immigration policy based on economic and labor market considerations[22] makes for an interest-driven use of family migration without losing the ability to control immigration.

IMMIGRANT LANGUAGE ABILITY

Stereotype
The willingness to learn the language of the destination country is generally seen as a central prerequisite for social integration.[23] The willingness of migrants to accept this requirement often meets with considerable public skepticism. The perceived inflexibility on the part of immigrants to learn the language of their new home country is considered one of the most serious potential hindrances to integration.[24]

Reality
The overwhelming majority of immigrants in Europe consider themselves to be bilingual or multilingual. For example, more than 90% of interviewed immigrants in a recent representative survey by the German Federal Ministry of Labor claimed proficiency in German.[25] Similar results can be found in a study by the German Youth Institute relating to young adults.[26] The widespread belief that immigrants are either unwilling or unable to learn the language of their adopted country has also been disapproved by empirical studies in other countries. Studies like the OECD Programme for International Student Assessment demonstrate that some education systems are quite successful in opening access to language training and other qualifications to immigrant children.[27] With regard to future immigration from the CEEC resulting from EU eastern enlargement, the need to improve immigrant language proficiency will be somewhat less in countries like Germany and Austria, since German is one of the most frequently taught foreign languages in many Eastern European countries.[28] As a consequence, the linguistic integration of immigrants after enlargement may be somewhat easier in these countries.

ENDNOTES

1 Welt am Sonntag, 22 April 2001.
2 See Thomas Straubhaar, "East-West Migration: Will It Be a Problem?" Intereconomics (July/August 2001): 168.
3 See Thomas Straubhaar, Ost-West-Migrationspotential: Wie groß ist es? HWWA Discussion Paper (2001), 137.
4 See Herbert Brücker, Parvati Trübswetter, and Christian Weise, "EU-Osterweiterung: Keine massive Zuwanderung zu erwarten," Wochenbericht (2000): 21.
5 Heinz Fassmann and Christiane Hintermann, Migrationspotential Ostmitteleuropa: Struktur und Motivation potentieller Migranten aus Polen, der Slowakei, Tschechien und Ungarn, Institut für Systemdynamik und Regelungstechnik Forschungsbericht, no. 15 (Vienna, 1997).
6 Hans-Werner Sinn et al., EU-Erweiterung und Arbeitskräftemigration: Wege zu einer schrittweisen Annäherung der Arbeitsmärkte, ifo

Beiträge zur Wirtschaftsforschung, no. 2 (Munich: ifo Institut für Wirtschaftsforschung, 2001).

7 See Johann Fuchs and Manfred Thon, "Nach 2010 sinkt das Angebot an Arbeitskräften," IAB Kurzbericht 4 (1999).

8 See Richard G. Miles, "Without Immigrants Germany Will Shrink Very Soon," *Wall Street Journal Europe*, 29 August 2000.

9 Fassmann and Hintermann assume that more than 75% of the immigrants from the CEEC following the eastern enlargement are not older than thirty-nine.

10 Straubhaar, "Ost-West-Migrationspotential," 7.

11 See Marlise Simons, "Resenting African Workers: Spaniards Attack," New York Times, 12 February 2000; Roger Cohen, "Europe's Migrant Fears Rend a Spanish Town," *New York Times*, 8 May 2000.

12 See Bernhard Santel, "Zwischen Abwehr und Normalität," in *Einwanderungskontinent Europa: Migration und Integration am Beginn des 21. Jahrhunderts*, ed. Klaus J. Bade, Beiträge der Akademie für Migration und Integration, vol. 4 (Osnabrück: Otto Benecke Stiftung e.V., 2001), 106.

13 See Santel, 112.

14 *Migration News* 3 (March 2000).

15 See Emilio Reyneri and Maria Baganha, "Migration and the Labour Market in Southern Europe," *IMIS-Beiträge* 17 (2001): 49.

16 See Dieter Oberndörfer, "Europa und Deutschland brauchen Einwanderer" (paper presented at Akademie der Diözese Rottenburg-Stuttgart, 10 April 2000).

17 See Heinz Fassmann, "EU-Erweiterung und Arbeitsmigration nach Deutschland und Österreich: Quantitative Vorhersagen und aktuelle Entwicklungstendenzen," *IMIS-Beiträge* 19 (2002): 76.

18 See Wolfgang Seifert, "'Alte' und 'Neue' Zuwanderungsgruppen auf dem Arbeitsmarkt 1990-1995," in *Neue Migrationsprozesse: Politisch-institutionelle Regulierung und Wechselbeziehungen am Arbeitsmarkt*, eds. Thomas Faist, Felicitas Hillmann, and Klaus Zühlke-Robinet, Arbeitspapier, no. 6 (Bremen: Zentrums für Sozialpolitik, Universität Bremen, 1996), 54; Wolfgang Seifert, "Neue Zuwanderungsgruppen auf dem westdeutschen Arbeitsmarkt," *Soziale Welt* 2 (1996): 180; Johannes Velling, *Immigration und Arbeitsmarkt: eine empirische Analyze für die Bundesrepublik Deutschland*, Schriftenreihe des Zentrum für Europäische Wirtschaftsforschung,

no. 6 (Baden-Baden, 1995); Joachim Frick and Gert Wagner, *Zur sozioökonomischen Lage von Zuwanderern in West-Deutschland*, Enquête-Kommission Demographischer Wandel, 13th German Bundestag, 1996.

19 See Jasso Guillermina and R. Rosenzweig, "Do Immigrants Screened for Skills Do Better than Family Reunification Immigrants?" International Migration Review 1 (1995): 85-111.

20 See Bernhard Santel and James F. Hollifield, "Erfolgreiche Integrationsmodelle? Zur wirtschaftlichen Situation von Einwanderern in Deutschland und den USA," in *Migration in nationalen Wohlfahrtsstaaten*, eds. Michael Bommes and Jost Halfmann (Osnabrück: Universitätsverlag, 1998), 131.

21 See Philip Martin and Heinz Werner, "Der amerikanische Weg: Ein Modell für Deutschland," *IAB-Kurzbericht* 5 (2000): 1.

22 In 1981 the American lawyer Edward P. Hutchinson stated that "it would be in fact difficult to determine where immigration policy ends and labor policy begins, the two are so closely interrelated." See Edward P. Hutchinson, *Legislative History of American Immigration Policy 1798-1965* (Philadelphia: University of Pennsylvania Press, 1981).

23 See Hans H. Reich, "Sprache und Integration," in *Rat für Migration: Integration und Illegalität in Deutschland*, ed. Klaus J. Bade (Osnabrück and Weinheim: Institut für Migrationsforschung und Interkulturelle Studien, 2001), 41.

24 See, for example, Andrzej Stach, "Multikultur funktioniert nicht," Die Welt, 8 October 1999.

25 See Ursula Mehrländer, Carsten Ascheberg, and Jörg Ueltzhoeffer, eds. *Repräsentativuntersuchung 95: Situation der ausländischen Arbeitnehmer und ihrer Familienangehörigen in der Bundesrepublik Deutschland* (Bonn: Bundesministerium fuer Arbeit und Sozialordung, 1996), 267-293.

26 Alois Weidacher, ed., *In Deutschland zu Hause: Politische Orientierungen griechischer, italienischer, türkischer und deutscher junger Erwachsener im Vergleich* (Opladen: Leske und Budrich, 2000), 85-91.

27 And some, like the German one, are less successful in this respect; see Jürgen Baumert et al., eds., PISA 2000: *Basiskompetenzen von Schülerinnen und Schülern im internationalen Vergleich* (Opladen: Leske und Budrich, 2001).

28 In Poland, German is one of the two obligatory foreign languages in school. In the Czech Republic, more than 98% of pupils are obliged to learn either English or German in school.

Conceptual and Political Approaches to Integration: A German Perspective

Dieter Oberndörfer

Towards the end of the 1950s, the booming German economy made it necessary to recruit a rapidly burgeoning number of workers from abroad. These workers were given limited contracts for a specific length of time and were thus known as guest workers. These "guests" were supposed to return home when their contracts expired, and it was not envisaged that they should remain in Germany. Most of the workers initially came from southern and southeastern Europe, and subsequently from Turkey. The guest worker policy resulted in mass inflows and outflows of migrants. Estimates suggest that more than 20 million guest workers were in Germany at one time or another.

The mechanization of manual work and a growing shortage of jobs, especially in those sectors of the economy where guest workers were particularly in demand, such as the iron and coal industries and shipbuilding, led in 1973 to the termination of immigration through a recruitment ban. In spite of considerable migrant outflows, the number of foreigners in Germany continued to increase as a result of family reunification, natural growth, and an influx of refugees. The foreign population subsequently doubled to reach 7.3 million. Currently, 9% of Germany's residents are "foreigners"—that is, per-

sons who do not hold a German passport. Of these, about 1.5 million were born in Germany. About 1 million people have acquired German citizenship by means of naturalization.

The political and social integration of foreign immigrants into German society did not form a part of the guest worker model. After all, foreign workers were not supposed to remain in Germany. Such a large-scale rejection of permanent residence and integration of foreign immigrants into German society was already in evidence in imperial Germany in the form of limited contract labor from the Polish part of the Russian Empire. It was also characteristic of the policy on foreigners pursued by the German Democratic Republic (East Germany), where limited contract workers from fraternal communist states were permitted to remain for only a specified period. Furthermore, contact with the East German population was restricted to an absolute minimum. Clearly, the ideological roots of the policy on guest workers lie in the tradition of construing the nation as a community of common ethnicity. This is also apparent in the fact that the preunification Basic Law expressly stated that immigrants from the German minorities in eastern and southeastern Europe were German citizens who had the right to live in Germany. Thus, it was possible to integrate 1.7 million ethnic Germans as citizens of West Germany prior to unification with East Germany in 1990.

Since the recruitment ban of 1973, German society's defensive attitude towards "foreigners" has become even more entrenched. It is true that, on the basis of what were called the recruitment ban exception regulations of 1984, foreigners were allowed to repeatedly enter Germany to fill vacancies for which, as in the health services (nurses), there were insufficient German applicants. However, the work permits that were issued were again granted only for limited periods. A fairly large number of permits were and continue to be issued. Thus, for example, in 2000 almost 350,000 work permits were granted, mainly for seasonal labor in the agricultural sector (ninety days). Within the green card framework of 2000, a special regulation which applied to the recruitment of information technology and communications technology specialists, work permits were again limited to a period of five years.

In 1991 a new naturalization law marked the first breach in the opposition to the permanent inclusion of foreigners in German society. Up to that point, naturalization could only be "granted" by means of a "discretionary" procedure based on the criterion of "public interest," for example, in the case of eminent scholars, artists, or sportsmen. Foreigners now possessed for the first time the legal right to request naturalization after a minimum of six years' residence in Germany.

In the wake of growing mass unemployment in the east of Germany and the resulting westward migration of East Germans, the immigration and integration of foreigners became an even more politically sensitive subject in the context of German domestic policy. On top of this came the influx of asylum seekers. By 1992, when 438,191 people arrived, the inflow had become a tidal wave, making it imperative that the provisions of the Basic Law relating to the legal asylum rights of victims of political persecution be curtailed. Furthermore, the collapse of communism in Eastern Europe marked the start of the mass migration of almost 3 million ethnic Germans from the territory of the former Soviet Union. Since their resettlement in the Federal Republic, in both ideological and constitutional terms, was not considered immigration, but was seen as a return to their homeland, the unrealistic phrase "Germany is not a country for immigrants" continued to constitute the political dogma of German domestic policy.

At the same time, the new arrivals were beset by the problems of high unemployment, social marginalization, and insufficient linguistic integration. Shortcomings in the educational system with regard to the teaching of linguistic skills and the acquisition of educational qualifications deprived large numbers of young foreigners of the opportunity to pursue a career and acquire social standing. Most asylum seekers and refugees were not allowed to work and were denied the permanent residence status that would have protected them from deportation.

At the end of the 1990s, these and other integration-related shortcomings were discussed for the first time in a wide-ranging and intense political debate. As a result, in 1998 the integration of foreigners into German society was depicted as an important task for the future by the new federal government under Chancellor Gerhard Schröder. As early as 1999, in a new law on aliens, the period of residence in Germany required to qualify for naturalization was reduced to eight years. The introduction of jus soli—that is, the automatic naturalization of the children of foreigners born in Germany—also provided an opening to German society.

At the same time, a number of publications drew attention to the forthcoming rapid contraction and aging of the German population and the associated danger this posed to prosperity and the social security system. There was a widespread political response. Certain suggestions on how to slow the process of contraction and aging by encouraging immigration led for the first time to a noticeable shift in the traditionally defensive attitude towards immigration and integration of foreigners. Thus, in 2000 and 2001, a broadly based consensus on the need for a policy on immigration and integration organized and implemented by the state emerged that enjoyed the support of all the political parties. Against this background the Minister of the Interior, Otto Schily, convened a commission of experts chaired by Rita Süssmuth, the former president of the German Parliament, in order to define the conceptual and practical guidelines for a new policy on immigration and integration.

The commission's report, known as the Süssmuth report, demonstrated that organized immigration was needed in order to secure Germany's prosperity and made suggestions for a policy on immigration and integration that took its lead from the needs of industry and demographics. On this subject the policies on immigration and integration pursued in the United States, Canada, and Australia provided numerous points of departure. In contrast to the recruitment of guest workers, the proposals were designed to attract technical and scientific specialists, who would also be granted residence permits. In the case of refugees, it was suggested that humanitarian tasks should be emphasized more strongly than in the past. The report's policy on integration proposals assigned a central role to funding the acquisition of German language skills, an absolutely essential prerequisite for the economic success and social integration of foreigners. Furthermore, orientation courses for foreigners were intended to provide them with information about their political and social environment. The broadly based political response to the Süssmuth report was very positive. Indeed, Germany seemed to be on the verge of becoming a country for immigrants. And such immigration would not constitute what amounted to unwanted seepage, but would be seen in a positive light and implemented in a manner that enjoyed broad social acceptance.

However, the political consensus about opening Germany to immigration and pursuing an innovative new policy on integration came to grief a few months later in the course of a bitter controversy between the government and the opposition on whether or not to pass immigration legislation on the basis of the Süssmuth report.

In the government proposals, certain aspects of how to manage immigration were given priority. The opposition, by contrast, referred to the high level of unemployment and emphasized the need to control and place restrictions on immigration. It also proved impossible to reach agreement on how to defray the costs associated with integration, such as language and orientation courses for immigrants. The opposition subsequently vetoed the law on immigration during consideration in the second legislative chamber, the Bundesrat. To date it remains unclear whether or not the law will be passed, and especially whether the legislation will make a clean break with the guest worker model and open Germany to a kind of immigration that takes into account not only the need to replenish the workforce, but also the constraints of demographic development. However, as a result of the new debate on terrorism and what continues to be the rather unsatisfactory development of the labor market, the chances for such a policy on immigration and integration are currently remote.

Conceptual and Political Approaches to Integration: An Anglo-American Perspective

Anja Rudiger

Integration of Migrants: Historical and Conceptual Background

British discourse and politics shifted away from an expressed concern about the integration of immigrants or migrants soon after the first stages of postwar immigration from the Commonwealth. Race riots and growing racist and anti-immigration sentiments in the late 1950s precipitated two major developments which to this day distinguish the British model from most continental European models of integration. First, while immigration policies increasingly aimed to curb nonwhite entry, a legal and institutional race equality regime began to emerge. The separation of these two policy areas was driven, however, by successive governments' assertions that good relations between Britain's diverse communities required restrictive immigration policies, thus portraying the presence of black and ethnic minority people as a challenge to cohesion. Second, and leading on from that, integration policy ceased to be about assimilating newly arrived individuals into a homogeneous society and instead turned to regulating the relations between distinct groups of people in a pluralist society.

Contrary to continental approaches, the focus in Britain has not been on how newcomers can blend into society, but on how society can achieve equal treatment of different groups-that is, how to balance difference and equality to maintain social cohesion. As these groups are largely identified through a political concept of race, this approach has become known as the race relations model, echoing the title of the Race Relations Act 1976, which sets out the principles of antidiscrimination and equal opportunities on which the British model is based. Britain's first race relations law was conceived in 1965, influenced by the US Civil Rights Act of 1964, and in its different versions and amendments has become the basis of a highly institutionalized equality regime. Both the British and the US equality frameworks were designed to address the situation of groups of people, not merely that of individuals.

In the United Kingdom successive administrations have placed considerable importance on the concept of community and the idea of managing community relations—to the effect that the British model is sometimes referred to as communitarian. However, contrary to value-based communitarian approaches, the British model is based on a pluralist conception of democracy in which the presence of different ethnic and racial groups is regulated through a management strategy. This approach can also be contrasted with the multicultural Canadian model, as the United Kingdom's multicultural strategy does not rest on a recognition of minority group rights but on a pragmatic facilitation of relations between different communities. As in the United States, the main tools of this approach are antidiscrimination laws and equal opportunities policies, as well as easy access to full civil and political rights. The emphasis is on promoting equality in all spheres, while protecting the exercise of different cultural practices.

While this has not succeeded in eliminating racism and social disadvantages, it has provided a framework for society to identify and address inequalities. For example, after a failed police investigation into the racist murder of black teenager Stephen Lawrence, a 1999 public inquiry report (the Macpherson report) raised awareness of racism to a new level by identifying many public bodies as institutionally racist. A subsequent amendment of the Race Relations Act brought police and law enforcement functions under the scope of the law and required public bodies to actively promote equality.

British multiculturalism has also managed to create a diverse citizenry with relatively little tension between national and group identities: the majority of British-born black and minority ethnic people feel comfortable affirming that they are both British and members of a minority ethnic group. However, conflicts can arise when differences within communities are disregarded or when particular groups are not acknowledged. A failure to recognize the specific needs

of religious communities and those of new immigrants and refugees has contributed to some competition between different groups. New immigrants are either subsumed under the category of ethnic minority or set apart from those who already belong. This failure to identify different needs generates social divisions, which rest less on cultural differences than on perceived differential access to scarce resources, such as jobs, education, and housing.

Such divisions are being increasingly addressed through an emphasis on social inclusion, which is a stated policy goal towards all social groups, not just migrants and minorities. Most recently, this has turned into a focus on community cohesion, as the latest incarnation of integration policy in the United Kingdom. Both inclusion and cohesion approaches have more in common with Canadian than US strategies, as they oblige the state to take an active role. The recently amended Race Relations Act requires public authorities to simultaneously promote equality and good race relations. Cohesion is thought to result from the interaction of different but equal communities that build a bond through the recognition of difference and interdependence.

A COMPARISON OF BRITISH AND US APPROACHES TO INTEGRATION

The United Kingdom and the United States both tend to separate immigration from integration or race relations issues. While in the United Kingdom the rationale for immigration measures often remains tied to their perceived impact on community relations, in practical policy terms there is hardly any mention of immigrants or migrants for whom integration policies would be devised, only different racial and ethnic groups whose interaction and access to opportunities need to be regulated. This race relations approach is mirrored in the United States, which has a black minority population that did not come to the country as immigrants, unlike the white majority which did. The United States has a significant contingent of racial and ethnic minorities without any, or any recent, migratory background, and it has largely been this native or previously enslaved population, and not the majority of white immigrants, that has been in need of integration policies. Thus, policies to promote equality and diversity were developed independent of immigration issues, and only the growth of nonwhite immigration over the last three decades has led to a gradual inclusion of immigrants as target groups of such policies. That Britain has, despite its different history, developed a similar approach, which acknowledges diversity as inherent to society rather than contingent on immigration flows, indicates to some extent a common basis in Anglo-American pragmatism and pluralism.

The advantages of this rights-based approach to addressing racial, ethnic, and cultural differences, as exemplified by the US Civil Rights Act and the UK Race Relations Act, are that the objective of equal opportunities for all groups is an integral part of mainstream policy-making and that belonging to, and participation in, society are not questioned at the policy level. While immigrants are not explicit targets of equal opportunities policies, they benefit as well, not least because a rights-based approach also implies relatively easy access to citizenship in both the United Kingdom and the United States.

However, complications arise regarding new immigrants who are not yet citizens. In the United States the treatment of newcomers resurfaced as a policy issue in the 1980s, mainly in the context of welfare expenses and competition for resources. A 1996 law made citizenship the threshold for access to many public services and benefits, thus erecting a new boundary between people that regulates inclusion into society. This exclusionary tendency, continued with restrictive measures under the new US Patriot Act, seems at odds with EU efforts to equalize the rights of third country nationals and EU citizens. At the same time, similar exclusionary measures can be found in UK asylum policies, which in rhetoric and practice exacerbate differences between new, settled, and native communities, instead of laying out a path for integration.

However, in both countries it is ultimately their strong antidiscrimination and equal opportunities regimes that might help counter processes of exclusion. Both the United Kingdom and the United States outlaw discrimination on grounds of national origin, and the United Kingdom even prohibits discrimination on grounds of nationality. Non-naturalized UK residents have far better employment opportunities than noncitizens in continental Europe, with most British public sector and civil service positions open to non-nationals. In the United States the Justice Department's Civil Rights Division has recently established a National Origin Working Group to help both naturalized citizens and recent immigrants better understand and exercise their legal rights. These include new immigrants' rights to equal treatment as well as special assistance through language training and other integration measures. This demonstrates that an equal opportunities approach can serve the needs of newcomers as well as those of settled and indigenous minorities, indicating a convergence of race relations and immigrant integration models.

At the same time, Anglo-American approaches to race relations remain less reliant on state intervention in the socioeconomic policy arena than continental or Canadian models. Government-led settlement policies practiced in Canada or Australia, based on established, though nowadays less explicit, multicultural tenets, find a more hands-off expression in Britain, and particularly the United States, where social policy interventions, such as targeted education and training measures, are less common.

The rights-based equality framework of the United States is, however, employed to indirectly influence socioeconomic outcomes for a range of minority groups, including non-naturalized immigrants, by means of affirmative action programs. While programs such as set asides for minority businesses, contract compliance mechanisms, and recruitment quotas were originally designed primarily as compensatory remedy for the descendants of African slaves, their eligibility criteria have long included national origin as well as race, with an increase over time of the range of national origins covered, to include

recent immigrants, often irrespective of citizenship status. Today, affirmative action has come to signify an effective, albeit controversial, tool to promote diversity. While the private sector has supplemented it with diversity management approaches, these have had less impact on increasing the representation and participation of minority groups.

Although Britain shares a similar legal and institutional framework for promoting race equality, the practical tools have been less outcome oriented, dominated by a narrower, compliance-driven approach concentrating on remedies for individual acts of discrimination. However, the identification of institutional racism in the Macpherson report has inspired a more proactive and positive strategy, in the form of the public duty to promote race equality. Although the public duty and other positive action measures remain below the threshold of enforceable quotas of participation and representation of disadvantaged groups, they signal a new willingness to encourage a real equality of outcome.

The recent emphasis of the United Kingdom on community cohesion also indicates a potential move towards a more interventionist stance. A communitarian vision of shared values appears to develop alongside the liberal emphasis on rights on which Anglo-American equality regimes are based. This could generate a closer attention to socioeconomic integration measures. Britain seems inclined to pursue more substantive interventions to promote equality and inclusion, in the form of American-style positive action as well as continental European socioeconomic support programs.

LESSONS FROM THE ANGLO-AMERICAN EXPERIENCE

Are there any elements in the Anglo-American experience that are essential to managing religious, racial, ethnic, or cultural differences in a constructive and peaceful way? The Anglo-American emphasis on diversity, which finds its institutional expression in race relations (the United Kingdom and the United States) or multiculturalism policies (Canada), appears to be a prerequisite for tackling exclusion, promoting equality, and maintaining social cohesion in Europe. In as far as racial, ethnic, cultural, and religious differences are perceived in relation to migration, the integration of migrants should be guided by the principles of equality and diversity, in the form of two-way processes of adaptation by migrants as well as receiving societies. At the same time, it is worthwhile to consider at least a partial decoupling of migration and integration issues, as practiced in the Anglo-American context. This could open up opportunities for recognizing long-term residents as belonging to the European societies they were born or raised in, and for including indigenous minorities, such as Roma communities, whose role will increase with EU enlargement. In pragmatic terms this would shift the location of integration policymaking from the areas of immigration, border control, and criminal justice to the socioeconomic field, where mainstream social inclusion strategies are already being designed.

This does not mean that migration policies, such as family reunion or work permit schemes, can be disregarded in their often negative impact on integra-

tion, but that integration policies must be able to address a variety of experiences and needs, based on migratory background as well as racial, ethnic, or religious differences. The prevalence of institutional discrimination in particular constitutes a key barrier to the integration of both migrants and racial or ethnic minorities without recent migratory background.

An equal opportunities approach as developed in the Anglo-American context can enable policymakers to tackle a range of barriers to inclusion. Its objective is to ensure that migrants and ethnic minorities can exercise equal rights and thus become full partners and participants in the development of a cohesive society. Such rights must create security for them as individuals, regardless of their particular background or origin, but also as members of minority groups. Continental policymakers tend to disregard the collective needs of people who share certain experiences and encounter similar barriers, by neglecting that these affect groups of people and not just isolated individuals. This reluctance to identify people as groups for the purpose of policymaking can diminish the effectiveness of policies, in so far as they fail to correspond to people's needs, as well as perpetuate the exclusion of migrants and ethnic minorities, whose needs remain unrecognized. Therefore, the Anglo-American system of monitoring group needs and performance is an essential tool for devising effective inclusion policies.

Anglo-American approaches also provide mechanisms for meeting the needs identified, by means of creating equal opportunities for people from disadvantaged groups. Anglo-American equality frameworks offer an array of formal and substantive measures, ranging from combating discrimination (through legal antidiscrimination provisions) and creating opportunities (equal opportunities policies) to positively influencing outcomes (positive or affirmative action). Such measures are supported by institutional machinery, such as the US Equal Employment Opportunity Commission (EEOC), established in 1964 by the Civil Rights Act. The EEOC is tasked to promote and enforce race, disability, and gender equality in employment and has been effective in combating institutional discrimination by means of class action suits and strong sanctions. Britain's Commission for Racial Equality (CRE), established in 1976 by the Race Relations Act, has a remit reaching beyond employment to include areas such as education, housing, public services, and law enforcement. Both the CRE and the EEOC are independent public bodies with a range of promotional, investigative, and enforcement powers. When implementing the EU Race Equality Directive, which requires the establishment of equal treatment bodies, EU Member States could learn from the extensive experience of these commissions, and indeed of others, such as those in Ireland and Canada, where the power to carry out equality audits into the practices of public and private bodies and to order enforceable remedial action has been particularly effective. Experience has shown that the stronger a commission's powers are to enforce laws and issue sanctions, the more effective they can be at challenging institutional barriers to social inclusion and participation.

Continental European policymakers tend to underestimate structural disadvantages and instead focus on human capital issues, such as improving an individual's educational qualifications and employability. This also prompts them to see migrants' and minorities' cultural and religious differences as obstacles to integration. However, by concentrating on individual adaptation and short-term conflict prevention, they forgo a long-term perspective on social cohesion built on the rights-based management of diversity. The strength of Anglo-American approaches lies in the recognition that inclusion can only be achieved if all people have equal access to and opportunities for participation in a society's resources, institutions, and democratic processes, with shared responsibility for shaping and contributing to society.

To achieve this, social institutions must be able to adapt to and manage the consequences of social change. Anglo-American equality frameworks were to some extent developed to support such change, through active measures to promote a culture of equal opportunities and diversity. This has been most successful when driven both by commitment at the top layers of decision making and through strong community involvement, with pressures exerted by minority-led nongovernmental organizations or movements. As long as continental Europe focuses on human capital development, the role of minority-led organizations as well as of public and private sector leadership is likely to remain marginal, as the onus for change will continue to be on migrant and ethnic minority individuals. From Anglo-American approaches continental policymakers can learn to facilitate the participation of all social groups in social, economic, and political processes, thus encouraging a cross-fertilization of cultures and identities that can generate social cohesion based on diversity and equality.

A Suggested Approach to Integration in the Enlarged European Union

Common Strategies, Guidelines, and Framework for EU 25

The Tampere European Council decided to pursue a more vigorous integration policy, and the European Commission put forward relevant directives as the legal building blocks for such a policy. It has also proposed general guidelines for Member States to develop comprehensive integration policies in partnership with civil society and other stakeholders. However, the commission appears to see its own role as limited to that of developing common standards for integration measures and facilitating information exchange.

In an enlarged European Union, this approach may be too limited. Member States' perspectives on integration differ widely, and national policies have proved less than effective. Blockages to integration progress at the national level often expose a lack of political will to accommodate diversity, while it is precisely such diversity that an enlarged European Union embodies. Therefore, integration impasses at the national level call for concerted action at the EU level. At the local level, many initiatives across Europe already

correspond and overlap, bypassing national frameworks in a range of policy areas. Such transnational initiatives, anchored in local practices, deserve more coherent and systematic support from the European Commission. By building on Member States' experiences, the commission can learn lessons from national approaches while overcoming national constraints, for example regarding issues of nationality or cultural differences. A coherent integration policy framework at the EU level could be based on the following three components:

First, with regard to recent migrants and third country nationals, all immigration policies should be checked for their potential negative impact on integration. The rights of third country nationals and European citizens should be equalized, initially by linking the acquisition of rights to residency as well as facilitating access to naturalization, and eventually by devising an inclusive form of European citizenship which confers substantive rights independent of nationality.

Second, an integration framework needs to move beyond an immigration perspective. The new Member States bring with them substantial indigenous minorities, who lack a recent migration background. EU integration policies must address the issue of equality and diversity in multicultural societies rather than classify groups of people according to their immigration status. Minorities—whether third country nationals or citizens—face similar problems in societies that lack effective protection from discrimination. Roma communities require equal rights as much as third country nationals and recent migrants, and integration policies could develop common strategies against the social exclusion of all of these groups.

Third, the promotion of equality must be at the heart of European policymaking. The European Commission should maintain the momentum generated by the Article 13 directives and carefully monitor their implementation, with a view to extending their scope in the future. It could also take a lead in ensuring adequate and appropriate ethnic monitoring procedures across the European Union to identify the need for policy interventions. Building on its antidiscrimination actions, the commission could pave the way towards a more substantive understanding of equality, learning from, and adopting where suitable, Anglo-American positive and affirmative action measures. Its leverage over a range of public procurement rules could provide a simple tool for requiring employment and service delivery practices to become more inclusive.

An EU integration policy framework consisting of the above components could only become operational reality if the objectives of equality and inclusion for migrants and minorities were mainstreamed throughout European Commission policymaking, programming, and practices. These objectives would have to become an integral part of employment, health, housing, and education policies, immigration and criminal justice initiatives, public consultation mechanisms, and many other policy areas. While some attention to integration is already reflected in the European employment strategy and the social inclusion objectives, as well as the European social agenda, a better integrated and more consistent focus on the inclusion of migrants and minorities would be needed. For example, social inclusion guidelines could require that specific targets for the integration of migrants and minorities be incorporated into national action plans on social inclusion, supported by dedicated EU funds.

A BRITISH PERSPECTIVE

To encourage a more active UK engagement in EU integration measures, integration would have to be conceived as at least partly independent from the immigration agenda. The United Kingdom has positively driven the antidiscrimination directives, but is much more hesitant with regard to initiatives under the immigration title. To take this into account the European Commission might consider building on and extending equality and inclusion measures for all minority groups, with a view of gradually mainstreaming these into all policy areas, including asylum and immigration. A strengthened overall focus on equality, inclusion, and diversity could improve the situation of all EU residents, irrespective of nationality or migration status. For the commission, this would require much closer cooperation between directorates-general, with a prominent role for the Directorate-General for Employment, Social Affairs and Equal Opportunities, especially in setting and monitoring targets for the implementation of social inclusion and employment guidelines.

From a British point of view, it is also essential that lessons learned in the

United Kingdom over four decades of experience with an evolving equality and diversity regime are taken on board in the European Union, if only to prevent the European Union from becoming irrelevant in this regard for Britain and its ethnic minorities. The British approach to race equality, which has already shaped the antidiscrimination directives, has much to offer to continental policymakers, especially concerning ethnic monitoring, equal treatment bodies, and innovative positive action measures such as the duty of public bodies to mainstream the promotion of equality and good community relations. Britain's legal antidiscrimination regime, based mainly on civil law, has proven modestly successful and generated a significant body of case law, compared to underused criminal law provisions in some other Member States. A heavy-handed interference by EU criminal justice initiatives could prove counterproductive. Most antidiscrimination provisions are more effectively implemented by civil law, with a lower threshold for bringing complaints. Where criminal law is necessary, a fair balance of rights (e.g., higher penalties for racially aggravated offences and outlawing incitement to racial hatred while respecting the principle of freedom of expression) can foster cohesion instead of resentment.

Finally, the European Commission is unlikely to gain acceptance as an actor in this field, at least not in British eyes, if it fails to lead by example. It should take steps to implement effective equal opportunities procedures in its own operations, including ethnic monitoring and positive action, to increase at all levels the number of employees from ethnic minorities. The exclusion of third country nationals from employment in EU institutions should be reconsidered, especially in the context of proposed measures to equalize the rights of citizens and third country nationals.

Conceptual and Political Approaches to Integration: A Central European Perspective

Krystyna Iglicka and Marek Okólski

Since migration and minority policies are designed and implemented in the context of socioeconomic, political, and cultural change, it seems justifiable to begin by elaborating the integration problems that exist among both old ethnic groups and new immigrant communities. The ongoing transition occurring in Central European countries has resulted in highly complicated processes of societal disintegration and reintegration, affecting the lives of all persons, irrespective of national or ethnic origin. Minorities, including immigrants, have played an important role in speeding the process of forming cohesive societies. Generally speaking, the incorporation of immigrants and minorities into changing societies may be easier than their incorporation into societies that are more or less static. On the other hand, it is also well known that the more homogeneous the society, the more difficult it is to create open and friendly attitudes towards strangers ("them") among local populations ("us"). For the last fifteen years, the countries of Central Europe have all been undergoing continuous transition. It is also well known that until 1989 the focus of official ideology in the region was on national (ethnic) unity and homogeneity. This gave rise to a number of dynamic phenomena or paradoxes of integration that are now observed in almost every country of the region.

On matters relating to issues of immigration and the integration of immigrants or ethnic minorities, one can observe two different trends within Europe. Though Europe is becoming more and more involved in ethnic issues, it is going in two opposite directions: first, there is the process of integration of nations within the EU structure and its future enlargement; and, second, there is the process of disintegration of multinational (postcommunist) states.

The social and political transformations initiated in 1989 have proved that national issues in Central and Eastern Europe have not been permanently solved and, although suppressed or concealed, that they were certainly not silenced in the decades of the social experience of real socialism. On the contrary, they became doubly significant and have since erupted as a result of repressed xenophobia and nationalism, as well as the delay in implementing processes creating civil societies.

Each of the region's countries has a diaspora of coethnics living abroad, usually in close proximity—a circumstance caused by past migration and multiple border changes over the course of the last century. There are, for example, 1.2 to 2 million ethnic Poles living in the former Soviet Union. Several hundred thousand coethnics resident in foreign countries are claimed by Romania (mainly in Moldova), the Czech Republic (mainly in Ukraine), and the Baltic States (across the ex-USSR). In 2002, for instance, 6,600 Romanians or ex-Romanian citizens were repatriated to Romania, the majority of them from Moldova.[1] The largest ethnic minority of the region, however, are Hungarians,[2] who live mainly in Romania, but also in Croatia, Slovenia, Slovakia, Ukraine, and the Federal Republic of Yugoslavia (according to Act LXII of 2001 on Hungarians Living in Neighboring Countries). All of the aforementioned Central European countries are concerned with repatriation of their coethnics and recently undertook to adopt specific laws intended to create specific institutions aimed at facilitating that process. In addition, some of them (e.g., Hungary and Poland) introduced measures to enhance, maintain, or revive ethnic identity among the coethnics living in the diasporas.

According to some researchers, the delay in creating modern nations in Central Europe has influenced the attitudes of the majority towards the minority and the ways in which the majority deals with a minority. Minorities living in Central Europe do not yet benefit from strong integration mechanisms. With the collapse of Communism, national emancipation, not only of minorities but also of the dominant national group, takes place in precarious circumstances, where decayed state structures are continuously rocked by economic and social difficulties.

Nevertheless, newly adopted constitutions in most Central European countries include provisions that recognize

minorities, whether they are ethnic, cultural, religious, or linguistic minorities. Usually, the principle of equality before the law has been established. Some states have gone further by granting specific rights allowing minorities to preserve their identities. These include the right of mother-tongue education for children (in addition to compulsory instruction in the official language); the right to use the minority language in relations with the government and government services; the right to receive and send information in the native language; the right to names and surnames in the minority language; the right to preserve the minority culture and to practice the minority culture religion; and the right of association.

Structures for dialogue between minority groups, and between ethnic or national minority groups and governments, have recently been set up in many Central European countries. Freedom to establish associations and civil organizations by members of ethnic or national groups has become a norm in the region. In some countries, minorities are entitled to official political representation and self-government. In Hungary, Poland, and Romania, constitutional provisions guarantee minority groups representation in the parliament (in Poland this applies exclusively to the German national minority). In Lithuania minorities enjoy the same rights as all citizens of the state, including the right to political representation (e.g., in the parliament). In Croatia members of minority groups that constitute more than 8% of the total population are represented in the parliament and other government bodies, while in Slovenia representation in the National

try to negotiate a place in a French multicultural model more or less imposed by regionalist and European trends. Integration is now used mainly to analyze the size of the populations of immigrant origin who have been settled in France for a long time and whose members are by large majority French citizens. This differs from the questions that arise from the flows of migrant populations resulting from the globalization of migration. In an old immigration country such as France, understanding the distinction between the problematic of population size and that associated with the flow of migrant populations is essential to dealing with integration.

MAIN CONCEPTS AND POLITICAL APPROACHES

Some concepts are dominant in the French approach to integration. Among the most important is citizenship, intended as a means to political inclusion. Citizenship has long been associated with nationality, although the two are not synonymous. Rediscovered by the French revolution in 1789, citizenship mainly refers to the contract (inspired by Rousseau's social contract) between the nation-state and the individuals living in that state and to the rights and duties that apply within a political community (the *communauté des citoyens* defined by Dominique Schnapper). The Third Republic provided citizenship with a foundation by linking it to nationality, thereby creating the political institution of the national citizen, a model taught in the new compulsory, free-of-charge, and secularized public school system and through military service (the blood tax). Challenged in

part by competing concerns (e.g., class struggle), since the 1980s citizenship has acquired an emerging visibility, and it is now at the center of political debates over integration. The associations created by second-generation immigrants have also tried to develop an alternate definition of citizenship: the new citizenship, rooted in inner cities, oriented towards grassroots activities that focus on participation in local affairs, without regard to nationality, aimed at all persons living in the country (*citoyenneté de residence*) or born in the country (placing greater emphasis on jus soli), and including multiple allegiances and multiculturalism.

But citizenship is challenged by the problems of political identity and by societal mechanisms of exclusion (political inclusion and exclusion), especially when traditional tools of socialization have lost most of their strength. Political discourse tends to focus on citizenship when referring to the failure to achieve integration among the youth of the inner cities (*incivilités, fracture sociale, zones de non droit, dangers du communautarisme, atteintes à la laïcité*). This problem of political identity is particularly relevant in France, where the nation-state has been defined by republican and universalistic values without reference to cultural or ethnic identity. The citizen is a member of the state, defined by his or her political rights and duties. But this formal definition of equality of rights does not easily account for inequalities of opportunity, social conditions, and access to rights and their collective expression. Antidiscrimination measures, imposed by the Treaty of Amsterdam in 1997 (Article 13), have been difficult to implement, given the French focus on formal political rights. The question of discrimination is particularly acute for Muslim second-generation immigrants from former colonies, who are thought of as outside the social contract, of dubious allegiance, and badly integrated.

The concept of second generation is very French, although the social phenomenon itself is difficult to label with any specificity due to the long-term settlement of immigrant populations mostly from the Maghreb. *Générations issues de l'immigration, jeunes d'origine étrangère, franco-maghrébins, jeunes des banlieues, beurs and beurettes*-all these terms have been used in the vast literature dealing with this subject. In fact, the term "second generation" does not neatly reflect the three characteristics which define immigrants: foreigners (first) who have migrated (second) for the purpose of seeking work (third) and whose legitimacy is dependent on this condition. How do immigrants define themselves? There have been several different phases with respect to the expression of identity: advocating for the right to difference (SOS racisme, 1985) and then the right to inclusion (France Plus, 1989); emphasizing a collective identity as Muslims (such as the recent party Muslims of France led by Abdelkader Latrèche), as French willing to be politically represented and to participate in the political system (electoral list *motivé(e)s* in Toulouse in 2002), as women of immigrant origin (*nanas beurs in the 1990s or ni putes ni soumises* today), or as members of an ethnic community (such as the Berbers). The term "*beur*" is itself a variation of the slang for "Arab" and is considered a Parisian word, not used in Lyons or Marseilles.

The 1981-1990 period was a turning point for the emergence of immigrants in French politics. Due to the right to form associations granted to foreigners in 1981 (some of them were still of foreign nationality in this period), under pressure from the National Front (which was suggesting immigrants lacked a proper sense of allegiance), and owing to the general difficulties they faced in life (the *galère*) and the insecurity of inner cities, immigrants found new forms of expression in political life. They created new social roles such as cultural mediators in urban areas and pursued interests based on collective identity (*citoyenneté de residence* and local political rights for their parents, a claim to both French and Muslim heritage, the abolition of *double peine* for persons with foreign citizenship sentenced for crimes committed in France and then deported to their countries of origin, and the fight against discrimination by the police, at work, and in terms of housing). The denial of political eligibility for immigrants has led some to call for the creation of political quotas (with the mobilization in February 2004 around Mohammed Dib in Seine-Saint Denis).

Another challenge that has arisen in French politics is the creation of "a French Islam." With 4 million Muslims, most of whom are from the Maghreb, France has the largest proportion of Muslims in its population of any European country. Attempts at bringing about an institutionalization of Islam began at the end of the 1980s and were aimed at making it more compatible with a secularized country—illustrated in the controversy over the wearing of headscarves, which first arose in 1989 and led eventually to the decision to prohibit headscarves at school by law. Most of the roughly 1,500 Islamic associations in France are subsidized by Morocco or Saudi Arabia. The two largest organizations, the Union of Islamic Organizations of France (UOIF) and the National Federation of French Muslims (FNMF), have obtained representation in the French Council of the Muslim Faith (CFCM) created in 2003. The visibility of Islam in public life is often viewed as a failure of integration, and the Montesquieu-like question of how can one be French and Muslim is raised in relation to the presence of mosques, new regulations mandating imams in jails and hospitals, the creation of separate Muslim sections in cemeteries, and the establishment of halal slaughterhouses.

As a rule, the overwhelming majority of French Muslims are politically loyal, with the exception of a very small minority who have been involved in terrorist activities (such as Khaled Kelkal in 1995 and Zacharias Moussaoui, the presumed twentieth pilot of 11 September 2001). Even if the failure of integration can lead to radical Islamism, the political challenge posed by securitization efforts stems in large part from the image of Islam as a religion of poor, colonized people, unable to adapt to modern ways of life. Suburbs where republican laws seem to no longer apply, a culture of violence and ethnic conflict encouraged by local *caïds*, the presence of transnational drug networks, and forced marriages of girls in the countries of origin are more the result of social exclusion and institutional discrimination than an illustration of a lack of integration, since most immigrants are very well integrated into the social group to which they belong, the ethnic working class.

The French debate about integration has been a misdirected one, focusing on the character of young people of Maghrebi origin without asking if the French model of *exception française* is sufficiently inclusive. The neocolonial approach to policy related to ethnic minorities, contradictory to republican values but nevertheless frequently applied, has led to various forms of ambiguity. These ambiguities have changed integration issues, in a bilateral dialogue and conflict (of love and hate) with French of Maghrebi origin, that consists of delegating to local mediators the management of collective identities and leading to perverse effects such as *communautarisation par défaut*.

The French approach differs from the approach to integration policy elsewhere, due to its close connection with the old assimilation strategy. The most appropriate term to describe the current French policy approach might be "living together," an objective of most European countries even though the precise nature of the tools employed may be different: in France, the territorialized policies of integration characterize the French model, while other countries prefer antidiscrimination policies, multiculturalism, or the granting of local political rights. The underlying aims are the same, however: social cohesion, political inclusion, participation, recognition of cultural identity, and social peace.

Part 2

Status Quo of Integration in an Enlarged European Union: Models and Indicators for Successful Integration

EUROPEAN COMMISSION
DIRECTORATE-GENERAL JUSTICE AND HOME AFFAIRS

Directorate A
Unit A/2 Immigration and Asylum

MIGRAPOL 21 rev1

6th Immigration and Asylum Committee
7 April 2003

Subject: Integration of immigrants; draft final synthesis report of answers received to the Commission questionnaire (MIGRAPOL 9) on policies concerning the integration of immigrants

---

Summary:

The Commission Services have received (by March 2003) 8 replies from Member States and 9 replies from accession countries to the questionnaire MIGRAPOL 9. This document syntheses and analyses the answers received.

Action to be taken:

For approval.

Draft Synthesis Report on Policies Concerning the Integration of Immigrants

Helene Urth

Replies to the Questionnaire from Members of the Immigration and Asylum Committee

Introduction

The Commission Services have received (by January 2003) 8 replies from Member States[1] and nine replies from accession countries[2] to the questionnaire MIGRAPOL 9. The replies vary greatly as far as the amount of information and details are concerned. However, it is clear that wide differences exist in integration policies not only with regard to accession countries but certainly also within the European Union itself. Some countries do not have integration policies for newcomers as such (Ireland, Latvia, Malta), and other countries have extensive legislation in this field (The Netherlands, Finland, Denmark). In this context it is important to recall that the questionnaire does not take into account legislation or special programmes designed for the integration of refugees (some countries have extensive integration programmes for refugees but not for immigrants). On the contrary, many countries do not separate their foreign populations into refugees and immigrants when it comes to integration, and in some countries the integra-

tion programmes described apply to both categories. The replies from Member States are synthesised below, and in the Annex to this report there is a summary of the replies from accession countries.

Executive Summary

In those countries where integration policies exist, there seem to be two trends, which become apparent. Either the Member State has set out a clear legal framework for integration of immigrants and a national integration programme, or Member States have an overall policy, which is implemented via different programmes on local and regional level or programmes for special targeted areas. In all Member States there seems to be a general high level of participation of immigrants in consultative or advisory bodies, and integration policies are well monitored. The main trends, which can be deducted from the replies given by accession countries, are that many countries have only recently started looking into issues related to the integration of immigrants. All accession countries do have legislation in place regulating the conditions for obtaining residence and work permits, and they have also—as a first step towards developing an integration policy—criminalised racism and discrimination.

However, policies on integration exist only in a very limited number of countries.

Synthesis of Answers Received to the Questionnaire

I Reception of New Immigrants

1.1 Objectives of the Integration Policies

Descriptions of objectives of the integration policies vary naturally, nevertheless it seems to be the general opinion in all Member States that the main objectives of their integration policies are on the one hand to enable immigrants to function independently and be self-supportive and on the other hand enable them to participate actively in all aspects of life (cultural, social, religious, political, etc.). The Portuguese Government has defined their overall objectives to be, firstly, to combat illegal immigration and, secondly, to integrate legal immigrants.

1.2 Description of Integration Policies

One thing which becomes evident when going through all the replies is that in those countries where specific integration programmes exist the integration problems are mostly related to the relatively high unemployment rate among immigrants and ethnic minorities and to the fact that most new immigrants are persons admitted under family reunification arrangements and conversely do not have a job offer when entering the country. These programmes therefore focus very much on language learning and integration in the labour market. In other countries these problems do not seem to be paramount, and problems seem to be more related to ensuring the proper infrastructure to integrate these people, such as access to housing, social services and health care.

Finland, Denmark and The Netherlands are countries where integration programmes exist and extensive integration laws were passed back in 1998 and 1999. Similar initiatives have been launched recently in Germany. Such integration programmes—which are compulsory to a certain extent—are in most cases tailored to the specific needs of the immigrant. The immigrant is invited for an interview, where the level of qualifications, education, practical experiences and language skills are examined. On the basis of this interview it is decided which components the integration programme should consist of. In general the three main components of integration programmes are first and foremost language training, which is considered a very important element, secondly orientation courses and thirdly occupational integration measures or vocational training. The specific content of the components of the integration programmes varies. In Germany, for instance, pursuant to the new Immigration Act, new immigrants will have a legal entitlement to attend an integration course which will comprise a basic and continuation language course plus an orientation course. The orientation course is intended to provide information about the legal system, culture and history of Germany, whereas in Denmark the orientation courses are directed towards a more practical approach of getting to know the new local community. Not all Member States have given information on the length of the integration programmes, and it seems to vary, but in most cases integration programmes last 2-3 years.

In some Member States specific legislation laying down a framework for nation-wide integration programmes does not exist (Sweden, Spain and Portugal), but nevertheless substantial efforts have been made to develop a national policy to promote integration. In Sweden the Government decided in 1997 to focus more on integration, and the policy is built on mainstreaming. The point of departure is equal rights, responsibilities and opportunities for everybody, and integration permeates all policy areas and should be implemented in the everyday operations of all sectors of society. In Spain the overall national policy has identified some target areas where they find a need for improvement of access for immigrants, e.g., health care, education, naturalisation procedures, family reunification. Special targeted national programmes have been set up for migrants who risk social and labour market exclusion, and these include an interview for estimating the particular needs of the immigrant in question and then four components, which are language learning, orientation, professional training and job consulting. In Portugal, as well, a number of initiatives have been taken by the newly established High Commission for Immigration and Ethnic Minorities, which is the national body which has assumed responsibility for development for integration policies in Portugal.

1.3 Compulsory Elements
In those countries where specific integration programmes exist, they in general entail compulsory elements. Failing to participate successfully in an integration programme could in Denmark have negative consequences for renewal of residence permits. This will also be the case in Germany when the new Immigration Act enters into force. In Germany and The Netherlands a certificate of successful attendance at an integration course is issued and this may—in the case of Germany—serve to shorten the period for naturalisation from 8 to 7 years. Also in the Netherlands the new government is examining the possibility of linking successful attendance with possibilities of obtaining a permanent residence permit. The Netherlands is also examining the possibility of letting the immigrant pay a sum of money towards the integration programme and returning half of the amount after successful completion.

In those countries (Finland, Denmark, The Netherlands) where the immigrant receives an allowance or social benefits while attending the integration programme, this will be reduced if the immigrant fails to participate. However, this applies equally to nationals and immigrants in those countries where immigrants are referred to mainstream services if they fail to participate in labour market activities.

1.4 Structure of Implementing Authorities
In all Member States it is the local or regional authorities that have the competence to implement the integration policy, whereas it varies a great deal who is actually paying for the measures/ programmes. In some countries both the regional and local authorities have competence in this area, and in some cases big cities have competence as well. In Germany the State provides

the integration courses, but they are conducted by public and private supporting organisations. The nation-wide integration programme, which sets out the integration services to be offered by the different stakeholders and gives recommendations for the development of these services, is developed in co-operation between state, federal governments and local authorities, as well as social partners and civil society. In Denmark and Finland it is the local municipalities which bear the overall responsibility for offering integration programmes, but the municipalities can decide to let other public or private organisations help them in conducting the programmes.

1.5 Funding of Policies

Some countries gave exact numbers on how much money is spent on a yearly basis implementing integration policies. However, the amount varies according to the number of new arrivals and the size of the country in question, and it is therefore not possible to draw any uniform conclusions from this. It is nevertheless possible to conclude that some countries are spending large amounts on the integration of immigrants, which gives a clear indication of how important the issue is.

1.6 Possible Future Action in the Field

With the changes of governments around Europe, a number of new initiatives have been taken concerning integration. The general approach is that efforts to integrate immigrants so far have not been sufficient, and improved action and more initiatives need to be taken.

1.7 Best Practices

In the reply to the questionnaire Finland mentioned the use of integration programmes tailored to the needs of the immigrant as a good practice. If an immigrant is unemployed, an individual plan for integration into the labour market is drawn up. This individual plan takes into account, besides professional competencies, the immigrant's previous experience, education history, language, hobbies and other skills in order to find work placement. If work cannot be found immediately, the plan will suggest which actions should be taken and how—e.g., a specific course or further language courses. (A similar system exists in The Netherlands, Denmark and Sweden.)

2 Medium- to Long-term Arrangements for the Integration of Immigrants

The Member States which replied to this question generally referred to the descriptions of arrangements for newly arrived immigrants. It has therefore not been possible to synthesise the answers under every heading for this question. However, this does not mean that Member States do not have policies in place for long-term immigrants.

Immigrants who have stayed in the country for a long time are often referred to mainstream services, e.g., unemployment services, and therefore policies directed towards this group are often project-based and addressing special needs. Initiatives mentioned in the questionnaire include measures within the field of education, employment, health and welfare, housing and the promotion of immigrants' participation in social, cultural and political life. Special measures focussing on targeted groups of long-term immigrants are undertaken in many countries. In The Netherlands programmes have been set up to avoid immigrants (ethnic minorities) becoming a less privileged group in society. In Germany occupational integration, in particular for young foreign nationals and women, has been undertaken, and different anti-discrimination and integration measures supplementing the mainstream services have been implemented.

A number of Member States mention that since the mid-1970s they have supported language courses for immigrants, and in most countries this has been free of charge. For best practices see above under 1.7.

3 INTEGRATION INTO THE LABOUR MARKET

When examining measures for improvement of integration into the labour market, it appears from the answers received from the Member States that there are great differences between the countries. These differences seem to be crucial for the approach chosen to deal with this issue. In most of the countries which have replied to the questionnaire, in particular The Netherlands, Denmark, Sweden and Finland, recent immigration has not been work related, and a high unemployment rate among immigrants compared to the rest of the population in these countries therefore exists. In a country such as Ireland all immigration is work related, and this disproportionate unemployment rate does not seem to exist. All migrants coming to Ireland virtually need to have an employment offer before coming.

3.1 Planned Measures

The integration of unemployed immigrants in the labour market is promoted in all Member States through individual integration plans or job seeking plans. In a number of Member States, insertion pathways are developed for young people, and programmes focus on the exploitation of employment possibilities especially suitable for immigrants as well as the organisation of movement within the country to take up unfilled job offers. Additional resources have been granted to Public Employment Services to enable them to contribute to the integration of immigrants.

Concerning the European Employment Strategy, there are no specific national targets on the integration of immigrants in the labour market. However, in The Netherlands, specific labour market policy is aiming at halving the difference of unemployment between ethnic minorities and persons who are of Dutch origin, which amounts to reducing unemployment of ethnic minorities to 10%.

3.2 Involvement of Social Partners

In most Member States that have replied to this question, the Social Partners are involved at the national and local level in the preparation and implementation of integration measures. In Spain, for example, the Social Partners are involved in the estimate of labour shortages in the country. In Finland labour market organisations participate at a national level in the integration of immigrants mainly through advisory bodies on which they are represented.

The cost of integration measures is mainly born by public authorities, but enterprises sometimes share in training expenditures for immigrants.

3.3 Coordination with Other Authorities

Typically, regional and local authorities are responsible for the implementation of integration policies concerning immigrants. In many Member States, overall guidance is given in a national plan, and measures are carefully co-ordinated.

3.4 Best Practices

The Netherlands has in their reply to the questionnaire highlighted the "SAMEN" Act as a best practice concerning labour market integration. In The Netherlands labour market policy is supported by this act, which obliges employers with more than 35 employees to register the number of ethnic minorities employed and report yearly on efforts undertaken to promote a multicultural environment in their companies.

Concerning integration of immigrants into the labour market, experiences in Finland, The Netherlands and Denmark clearly show that on-the-job training in combination with language instruction (dual path), preferably in the very initial stage of the immigrant's stay in the country, makes it significantly easier for the immigrants to find a job on the open labour market.

4 Immigrant Participation

In almost all Member States immigrants generally have free access to social and cultural life, including free access to education. Immigrants are able to become active in the political field, in political parties, associations, societies and organisations.

Only in Denmark, The Netherlands and Sweden are immigrants allowed to vote at local elections and stand for election, typically after three years of legal residence.

4.1 Special Advisory or Consultative Bodies

Almost all countries have established special advisory bodies for immigrants at both the national and local level, although none of them has any direct decision-making competence; they are true advisory bodies. In some countries like Sweden, Denmark, The Netherlands and Germany, there is a long tradition for involving immigrants and their organisations in decision making processes.

In Portugal a Consultative Council for Immigration Matters has been created to ensure that associations representing immigrants, social partners and institutions of social solidarity participate in defining the policies of social integration, and the struggle against exclusion.

In Denmark all municipalities must establish an integration council if requested by more than 50 people. The integration council may give advisory opinions on the general effort of integration in the municipality, and up until today around 40 integration councils have been established. The members of the local integration councils elect a national Council for Ethnic Minorities, which advises the Minister of Integration on issues related to integration.

In Finland an Advisory Board for Ethnic Relations has been set up and affiliated with the Ministry of Labour. On the board both immigrants and

Finland's traditional ethnic minorities are represented, as well as different ministries and associations such as the social partners and the Finnish Red Cross. The board monitors matters related to integration and gives expert opinions.

4.2 Level of Participation
Immigrants are in almost all Member States frequently represented on the advisory bodies for immigrants. In some countries the organisations representing immigrants and ethnic minorities are checked on their representativeness. In Spain around a third or a fourth of the representatives on the advisory bodies are migrants themselves. In Denmark currently all elected members of the Council for Ethnic Minorities have an ethnic minority background.

4.3 Best Practices
Portugal has in their reply to the questionnaire highlighted the moveable booth which offers information to immigrants (Ciberbus) as a best practice. A bus has been transformed and adapted to be moved to areas of high density of immigrants and is available there for consultations on the internet, distribution of leaflets and other information. A team of three instructors able to communicate with the immigrants will assist.

5 ANTIDISCRIMINATION AND EQUALITY

All Member States are currently in a process of revising their legislation concerning anti-discrimination or enacting new legislation in order to implement the so-called article 13 directive (2000/43) on anti-discrimination.

In order to promote integration and combat racism, awareness raising campaigns and special programmes seems to be a part of the ongoing activities in almost all Member States. In some countries special initiatives have been taken as a result of preparations for the World Conference against Racism, held in Durban, South Africa, 2001. In The Netherlands a national platform has been provided to give input to a National Action Plan against Racism, in Finland a National Action Plan to Combat Racism was adopted in 2001, and in Ireland an Action Plan is also on its way. Several countries ran anti-discrimination campaigns in 2001 and some countries such as Sweden and Germany have allocated money for campaigns combating racism and promoting equality in particular for children and young people.

Several Member States also have special bodies to monitor or advise in equality or discrimination matters; e.g., in Ireland the Equality Authority provides information and advice to anyone who feels that he/she may have been discriminated against.

6 SUCCESSFUL INTEGRATION

6.1 Official Definition
No Member State has a uniform definition of integration, however they do to a certain extent agree that integration is composed of different elements and is to be looked at as a two-way process. In those countries where specific legislation for integration exists, integration may be defined within the framework of the act, but also in these cases integration is referred to as a process, which has some core elements.

The elements which are mentioned in the replies of the Member States could generally be summarised as including

- respect for fundamental values in a democratic society;
- the right to maintain his or her own cultural identity;
- rights comparable to those of EU citizens and corresponding obligations;
- active participation in all aspects of life on an equal footing (economic, social, cultural, political, civil).

6.2 Key Factors in Successful Integration

In most countries there exist no instruments for measuring integration or an established standard for successful integration. According to the replies, integration takes place gradually and proceeds differently in each individual case.

In The Netherlands the key factor for successful integration is when the immigrant is self-supportive.

6.3 Main Barriers to Integration

All Member States which have replied to the questionnaire emphasise that a major barrier for successful integration is the lack of sufficient language skills. The lack of education or formal skills is also mentioned as a barrier together with the difficulties in assessing and approving immigrants qualifications— e.g., recognition of foreign exams and diplomas. Some countries also mention that one of the major barriers to successful integration is the fact the immigrant is unemployed, thereby implying that employment is the best possible way of integrating immigrants in society. The Netherlands recognises that poor knowledge of the language can also leave the

children of ethnic minorities in backward positions. Finland mentions that the attitude of the population has a strong impact on how welcome the immigrants feel as members of the Finnish society and that racism and discrimination play an important role when it comes to integration.

6.4 Best Practices

In Germany migrant organisations and associations play an important role in promoting integration. Organisations run by and for foreign nationals carry out highly committed work in many areas. In Germany this system of inclusion and co-operation has proved its worth in tackling particular problem areas in integration such as the naturalisation of foreign nationals, advice on the law in relation to foreign nationals, integration of women, girls and single parents, tackling segregation and co-existence in residential areas, intercultural conflict management and the integration of young Muslims.

7 Monitoring Integration Models

7.1 Special Monitoring Bodies

In almost all Member States monitoring plays an important role, and special schemes for monitoring have been set up. All Member States have one way or the other been monitoring the integration process, and many countries give special yearly reports, which are discussed in the national parliaments. In those countries where special legislation on integration exists, progress on implementation or revision of legislation is discussed by Parliament.

Denmark has tried to develop special integration indicators on how integration can be measured, and in The Netherlands a special integration monitor (research with facts and figures) gives an overview of the position of ethnic minorities on three dimensions: social-structural, social-cultural, and political-institutional levels. Finland examines employment rates, living conditions, education, position of children, young people and women, and social services provided.

In Germany, pursuant to the new Immigration Act, a special body of experts will be set up, and it will have the task of observing domestic capacities for reception and integration and the current trends in migratory movements.

7.2 Responsibility for the Monitoring Process
In all Member States, competence to monitor the integration process is decentralised to local and regional or city authorities, as well as responsibility for implementation of integration policies. But as mentioned above, some countries discuss in Parliament the integration progress in their country, and national ministers often have the overall responsibility for integration policies and therefore also naturally for the monitoring process and evaluation of policies to ensure the desired results are obtained.

ANNEX

DRAFT SYNTHESIS REPORT ON POLICIES IN ACCESSION COUNTRIES CONCERNING INTEGRATION OF IMMIGRANTS

REPLIES TO THE QUESTIONNAIRE FROM ACCESSION COUNTRIES

INTRODUCTION

For the purpose of this questionnaire on integration of immigrants, 9 accession countries replied to the questionnaire.[3] The replies from accession countries vary even more in length and detail than replies from Member States. Most

countries found the questionnaire far too detailed or not relevant to describe their policies. Most countries therefore chose to give a more general overview of recent developments and policies in the field of integration or just replied to the more relevant questions. In light of the replies received, it therefore seemed more appropriate to give a brief summary of the replies to some of the more relevant questions than going through the replies question by question, as it was done with regard to the Member States. This approach will not give justification to all 9 replies received in terms of details given; it will, however, give a more general overview of the efforts undertaken in the field of integration in the accession countries.

In relation to the accession countries it must also be recalled that the questionnaire does not deal with the integration of refugees and special efforts taken in this regard.

DESCRIPTION OF INTEGRATION POLICIES

For all countries there is legislation governing residence permits and work permits for immigrants, and most countries also have legislation by which immigrants are entitled to some basic social rights and benefits.

Czech Republic, Slovak Republic, Romania and Bulgaria describe, for example, their extensive legislation determining when residence and work permits can be granted to immigrants and under which conditions. The starting point for any policy on integration of foreigners is security of residence, and countries cannot even begin to establish successful integration policies unless the persons who are the objects of that policy have security of residence. This is therefore a very important first step towards developing an integration policy.

When it comes to actual integration policies and programmes, only a very few countries have policies or programmes in place.

Latvia clearly indicates that they do not have any programmes related to the integration of immigrants, because up to now the number of new immigrants is very low (approximately 0.5% of the population), and a part of these people are already successfully integrated, as they have lived in Latvia as citizens of the former Soviet Union and have now returned. The same more or less applies to Malta, which does not receive any new immigrants but only a few returning migrants who have worked outside of Malta for some time and decided to return. Malta has therefore not found it necessary to develop an integration policy, and migrants, who are Maltese citizens or married to Maltese citizens, are in general referred to mainstream services.

Romania mentions that they have only just very recently started to develop a national policy and special programmes for the integration of immigrants. Their new policy, which has not been finally decided upon, may include language training, professional training, information courses regarding rights and obligations of the immigrant, history classes and facilitation of meetings with Romanian citizens. A public awareness raising campaign will also be launched.

Another approach has been taken by, for example, Estonia, which declares that it does not have any policies for newly arrived immigrants; however, integration policies exist. In opposition to most other countries, the population of Estonia as a whole is defined as the target group for integration policies rather than immigrants. The main objective of the integration policy is to remove the remains of repellent attitudes towards ethnic minorities. Some of the major cities in Estonia have also adopted their own integration programmes, but

Assembly is guaranteed to "important and long-standing minorities." Moreover, in several countries (e.g., Latvia, Lithuania, and Romania) minorities form part of a national organization that must be consulted in the decision-making process on matters affecting minorities. The case of Slovakia might be particularly illuminating in this respect. Since the early 1990s, national minorities there have had permanent representation in the parliament. In November 1998, the state administration created a structure to address the problems of minorities, with provisions for their direct participation in decision-making processes. A deputy prime minister for human rights, national minorities, and regional development was appointed. The government has set up the Council for National Minorities and Ethnic Groups, through which the representatives of minorities have a major voice.

Isolated during much of the post-World War II period, Central European countries are now in the preliminary stages of an inflow of immigrants from outside the region, which leads in many cases to the formation of new and different diasporas. These new groups of immigrants (e.g., Vietnamese, Chinese, and Armenians) arrive through various channels-illegally, through temporary stay, through arranged marriages, as entrepreneurs, or through permanent settlement. The communication networks and the very high mobility of Chinese migrants (particularly vibrant in Hungary) enable them to maintain a transnational community within which they can easily shift from one country to another within Central Europe and elsewhere and can assume various social roles (e.g., from student to trader to worker), if doing so is economically expedient. Similarly, Vietnamese immigrants also carry on lively economic activities and express feelings of well-being within the Central European region (in Poland and the Czech Republic especially).

In contrast to the Chinese and Vietnamese, Armenian immigrants arrived in Central Europe mainly as asylum seekers. Their arrival was a result of the convulsions that shook the Caucasus, beginning in the early 1990s. However, contrary to other asylum seekers, who treat Central Europe mainly as a short stopover on the way to Western Europe, Armenians extended their stay and, in many cases, settled in the region. In response to the undefined status of the large but undocumented number of immigrants from Armenia, Poland, which hosts a significant group of Armenian refugees and exiles, launched a regularization program in 2003 aimed at bringing about the full integration of those persons (as well as other foreigners) resident in Poland since 1997.

Another recent problem has to do with trafficking and smuggling of migrants through Central Europe into Western Europe. In the 1990s, the Central European region became one of the major transit areas in Europe for hundreds of thousands of smuggled persons, mainly from India, Afghanistan, Sri Lanka, and Bangladesh. A large majority of those persons who reached Western Europe, or who were apprehended in transit countries or readmitted there from the West, have decided to seek refugee status in Central Europe and consequently have become immigrants there (many of them illegally). As yet, it is hard to draw any broad conclusions for the region regarding either the features of immigration or the reactions of government and local communities to this phenomenon.

There is no common approach regarding immigrant or ethnic minority integration policy in the Central European countries. Governments in those countries new to immigration are gradually recognizing that many newly arrived foreigners might, in fact, remain in their countries. They have thus (to varying degrees over the last few years) begun to develop policy and other responses on integration and community relations, along with policies regulating the admission of returning nationals, immigrants, and refugees. The development of integration policies is a part of, and profits from, changes in these countries' overall legal frameworks, including constitutional changes. Provisions outlawing discrimination on the basis of race and skin color, national or ethnic origin, and religious practice are being inserted into national laws in many of these countries. Specific integration programs are, if at all, primarily designed for "returning" nationals, deportees, or refugees. Several countries are reviewing their existing legislation on nationality and citizenship, not only to respond to the immigration situation, but also to address the issue of national minorities and stateless persons. In some newly created states, the process of developing an independent citizenship policy is still underway and has not yet been finalized.

The approach taken to integration in most countries of Central Europe can probably best be characterized as selective. Certain specific groups of immigrants or limited aspects of integration are being targeted first, and as a rule the criteria of small scale and low cost are applied. Therefore, integration programs start from small groups of immigrants, usually refugees, and narrowly defined areas, such as courses in the official language of the host country. There are several reasons for this, primarily having to do with the many competing priorities and generally low level of affluence (and the scarcity of resources) in Central European countries.

In relative terms, the Czech Republic hosts the largest number of immigrants in the region, and it is by all means further along in the development of integration policy than any other Central European country. The programs on integration of foreigners in the Czech Republic were in the course of the 1990s directed towards three main groups of immigrants: persons who were granted asylum, persons with the status of temporary protection, and re-emigrants. As far as the integration of compatriots is concerned, during the period of 1991 to 1993, over 1,800 ethnic Czechs returned to the Czech Republic from Ukraine—largely from the region affected by the Chernobyl nuclear accident. In 1991 the Czech government offered residence in the Czech Republic to all those in the affected region who could show Czech descent. They were allowed to immigrate with all members of their families. In 1995 and 1996 some five hundred ethnic Czechs arrived from Kazakhstan and other countries. Their resettlement was organized, regulated, and supported by governmental bodies, and they were provided with transport, accommodation, and other financial, health, and social assistance. They generally settled in small communities in the countryside or in small towns. The first group of ethnic Czech resettlers from Ukraine might also be termed ecological migrants.

A turning point in the integration policy of the Czech Republic came in 1999, when the government adopted a resolution on the Principles of the Alien Integration Strategy. These principles create the conditions for goal-directed and systematic development of "good" relationships between communities and represent an indispensable precondition for adequate protection of rights of immigrants within the Czech Republic's territory. In 2000 the government of the Czech Republic adopted another important document dealing with the principles: the Alien Integration Strategy in the Czech Republic. The aim of the strategy has been the gradual harmonization of Czech legislation with that of the European Community and the development of a common integration policy, equalizing the legal status of long-term and legally residing foreigners in the Czech Republic with that enjoyed by Czech citizens themselves. Improving efforts aimed at promoting better relations between foreigners and Czech nationals, establishing a basis for mutual cooperation of all institutions involved in immigration and integration, and supporting measures directed at combating illegal migration have been the other main goals of the strategy.

ENDNOTES

1   Between 1997 and 2002, 45,300 Romanians were repatriated from Moldova.
2   Numbering 1.6 million to 6 million, depending on the estimate.

Conceptual and Political Approaches to Integration: A Mediterranean Perspective

Anna Terrón i Cusí

Southern European countries—most notably Spain, Portugal, Italy, and Greece-are relatively "new" immigration countries, and there is no doubt that their integration mechanisms, legal and otherwise, are not as advanced as those of the "older" immigration countries. France offers the clearest contrast in this regard. For several decades, a large share of the French population has been of foreign origin, many having emigrated from France's former colonies. As a result, integration policies have tended to focus on persons (and their families) long established on French soil, rather than on helping newcomers become acquainted with their new societal and cultural environment. For the French, integration has been linked with naturalization: between 1990 and 1999 alone, over one million "foreigners" acquired French nationality. At present, French integration policy is focused mainly on fighting racism and xenophobia and on granting all French people the right to enjoy all individual and collective rights.

In those southern European countries where immigration is a more recent phenomenon, however, the influx of new immigrants has radically altered the landscape of certain parts of their territories and cities over the course of the last few years. Not that long ago, Spain, Italy, and Portugal were net exporters of workers, notably towards northern European countries, and they faced serious unemployment problems. The flow of migrants towards these now relatively prosperous countries has taken local populations by surprise, a phenomenon due in large part to their failure to grasp the extent of their own relative well-being. As emigration countries themselves, they were lacking proper immigration legislation. They have therefore made successive efforts at creating legal norms for dealing with the new situation. Unfortunately, integration concerns have taken a backseat to more pressing concerns, while other issues have been even less developed in legal and societal terms. There is, for instance, not only no tradition of political asylum in these "recent" democracies, the issue also lacks clear definition within the current political landscape.

The most noteworthy case thus far is the Italian law passed in March 1998. It sets the main guidelines for integration, including new and enhanced responsibilities granted to regional authorities, the establishment of heavy fines for discrimination, and the creation of a national fund of 60 million euro annually for the promotion of integration activities. The law emphasizes both coordination and decentralization: an integration committee has been created with a view to outlining yearly priorities, and to harmonizing the efforts of the state, the regions, and the private sector.

The Spanish picture is less clear. Spain's new law, passed after an intense national debate in early 2000, was meant to deal both with immigration as well as with the integration of migrants. And yet the subsequently approved Global Program to Regulate and Coordinate Foreign Residents' Affairs and Immigration in Spain (GRECO), containing the operative aspects of this task, is still not operational. This plan seems to consist of a package of comprehensive, well-intentioned measures without practical substantiation. Portugal and Greece have made even more recent efforts to provide the necessary legal frameworks to enhance the integration of migrants.

For each of these European Mediterranean countries, national history plays a meaningful role in shaping migration trends. A considerable number of migrants originate from the former colonies and dependent territories. The picture here is very mixed, as is demonstrated by the cases of Spain and Latin America, Portugal and its former colonies in Africa, and France and Algeria. In each of these cases, there are differences in the attitudes and perceptions on the part of native citizens and the state. For some, this kind of immigration is more desirable, as newcomers already know the local language upon arrival and sometimes even share cultural norms, including religion. Spain, for instance, has chosen to give priority to citizens with these characteristics. For others, these societal features have not had any impact on policy.

The geographical location of Spain, Italy, and Greece should also be taken into account. These three countries lie in relative proximity to nations in the southern Mediterranean whose wealth and income levels are far below European standards. The resulting situation is not easy to manage. The continuous arrival of *sans papiers* on their shores creates a sense of vulnerability, although the real victims of this situation are those who flee their countries for the European Union. Often, the reactions of those states to which the immigrants are fleeing serve only to increase the public's perception of threat. This is not surprising when one considers that these countries lie at the border between two Mediterranean worlds—European and Muslim-Arab— and that the conflict reigning between these two worlds throughout history has been dramatically exacerbated by recent events.

The media has always paid close attention to racist incidents of varying gravity. At the same time, strong solidarity networks have been developed to receive migrants in southern Spain, Italy, and Greece. Not directly exposed to the pressures of the media, these networks have worked consistently and quietly. The high rate of victimization among those trying to reach European shores is a taboo subject for the countries of origin and a source of widespread unease among local citizens, who watch powerlessly as this tragedy repeats itself with insistent regularity.

One last factor to be taken into account when assessing attitudes and perceptions is that these countries are highly homogeneous in ethnic, cultural, and religious terms. Spain offers an extremely clear case in this respect, while Portugal serves as a partial exception given its colonial past. Consequently, there is a lack of solid, well-established models to manage societal differences.

Again, approaches to integration vary according to these different historic and conceptual frameworks. Thus, France's integration policy is based on its legislation on nationality; both concepts are closely related, and naturalization is the primary means of integration. In taking on French nationality, immigrants gain the same rights and obligations as all other citizens, including participation in political and societal institutions. Persons originating in French Overseas Departments and Territories—who already have French nationality—and those from former French colonies are favored over other immigrants with regard to naturalization, family reunification, and employment. French immigration policy is generally characterized as assimilationist, with a secular state based on the consent of free citizens and not, for example, on common ethnic ancestry. This means that the civil rights as laid down in the French Declaration of the Rights of Man apply to every citizen, and every citizen can exercise these rights. Citizenship and nationality are one and the same. Minority does not exist as a legal concept, and the formation of such minorities is seen as the failure of integration. Individuals fail to be absorbed into society on account of certain characteristics such as national origin or skin color, or they make such entry impossible by permanently clinging to these characteristics. This leads to segregation and social disintegration.

The remaining southern European countries take a rather different, less fundamental approach. In these countries, the core of immigration legislation is based on assumptions and considerations linked with migrant labor and economic activity. Naturalization is a secondary means of integration, since it is assumed—in accordance with the general European belief and practice— that migrants will wish to, or otherwise be forced to, return to their countries once this economic activity ends. Family reunification is nonetheless a basic right granted to legal residents. With the concept of assimilation long discarded, the debate is now centered on notions like tolerance and interculturalism or multiculturalism, though the respective meanings of these terms are not always clear. In some specific instances—like the Spanish policy towards Latin Americans—naturalization is relatively easy and is the fastest way to integration.

Managing religious differences remains difficult, however, most notably when it comes to dealing with Muslims. Most countries face similar experiences, with both state administrations and local populations finding it hard to accept different religious centers, such as mosques. It is unclear whether this stems from a reluctance to allow religious practices that differ from those of the majority or from a desire to defend a hard-won secular state.

The Mediterranean countries of Europe (France excepted) share certain common denominators with regard to integration:

- Their legislation puts more emphasis on the management of migration flows than on reception and integration.

- Immigration is always present on the political agenda in some form or another. There is a lack of appropriate terminology to refer to the integration of migrants of different origins. Terms like immigration and integration serve to cover the whole range of issues. This will unquestionably change when these populations settle permanently—as is already taking place—and progressively become nationals.
- There is a great deal of pressure on lower administrative levels to take measures to improve social integration and coexistence (for example, with respect to regional and local governments, the public school system, and social services).
- There is strong competition for resources between newcomers and the weakest segments of the local population in those countries where social benefits are among the lowest in Europe.

The only migratory model present in southern European societies derives from the historic memory of their own migration towards richer, more industrialized European countries in the decades after World War II. Nevertheless, attempts to draw comparisons between this experience with that of the current wave of newcomers are generally rejected. Although southern European migrants also left home to search for employment abroad, the idea that today's newcomers are responding to the same needs and patterns does not enjoy widespread public acceptance. This subjective perception is reinforced by the existence of a black labor market

employing many migrants, some of them without documents.

Any attempt to build a solid and effective EU policy in the field of migration must go hand in hand with efforts to improve integration. The European Year against Racism and Xenophobia, 1997, was a landmark in EU efforts to combine both lines of policy development. Moreover, it pointed to an interesting turn of events, namely that the promotion of human rights in Europe also stimulates greater attention to migration-related issues. In 2000, the European Commission undertook new initiatives toward this end, adopting a package of measures to fight discrimination and social exclusion. This package against discrimination consists of two directives: one implementing the principle of equal treatment irrespective of racial or ethnic origin and the other establishing a general framework for equal treatment in employment and occupation. Another landmark was the creation of the Community Action Programme to Combat Discrimination (2001-2006), which dedicates EU funding to transnational actions aimed at developing the capacity and effectiveness of key players involved in combating discrimination. This is to be achieved by strengthening the means of action available to responsible organizations through greater exchange of information and best practices and through increased networking at the European level, all the while taking into account the specific characteristics of different forms of discrimination.

European Mediterranean countries share a common vision of the global dimension of migration, as well as a strong demand that measures be taken at the EU level. EU countries have agreed to establish a zone of freedom, security, and justice in the European Union that includes, among other main issues, common migration policies and common individual rights. Progress in this endeavor should pave the way for advancement in other areas as well, such as in European measures against exclusion and the creation of norms on social integration. Those countries now facing increased levels of immigration could benefit greatly from such norms, as well as from the exchange of information and best practices with those European countries that possess more extensive experience in dealing with integration issues.

Conceptual and Political Approaches to Integration: A Scandinavian Perspective

Ulf Hedetoft

Background and Commonalities

The Scandinavian[1] countries are small, highly developed nation-states, which perceive of themselves as possessing a high degree of cultural homogeneity, social trust, and political consensus, and traditionally cultivate a self-image of tolerance, friendliness, and internationalism. Since World War II, Scandinavians have developed a very specific form of universalistic welfare state, based on a high level of public assistance (health care, education, unemployment benefits, old-age pensions, etc.), accessible to all citizens and others resident in those countries. These welfare state structures entail both a significant degree of state regulation and extensive intervention in the public and private realm. Unlike the systems used in many continental countries, they produce significant levels of socioeconomic redistribution across social groups and classes. These structures are costly to operate and are based on ideological conceptions of social egalitarianism and universalism (as opposed to freedom and initiative), but also on the assumption that citizens earn their entitlements by contributing (through taxation) to the maintenance and growth of the national wealth through a lifetime of active work. In the Scandinavian context, cultural

acceptance and access to political rights are thus intertwined, with equality interpreted to mean both cultural similarity and political sameness (with respect to civic rights).

The keys to understanding the politics of immigration or integration and its conceptual foundations in the Scandinavian welfare states lie, on the one hand, in the prevailing concepts of cultural homogeneity and, on the other, in the universalistic structures and ideological presumptions that underlie these welfare systems. (The same is also crucial for understanding the major differences between the EU Member States.) Immigration has consistently been regarded as a responsibility of the state, which has set up formalized integration programs offering courses in language, civics, and history, and which provides for the same (or at least similar) levels of public assistance to immigrants and native citizens alike. It should be noted, however, that the continued acceptance of refugees from the late 1970s onward was a result of efforts to comply with international conventions and ran counter to the official and still active freeze on immigration resulting from the oil crisis in the early 1970s.

Emphasis thus far has been on trying to acculturate immigrants as speedily as possible by means of public control and regulation, as well as on extending egalitarian universalism to cover both native-born citizens and newcomers. In this sense, the welfare state has been viewed as an opportunity and an instrument for smooth integration.

Over time, however, these two historical staples of Scandinavian societies (homogeneity and equality) have increasingly come to be seen as obstacles to integration as immigrants increasingly came to be seen as an unwelcome burden; cultural assimilation revealed itself to be more difficult than originally imagined; calls for multicultural policies grew louder; and native-born citizens and political actors came to realize the extensive financial burden that newcomers placed on the welfare system.

These developments have led to an increase in negative immigrant stereotyping: refugees are routinely branded as "welfare scroungers" or "refugees of convenience," who illegitimately take advantage of a system never intended for their benefit.

Concurrently, the relatively high level of welfare benefits and the overall approach to integration currently operating seems to work as a barrier to the integration of immigrants into the labor market, since many immigrants stand to gain little or nothing in terms of real income by getting a job; the state-regulated induction programs seem to have a pacifying effect and often impede geographical mobility; the close-knit nature of Scandinavian societies tends to exclude culturally distinct immigrants from the social and informational networks that are frequently the gateway to participation in both the labor market

and in civic and political institutions; and the readiness to accept and utilize the social and educational skills immigrants have to offer is generally rather low (especially among employers). These skills (e.g., bilingualism) are frequently stigmatized as an obstacle to, rather than a means for, better integration.

DIFFERENCES AND DIVERGENT OPTIONS

Although the context and political-ideological presumptions are relatively similar across Scandinavia, there are nevertheless notable differences between the three countries. These can be discerned in four salient and to a large extent interconnected areas: first, the composition and size of the immigrant population; second, the financial structure of the welfare state, particularly the distribution of the tax burden; third, political acceptance of cultural diversity and international humanitarian obligations toward refugees; and fourth, the structure of labor markets, qualifications, and wages.

With respect to the first area, the composition and size of the immigrant population, depending on the precise statistical categories applied, the size of the immigrant population in Finland is now around 2% of the total population, while in Denmark and Sweden it is in the 7% to 10% range. This indicates that, for a number of reasons, Finland has been a closed, inward-directed society for a longer period than either Denmark or Sweden. Finland did not start to receive economic migrants or refugees until after the end of the Cold War, and the size of the migrant population is currently at a level similar to that in Denmark in 1980. Since numbers do matter in immigration politics, this means that public debate and the formulation of public policies in Finland have been much less concerned with migration issues than in either Denmark or Sweden. The latter two countries, despite being relatively recent immigration countries, have experience with immigration and migration-related policies going back to the late 1960s, when guest workers started to arrive from Turkey, Pakistan, and, in particular, the former Yugoslavia. Finnish experience in this area has mainly been directed at problems associated with the Swedish-speaking minority in the South (and related migratory flows between Finland and Sweden) and the Sami population in the North. Moreover, since 1990, the main immigrant groups have been Russians and Estonians, many of them so-called ethnic Finns or *Ingermannlanders* (comparable to ethnic Germans in Eastern Europe) engaged in what officially is designated return migration. There are currently many other ethnic groups in Finland (Somalis are the largest among the non-Europeans), but they are all very small and are not seen to constitute a challenge to the welfare state or to Finnish national identity.

The significant differences in the second area, the financial structure of the welfare state, relate to Denmark and Sweden. In both countries, the welfare state demands a very high level of taxation. But the financial burden imposed on private corporations in the form of taxes and duties is more substantial in Sweden than in Denmark, where a heavier onus is placed on the taxation of private citizens while corporate taxes remain lower. This indicates that Denmark may constitute a more fertile breeding ground for negative welfare-based stereotypes of immigrants, since the extra costs associated with the extension of welfare benefits to non-Danes or new Danes—costs currently estimated to be between 1.5 and 2 billion euro annually—are carried directly by the private taxpayer.

Denmark and Sweden also evince a notable difference in the third area, political acceptance of cultural diversity and international humanitarian obligations toward refugees, as well (with Finland leaning toward the Swedish model). In spite of these countries' homogeneous ethnic compositions, political strategies and preferences relative to cultural diversity and multicultural policies have differed markedly. Whereas the Danish approach insists that Denmark is a country of cultural and historical homogeneity and refuses to implement multicultural discourses and policies, Sweden has gradually come to define itself as a multiethnic nation-state. Despite recent rifts and controversies, there is still extensive consensus across the Swedish political spectrum that immigration is something to be welcomed, that discrimination is morally reprehensible, and that it is wrong to canvass voters or seek public sympathy for an anti-immigrant platform. Hence, unlike in Denmark, there is no anti-immigrant party represented in the Swedish Parliament—though this is often no longer the case in local and municipal councils.

In Denmark, migration issues have, during the course of the 1990s, come to be placed squarely at the center of politics, both as hotly contested issues in their own right and as issues around which other debates (domestic and international) have clustered (e.g., supplementary cash benefits, international security issues, employment policies, European integration issues). Furthermore, the Danish media has played a more divisive role in the formulation of policy and the shaping of public opinion than in either Sweden or Finland. Inflammatory imagery in the media there, where "foreigners" are regularly portrayed as criminals, welfare abusers, or a threat to Danish culture and identity, has worked to the detriment of interethnic harmony. This has made for a polarized climate of debate unconducive to the formulation of a balanced integration policy.

The status of the Roma in the three countries may be taken as representative of the two different models: in Sweden (and now also in Finland), the Roma have gained the status of an accepted ethnic minority with appropriate political representation and civic rights. Not so in Denmark, which does not formally recognize any ethnicity other than Danishness—with the exception of the German-speaking minority in South Jutland and the extraterritorial citizens in Greenland and the Faeroe Islands, who are represented in the Danish Folketing.

Concerning the fourth area (the structure of labor markets, qualifications, and wages), immigrants and refugees—particularly the first-generation cohort—in general and as compared with the indigenous population, are poorly integrated into the labor market. Those who have managed to get jobs receive, on average, lower wages. This is true for all three countries. It is also true that the high level of welfare benefits tends to work as a disincentive to employment, because the economic benefits of working are often marginal since the gap between welfare payments and the minimum wage is insignificant. That said, the situation in this regard seems to be most acute in Denmark, where both the employment frequency (47% as compared to 76% of the indigenous population) and the occupational frequency (53% as compared to 80%) are markedly lower among immigrants. This is particularly pronounced as regards female employment, where Denmark otherwise ranks high in international comparisons. The average income for immigrants is 84% that of the indigenous population. However, the employment frequency has improved since 1994, as second- and third-generation immigrants become better integrated than their parents and grandparents, and younger people better than older ones. Importantly, there is a direct correlation between educational skills and the level of integration in terms of both employability and political participation as well as perceptions of social acceptance.

Another difference may be—although this has still to be conclusively demonstrated—that Denmark, more than the other two countries, contains an industrial sector with few remaining jobs for unskilled workers—as well as a trade union structure which has jealously guarded the privileges of indigenous members. Both these factors have worked as barriers to the successful integration of immigrants into the labor market—an area that has increasingly been perceived as a panacea for dealing with the integration dilemma.

There has been gradual movement in recent years in all three countries—though most conspicuously in Denmark—away from the old concept of integration (i.e., integrating immigrants into and by means of welfare state strategies and controlled induction programs) and toward a concept more clearly informed by liberal and individualistic thinking. This approach ascribes more significance than hitherto to labor market integration and ethnic entrepreneurship strategies. Along with this trend (again most markedly in Denmark) have come increased references to duty and demand, which challenge egalitarian and humanistic discourse. Immigrants are in many ways treated as second-class citizens, and political actors favor a linkage between restricted entry and successful integration. Nevertheless, there is still widespread reluctance on the part of political elites (less so among business leaders) to couple the sensitive refugee question too closely with that of future demographics and the predictable need to import skilled labor in the future.

LESSONS REGARDING THE WELFARE STATE-IMMIGRATION NEXUS

The most important lesson has to do with the social carrying capacity of the existing welfare system. While the welfare state is excellent at receiving and caring for refugee immigrants, it is vulnerable when the public's humanitarian consensus reaches its cultural limits and fragile when it comes to integrating immigrants into the labor market, the educational system, or civic/political institutions. Even in Sweden, which has gone furthest toward defining itself as a multicultural society, the success rate in these areas is at best only marginally higher than in Denmark.

There are three kinds of major barriers: political, cultural, and economic. Politically, the welfare state depends on a long history of "vertical trust" between state and society—a bond now seen to be threatened by large-scale immigration. Culturally, the welfare system engenders a host of negative immigrant stereotypes, all based on the suspicion that the newcomers may not be "real refugees." These negative images, in turn, provide material for both the national media and populist politicians to portray immigrants generally as "a problem." And in economic terms, there is a discrepancy between the skills structure of the labor market and that of most immigrants—which is not surprising, since the majority have entered as refugees and not as economic migrants.

Political, cultural, and economic factors also interact with one another. Compared with the minimum wage levels, the level of welfare support serves as a disincentive to employment. Employer unwillingness to hire immigrants is partly due to cultural considerations of social cohesion and linguistic interaction in the workplace. Assumptions of ethnocultural homogeneity inspire assimilationist strategies and are an obstacle to the acceptance of difference and the institutional elasticity required for successful integration, and government-controlled induction programs have sometimes developed into social incubators, insulating immigrants from society rather than preparing them for it. It would seem that the more extensive and universal the social benefits—and the more regulated the educational institutions and the labor market—the more difficult it is for immigrants to enter these institutions and, subsequently, the labor market on an equal footing and in the same proportions as the indigenous populations. Thus, in the Scandinavian welfare states, the core value of equality impedes not only more liberal integration measures, but to some extent also engenders its own inequalities and disparities—especially since these societies have difficulty coping adequately with cultural and social differences that fall outside the parameters of the traditional political compact between government and citizens.

ASSESSMENTS AND RECOMMENDATIONS

The problems that the Scandinavian welfare states now face in terms of integrating immigrants are rooted in two interconnected phenomena: First, this type of nation believes that its viability and stability depend on it being both culturally homogeneous and politically autonomous—neither of which apply any longer. Second, policies of entry and integration have been inadequately geared to distinguishing between different categories of immigrants (economic migrants versus refugees; immigrants with varying educational, religious, and geographic backgrounds; male versus female immigrants; and so forth) and have also been unprepared for the increase in the number of asylum seekers.

Both problem areas are linked to the challenges posed to traditional welfare states by both global developments and EU integration. All EU Member States, not least the Scandinavian countries, need to find new avenues toward functional cohesion, to adapt their policies to less neatly bounded ethnopolitical structures, and to cope with diversity in ways that promote intercultural trust—within each nation-state as well as across the EU cultural landscape. This is obviously a major challenge, which will require both hands-on policy experimentation as well as more focused research.

In light of the above analysis, action on all or some of the following points is called for. (Some recommendations would be appropriate for the entire EU area; others are more directly targeted at the Scandinavian situation.) Recommendations are as follows:

General Principles and Instruments
- Allow for institutional flexibility and openness to new human skill-sets.
- Employ positive action measures as temporary instruments.
- Treat immigrants as individuals rather than as groups.
- Promote self—reliance-the culture of public dependency must be tackled.
- Facilitate access to citizenship, which tends to fosters participation and feelings of belonging.
- Promote republican rather than ethnic solidarity.

Education
- Focus on education and educational resources (providing newcomers

with usable qualifications, but also educating the majority population on living with difference).

■ Transform induction programs into differentiated instruments for social integration (must promote and not hamper mobility; teachers must be knowledgeable about backgrounds, languages, and needs of different immigrant groups).

Labor-Market Policies
■ Create better linkages between refugee influxes and labor-market needs.
■ Revoke the official immigration stop while formulating proactive migration policies.

Refugees: Numbers, Attitudes, and Real Crunches
■ Maintain humanitarian responsibility for refugees and target the use of welfare assistance (it is unrealistic, for instance, to imagine that all categories of refugees can or should be integrated into and by means of the labor market);
■ Step up antidiscrimination measures and tighten legislation—as regards the media and their civic responsibility for social cohesion, but also to counteract discrimination in the housing and labor markets.
■ Better coordinate EU policies, and distribute immigration inflows into the EU area more fairly.
■ Tackle problems relating to patriarchal structures, gender inequalities, etc. —acceptance of diversity should not imply rubber-stamping ethnic insularity among newcomers or their descendants.

ENDNOTES

1 "Scandinavia" will in this chapter designate the EU members Denmark, Sweden, and Finland, although Finland does not normally belong to this typology. "Immigrants" refers broadly to different groups of third country nationals (and their descendants) having entered the three countries over the past thirty years or so, whether as refugees or asylum seekers, economic migrants, or relatives (family reunification).

Conceptual and Political Approaches to Integration: A French Perspective

Catherine de Wenden

Historical Background

Integration has been a major concept in social sciences since Emile Durkheim and a central issue in political life since the 1980s, with particular significance placed on immigration. But the French word "integration" was previously used in reference to colonial areas (e.g., Algeria before 1962) and defined as a place in which indigenous populations lived under French rule. The term was rediscovered in 1974, when a state secretary for immigration appointed by President Giscard d'Estaing, Paul Dijoud, decided to direct a policy of integration towards those who were still living in France after the French labor market was closed to additional foreign job seekers.

The word "integration" was in fact a reinterpretation of the old French concept of assimilation, implemented during the previous decades with regard to Italians, Poles, and refugees. It was based on the myth of a homogeneous French population and required acceptance of French public values (freedom, equality, fraternity, justice, secularism, citizenship, and democracy), along with the relegation of the cultures of origin (including language and religion) to private life. Until the 1980s, the world of work was for most foreigners a valuable socialization tool, due to trade unions, collective housing for foreign workers (foyers), and the closed universe of the businesses, coffee shops, and associations oriented towards (or against) the countries of origin. But French society required little allegiance from these foreigners, especially since they were considered a provisional labor force who intended to return to their home countries once their work time in France was over. A concept of insertion was employed for thirty years (1945-1975), aimed at achieving a functional relationship with the welcoming country, but it rapidly became inoperative. Family reunification as well as the closing of the borders were the most difficult issues for foreigners, which meant that the concept of integration became an increasingly urgent matter for public policymakers as well as for research.

Integration is supposed to contribute to social cohesion, to bridge social disparities (*la fracture sociale*), and to allow *mixité sociale* without requiring populations of foreign origin to abandon their identities but asking them to limit expression of these identities to private life. Collective expressions of language or ethnic identity as well as the practice of imported religions are prohibited as contrary to the republican definition of France (*une et indivisible*). These must

they follow the structure of the State programme, Integration in Estonian Society 2000-2007, which is a strategy aimed at achieving linguistic-communicative, legal-political as well as socioeconomic integration. The term "integration" must, according to Estonia, be understood as the removal of barriers, which hinder many non-Estonians from participating fully in society, without changing their ethnic identity. An integration foundation was established in 1998, and it is responsible for facilitating projects related to integration; more than 60 different activities were launched in 2001.

The Czech Republic has a similar approach to the one of Estonia, although it seems to have gone a little further in developing a national policy on integration. Also in the Czech Republic there are no specific programmes targeted at newly arrived immigrants; however, policies on integration exist for the benefit of the country as a whole.[4] Since 1998 the Czech Republic has given integration considerable attention, and on the basis of National Round Tables held in co-operation with the Council of Europe (and with the participation of NGOs, social partners, immigrants association, etc.), the new fifteen-points programme of principles, The Principles of the Concept for Integration of Foreigners, has been developed. These principles were the starting point in a longer process, which led to development of Integration Policy Plans in a number of ministries in order to mainstream integration measures into all levels of society. The overall aim of the integration policy is to approximate the position of long-term resident foreigners to the legal position of citizens and in general to improve access to housing, employment, language, culture, education and participation in political life. According to the Czech Republic, integration is an individual process of gradual inclusion of foreigners into the majority society (it is, however, recognised that the society is multicultural). It is also noted that integration is not always exclusively conditional upon the legal position of the foreigner. The integration policy will be evaluated by the end of 2002, and in light of the accession process to the EU, new measures may be initiated.

In Slovenia the integration policy is, due to its history, very linked to citizenship and cultural rights. The country consists of a number of ethnic minorities, of which some have a special constitutional status, which has been given special cultural rights. Special arrangements have been made to integrate the former citizens of the other republics of Yugoslavia by giving them access to a permanent residence permit which entitles them to the same rights as citizens with regard to labour market, social benefits and economic rights and access to naturalisation procedures. The overall aim of integration activities is, according to a 2001 resolution on migration policy, to give rights and obligations which, in accordance with the length of residence, will make immigrants entitled to more equal status in relation to nationals. After one year aliens are given immigrant status. Slovenia adopted in 1999 an Aliens Act, according to which the Government shall ensure conditions for inclusion of aliens by organising language tuition, courses and professional training, providing information about Slovene society, acquainting aliens with

Slovene history and organising joint events to promote mutual understanding.

Language Learning

Very little information was given on language tuition. In those countries which have special language tuition, it is often targeted at children of immigrants.

In Romania all compulsory education and Romanian language instruction courses for children of migrant workers are free of charge. The same applies to Malta, where all children of migrant workers are given free language instruction.

Estonia emphasises in its reply that the lack of knowledge of the Estonian language constitutes a major barrier for successful integration in the labour market. Special programmes in certain vocational areas therefore provide language learning opportunities for adults, who do not have a basic command of the language.

Fight against Racism and Discrimination

The fight against racism and discrimination is clearly an area which most accession countries emphasise. This is not surprising, as once immigrants have a secure residence status they are able to participate in the civil, economic and private life of their host state, and they then need protection against racial hatred. Combating racism and discrimination as well as promoting equal opportunities are therefore important steps towards developing a comprehensive integration policy.

In all countries which have replied to this question, anti-discrimination legislation has been enacted. Some countries have gone a little further than criminalising racism and discrimination and have allocated financial support to special awareness raising campaigns.

In the Slovak Republic the two anti-discrimination EC directives implementing art. 13 of the EC Treaty are being implemented into Slovak legislation, and the transposition will be completed by the end of 2003. Also, the Czech Republic has made efforts to start the implementation of the EC Directives on anti-discrimination.

In light of the World Conference against Racism and the preparatory European events, the Slovak Republic has prepared action programmes, which are currently being implemented, and a special minority tolerance programme has also been developed to increase tolerance through public information campaigns towards minorities, including the national Roma minority.

Institutions, Advisory Bodies and Monitoring

A number of countries are still in a process of establishing institutions as a part of development of integration and immigration policies. Very little information is given on the participation of immigrants in these institutions and bodies. Those countries, such as Estonia and the Czech Republic, which have developed more extensive policies are also monitoring these policies either through the responsible ministry or special bodies.

Bulgaria is envisaging the establishment of a National Migration Service and the creation of a centralised register to register all foreigners staying in the country. Latvia has recently established a Department of Society Integration under the Ministry of Justice and a nongovernmental Fund of Society Integration.

In the Czech Republic the Commission of the Minister of the Interior plays the role of an advisory body and ensures the preparation and implementation of the integration policy. Furthermore, 73 local advisory bodies have been established primarily to monitor and analyse the situation of foreigners.

Estonia has also established a governmental expert committee which is dealing with questions concerning integration of immigrants (7 of 23 members belong to an ethnic minority). A Presidential Roundtable on National Minorities, which holds discussions on matters of political and public life including issues related to ethnicity, has also been established (half of the members belong to an ethnic minority).

ENDNOTES

1   These countries are Ireland, The Netherlands, Denmark, Finland, Germany, Portugal, Spain and Sweden (partly).

2   These countries are Czech Republic, Romania, Slovak Republic, Slovenia, Lithuania (partly), Bulgaria, Latvia, Estonia and Malta.

3   These countries are Czech Republic, Romania, Slovak Republic, Slovenia, Lithuania (partly), Bulgaria, Latvia, Estonia and Malta.

4   However, a number of projects which are aiming at removing systemic and practical obstacles for aliens and improving integration do also exist.

Synthesis Report on National Integration Policies

Helene Urth

1. Introduction

At the informal Justice and Home Affairs Council meeting in Veria on 28-29 March 2003, Member States agreed that the Commission should prepare a synthesis report on national integration policies in view of the forthcoming European Council in Thessaloniki on 20-21 June 2003.

This synthesis complements the Communication on immigration, integration and employment by being a fact-finding survey on integration policies in Member States and provides clear evidence that there is scope for reinforcing policy co-ordination in the field of integration. The synthesis report has been prepared on the basis of a questionnaire concerning the integration of immigrants,[1] which was sent to both Member States and acceding countries. The Commission received 13 replies from Member States[2] and 8 replies from accession countries to the questionnaire. The replies vary greatly as far as the amount of information and details provided are concerned. However, it is clear that wide differences exist in integration policies not only with regard to acceding countries[3] but also within the European Union itself. This is not surprising as the migration history of the European countries varies greatly.

2. Synthesis of Answers Received to the Questionnaire

2.1 Reception of New Immigrants

National integration programmes are dominant in those countries where the main immigration tends to be primarily of a family reunification or of a humanitarian nature and where new immigrants consequently do not have a job offer before entering the country and rarely speak the language of the host society upon arrival. Furthermore, these countries tend to have highly developed social welfare systems. In other countries these issues do not seem to be paramount, and problems seem to be more related to ensuring the proper infrastructure to integrate labour migrants, such as access to housing, social services and health care.

2.1.1 Objectives of the Integration Policies

Descriptions of objectives of the integration policies naturally vary, nevertheless there seems to be a general consensus that the main objectives of Member States' integration policies are, on the one hand, to enable immigrants to function independently and be self-supportive and, on the other, to enable them to participate actively in all aspects of life.

2.1.2 Description of Integration Policies

In countries such as Finland, Denmark and The Netherlands, national legislation on integration was passed in 1998 and 1999, and in Austria and Germany initiatives in this respect have also been taken recently. The legislation provides a general national integration framework within which the different actors may devise measures, which are appropriate to particular local circumstances and individual needs. The national integration programmes consist in general of three main components: language tuition, orientation or introduction courses and professional labour market training. The programmes—which are compulsory to a certain extent—are in most cases tailored to the specific needs of the immigrant. The immigrant is invited for an interview, where the level of qualifications, education, practical experience, and language skills are examined. On the basis of this interview it is decided which components the individual integration programme should consist of. Not all Member States have given information on the length of their integration programmes, and it seems to vary, but in most cases they last 2-3 years. In Germany, for instance, pursuant to the proposed Immigration Act, new immigrants will have a legal entitlement to attend an integration course comprised of language tuition and orientation. The orientation course is intended to provide information about the legal system, culture and history of Germany. In Denmark the orientation course is an integral part of the language tuition, which is free of charge to all immigrants.

In the remaining Member States legislation laying down a framework for nation-wide integration programmes for immigrants does not exist, but nevertheless efforts have been made to develop a national policy to promote integration.

In Sweden[4] the government decided in 1997 to focus more on integration, and the policy is built on mainstreaming. The point of departure is equal rights, responsibilities and opportunities for everybody, and integration permeates all policy areas and should be implemented in the everyday operations of all sectors of society. A very similar multicultural approach to integration has been taken, based on race and race relations, in the United Kingdom, which has a long-standing history as a country of immigration. In parallel with immigration policy, a number of legal instruments and norms which mainly promote racial equality and equality of opportunity in a number of different areas—employment, education, housing and welfare—have been introduced, and this affects the life chances of migrants and their descendants. In Ireland an approach very close to that of the United Kingdom has been chosen. In this context it should be mentioned that so far all immigrants coming to Ireland have a job offer before coming, and integration takes place largely with the labour market at its axis.

As part of its national migration policy, Greece has recently started implementing an Integrated Action Plan (2003-2006) for the social integration of all legally residing immigrants. The Action Plan covers different measures in six main areas: information, labour market, culture, education and language, health services and temporary housing. As part of the labour market initiatives, Greece is creating a recording mechanism of professional skills of migrants, and action is being taken to foster entrepreneurship.

Spain is also currently implementing a national plan for integration: the Global Programme for Immigration (2001-2004). This programme has identified some target areas to improve integration: ensuring immigrants full exercise of their rights (medical care, access to the school system, family reunification, religious freedom), access to citizenship, access to the labour market, temporary housing measures, improving the national structure for integration issues (setting up mechanisms for increasing dialogue between public national, local and regional authorities, NGOs and civil society) and combating racism and xenophobia. Beside national efforts, a number of Regional Governments implement immigration programmes including measures for integration of migrants, and all major cities in Spain have integration programmes.

In Portugal a number of initiatives have been taken by the newly established High Commission for Immigration and Ethnic Minorities, the national body which has assumed responsibility for the development of integration policies in Portugal. In particular efforts have been made to increase information to newly arrived immigrants. In general NGOs in Portugal play a major role in providing integration measures, running a number of integration projects and providing language tuition and help to find accommodation.

In the implementation of the national integration policy, Italy, like Portugal, relies very heavily on civil society and the large NGO community in particular, who are key providers of basic social assistance services, including housing. A number of integration projects have been initiated at the national, provincial and local level with financial support from the government.

In 1993 Luxembourg approved an Integration of Aliens Law, which set up co-ordinated programmes to facilitate social, economic and cultural adaptation of foreigners. The proportion of foreigners in Luxembourg is far greater than in any other country in the EU, and the country has three official languages. Major emphasis has been put on developing a programme for integration of foreign children (immigrant children represent 38% of the total school population) based on the principles of common education, trilingualism and equal opportunity.

2.1.3 Compulsory Elements

In those Member States where national integration programmes exist, they generally entail compulsory elements. In Denmark and Austria immigrants are required to enter into and comply with an integration agreement (if the migrant successfully follows the national integration course, they will be able to comply with this agreement). Failing to meet the requirements stipulated in the agreement has negative consequences for renewal of the residence permit. In Austria the immigrants have to bear the cost of the integration programme, and up to 50% may be reimbursed by the Government if the migrant complies with the integration agreement within

18 months. In Germany, when the new Immigration Act enters into force, migrants will also be asked to contribute financially (according to personal means) to the integration programme, and if they fail to follow the programme, this may have negative consequences for renewal of the residence permit. Both in Germany and The Netherlands a certificate of successful attendance at an integration course is issued, and this may—in the case of Germany—serve to shorten the period for naturalisation from 8 to 7 years. Sanctions for not participating in the integration programmes exist generally in those countries where immigrants are entitled to social assistance during the programme, sanctioned with a reduction in these entitlements or—in the case of migrants who are self-supporting—with an administrative fine.[5]

2.1.4 Structure of Implementing Authorities

In all Member States it is the local or regional authorities which have the competence to implement integration policies, whereas it varies a great deal who is actually paying for the measures/ programmes. In some countries both the regional and local authorities have competence in this area, and in some countries, such as Spain and The Netherlands, big cities also have competence. In Germany the State sets out guidelines for the integration courses, but they are conducted by public and private organisations. The nation-wide integration programme within which the integration services to be offered are set out is to be developed in co-operation between the State, Federal governments and local authorities as well as the social partners and civil society. In

Denmark and Finland it is the local municipalities which bear the overall responsibility for offering integration programmes, but the municipalities can decide to let other public or private organisations help them in conducting the programmes.

2.1.5 Funding of Policies

Not all Member States gave exact figures as to how much money is spent on a yearly basis implementing integration policies. As the table shows, some countries are spending large amounts on integration of immigrants; however, as information is not given on what the amount exactly covers and it varies according to the number of new arrivals and the size of the country in question, it is difficult to compare the numbers, and it is therefore not possible to draw any uniform conclusions.

2.2 MEDIUM TO LONG-TERM ARRANGEMENTS FOR THE INTEGRATION OF IMMIGRANTS

The Member States which replied to this question generally referred to the descriptions of arrangements for newly arrived immigrants (described above) as integration measures applying equally or partly to this group as well. Nonetheless, immigrants who are no longer newcomers are generally included in mainstream services, e.g., public employment or social services. Therefore, policies directed towards this group are often project-based, targeted at specific groups and addressing special needs. Initiatives include measures in the field of education, employment, health and welfare, housing and the promotion of their participation in social, cultural and political life. In The Netherlands

Member State	Year	Budget
Austria		N/a
Belgium		N/a
Denmark	2002	Total budget for running the national integration programme for both refugees and immigrants: € 493 mill.
Finland		N/a
France		N/a
Germany		Federal Budget for national integration courses: € 169 mill. Additional funding at Länder level
Greece	2003	Yearly budget to finance the new Integrated Action Plan: € 65 mill.
Ireland		N/a
Italy	2002	Social Integration Fund for project at all levels: € 42 mill.
Luxembourg		N/a
Netherlands	2002	Integration budget for newcomers: € 165 mill. Budget for "oldcomers": € 100 mill.
Portugal		N/a
Spain		N/a
Sweden	2002	Refugee and newcomer reception: € 219 mill.
United Kingdom		N/a

special programmes have been set up to avoid ethnic minorities becoming the new underprivileged group in society. Sweden and Germany mention that since the mid-1970s they have supported language courses for all immigrants who do not speak the language properly, and this service has been free of charge.

2.3 INTEGRATION INTO THE LABOUR MARKET

When examining measures for improvement of integration into the labour market, it appears from the answers given that there are wide variations between the Member States due to the very different immigration patterns and labour market demands. Some Member States have a demand for highly skilled labour and others only for un-skilled. At the same time many Member States must deal with a relatively high unemployment rate among immigrants, in particular those of the 2nd and 3rd generation. These differences seem to be crucial for the approach chosen to deal with this issue.

2.3.1 Planned Measures

The integration of unemployed immigrants in the labour market is promoted in all Member States through either general policies or individual integration or job seeking plans. In Germany insertion pathways are developed to tackle youth unemployment, especially among immigrants. In Spain programmes focusing on the exploitation of employment possibilities especially suitable for immigrants as well as the organisation of movement within the country to take up unfilled job offers are organised.

The Netherlands has in accordance with the European Employment Strategy set specific national targets concerning integration. Specific labour market policy is aiming at halving the difference between the unemployment rate of ethnic minorities and persons who are of Dutch origin, which amounts to reducing unemployment of ethnic minorities to 10%. Finland also targets have been set concerning combating discrimination and promoting social rights in order to find additional resources for vocational training of immigrants.

A few Member States, namely Austria and Italy, have special quota systems for labour migration, and the United Kingdom is intending to introduce new schemes to bring in temporary workers at the low skilled end of the labour market as a need for labour migration has emerged in certain sectors. Austria has schemes with a yearly quota to bring in workers for the labour market for both highly skilled and seasonal workers. In Italy the employers who employ immigrants via the quota system must guarantee not only a job, but also accommodation and travel costs.

2.3.2 Involvement of Social Partners

In some Member States, the social partners are involved at the national and local level in the preparation and implementation of integration measures. In Spain, for example, the social partners are involved in the estimate of labour shortages in the country. In Finland labour market organisations participate at a national level in the integration of immigrants mainly through advisory bodies on which they are represented. In Denmark an agreement concerning integration measures on the labour market has been concluded between the government and the social partners underlining the concerted responsibility for integration. According to the agreement, exceptions to the Collective Agreements can be decided locally for the purpose of increasing the integration of immigrants in the labour market.

2.3.3 Coordination with Other Authorities

Generally, regional and local authorities are responsible for the implementation of integration policies concerning immigrants. In many Member States, overall guidance is given at the national level, and measures are carefully coordinated, often with the involvement of the social partners.

2.4 IMMIGRANT PARTICIPATION

Immigrants generally have free access to social and cultural life, including access to education, and they are able to become active in the political field, in political parties, associations, societies and organisations. Around half of the Member States have granted some kind of political rights to third country nationals. After a certain period of legal residence (between six months and five years), immigrants are allowed to vote or stand for elections at the local or municipal level.

2.4.1 Special Advisory or Consultative Bodies

In some countries there is a long tradition of involving immigrants and their organisations in the decision-making processes, and all Member States have established special advisory bodies for immigrants, although none of them has any direct decision-making competence. The advisory bodies are very different in structure, and mandates differ considerably.

In Portugal a Consultative Council for Immigration Matters has been created to ensure that associations representing immigrants, the social partners and institutions of social solidarity participate in defining the policies of social integration, and of the struggle against exclusion.

In Luxembourg the National Council for Foreigners gives advice to the Government on all relevant policy proposals. The council also has the right to submit proposals, which are aiming at improving the situation of foreigners, to the Government. Half of the members of the council are foreigners elected by their own associations. At the local level municipalities with more than 20% foreigners are obliged to set up a special advisory commission.

A similar principle is used in Denmark, where all municipalities must establish an integration council if requested by more than 50 people. The integration council may give advisory opinions on the general effort of integration in the municipality. The members of the local integration councils elect a national Council for Ethnic Minorities, which advises the Minister of Integration on issues related to integration.

In Finland an Advisory Board for Ethnic Relations has been set up and has been given the task of monitoring matters related to integration and of giving expert opinions. Both the immigrants and Finland's traditional ethnic minorities, as well as different ministries, the social partners and NGOs, are represented on the board.

Greece does not have a consultative body as such, but the Institute of Migratory Policy has been set up recently, which besides the task of compiling information and doing research, also has the task of supervising relevant projects and activities.

In Italy there are a number of different consultative bodies. The National Organisation for the Co-ordination of Integration Policy for Migrants, which gives advice on integration policies, has among its representatives local authorities, immigrants and social partners. At the local level a Special Counsellor elected by the immigrant community represents their interests with respect to local initiatives.

2.4.2 Level of Participation
In almost all Member States, immigrants are represented on the advisory bodies for immigrants. In Spain around a third or a quarter of the representatives on the advisory bodies are migrants themselves. In Denmark currently all elected members of the Council for Ethnic Minorities have an ethnic minority background.

2.5 ANTI-DISCRIMINATION AND EQUALITY

All Member States are currently in the process of revising their legislation concerning anti-discrimination or enacting new legislation in order to implement the Article 13 directive (2000/43) on anti-discrimination, which must be transposed into national law by the end of 2003.

In order to promote integration and combat racism, awareness raising campaigns and special programmes seem to be a part of the ongoing activities in almost all Member States. In some countries special initiatives have been taken as a result of preparations for the World Conference against Racism, held in Durban, South Africa, in 2001. In The Netherlands a national platform has been provided to give input to a National Action Plan against Racism, in Finland a National Action Plan to Combat Racism was adopted in 2001, and in Ireland an Action Plan is also on its way. Several countries ran anti-discrimination campaigns in 2001, and some countries such as Sweden and Germany have allocated money for campaigns combating racism and promoting equality in particular for children and young people.

Several Member States also have special bodies to monitor or advise on equality or discrimination matters; e.g., in Ireland the Equality Authority provides information and advice to anyone who feels that he/she may have been discriminated against.

2.6 SUCCESSFUL INTEGRATION

2.6.1 Official Definition
No Member State has a uniform definition of integration; however, they do to a certain extent agree that integration is composed of different elements and that it must be a two-way process involving both immigrants and their local community. In those countries where specific legislation for integration exists, integration may be defined within the framework of the act, but also in these cases integration is referred to as a process, which has some core elements.

The elements, which are mentioned in the replies of the Member States, could generally be summarised as including

- respect for fundamental values in a democratic society;
- the right to maintain his or her own cultural identity;
- rights comparable to those of EU citizens and corresponding obligations;
- active participation in all aspects of life on an equal footing (economic, social, cultural, political, civil).

2.6.2 Key Factors in Successful Integration

In most countries there exist no instruments for measuring integration or an established standard for successful integration. According to the replies, integration takes place gradually and proceeds differently in each individual case.

In The Netherlands the key factor for successful integration is when the immigrant is self-supportive. Both the United Kingdom and Austria highlight that becoming a citizen is significant and indicates a successful integration.

2.6.3 Main Barriers to Integration

The vast majority of Member States emphasise that a major barrier for successful integration is the lack of sufficient language skills. The lack of education or formal skills is also mentioned as a barrier together with the difficulties in assessing and approving immigrants qualifications—e.g., recognition of foreign exams and diplomas. Some countries also mention that one of the major barriers to successful integration is the fact that the immigrant is unemployed,

thereby implying that employment is one of the key ways of integrating immigrants in society. The Netherlands recognises that poor knowledge of the language can also leave the children of ethnic minorities in backward positions. Finland mentions that the attitude of the population has a strong impact on how welcome the immigrants feel as members of Finnish society and that racism and discrimination play an important role when it comes to integration. Austria mentions that religion may also constitute a barrier to integration, particularly for women.

2.7 Monitoring Integration Models

2.7.1 Special Monitoring Bodies

In almost all Member States monitoring plays an important role, and special schemes for monitoring have been set up. All Member States have, one way or the other, been monitoring the integration process, and many countries issue special yearly reports, which are discussed in the national parliaments. In those countries where national legislation on integration programmes exists, the implementation progress or the revision of legislation is discussed in Parliament.

In The Netherlands a special integration monitor (research with facts and figures) gives an overview of the position of ethnic minorities on three dimensions: social-structural, social-cultural and political-institutional. In Denmark a think-tank has been set up to develop benchmarks for integration. Italy issues an annual report on the integration situation of immigrants, which is presented to Parliament. Finland examines on a yearly basis the employment rates, living conditions, education, position of children, young people and women, and social services provided. In Germany, under the proposed new Immigration Act, a new special body will have the task of observing domestic capacities for reception and integration and the current trends in migratory movements.

2.7.2 Responsibility for the Monitoring Process

In all Member States, competence to monitor the integration process is decentralised to local and regional or city authorities, as well as the responsibility for implementation of integration policies. But, as mentioned above, some countries discuss in Parliament the integration progress in their country, and national ministers often have the overall responsibility for integration policies and therefore also naturally for the monitoring process and evaluation of policies to ensure the desired results are obtained.

ENDNOTES

1 The questionnaire did not take into account integration of refugees. It should be noted that in many countries refugees and immigrants are not treated as separate categories for integration purposes.
2 Belgium and France did not reply to the questionnaire.
3 Poland and Hungary did not reply to the questionnaire.
4 It should be noted that an integration programme for refugees similar to those existing for immigrants in Finland, Denmark and The Netherlands does exist in Sweden.
5 However, this applies equally to nationals and immigrants in those countries where immigrants are referred to mainstream services if they fail to participate in labour market activities.

PART 3

BUILDING A FRAMEWORK FOR A
COMMON POLICY APPROACH

Elements for an EU Framework for Integration Policies for Immigrants

Rinus Penninx

The Need to Rethink Integration Policies in EU Member States

European states try to handle international migration, rooted in global developments, in a framework that is essentially based on nation-state premises. In such a framework, the world is divided into separate political communities, each with its own national citizens and territory, where migration across political borders is an anomaly. As a consequence, migration policies have been primarily defensive and control-centered rather than proactive, while integration policies for immigrants have been reactive, if not absent. These two phenomena reinforce each other, and the lack of a consistent and transparent immigration policy is an impediment to effective integration policies. The absence of consistent integration policies and the real or perceived blockage of integration processes for newcomers of increasingly diverse origin lead in turn to predominantly negative perceptions of migration and immigrants, and hence reinforce defensive immigration policies.

This situation pertains particularly to northwest European countries that have a longer (postwar) tradition of immigration. This set of problems is reflected in the cumbersome process of establishing migration and integration policies at

the EU level. A communitarian migration policy (as decided in the Treaty of Amsterdam) is often thought of as running counter to perceived national interests or is seen as a threat: "If we have more lenient immigration policies than our neighbours, the Netherlands is going to become the waste pipe of Europe," as one Dutch politician once said. Integration policies at the EU level have been formulated primarily in a negative fashion: combating exclusion, racism, xenophobia, and discrimination.

On a positive note, however, it seems that a solid, comprehensive, and proactive framework for creating an EU policy on migration and integration is the only way out of the stalemate that, in particular, the northwest European states have created for themselves through their national immigration policies. It is also not surprising that those EU members that have experienced immigration more recently seem generally more supportive of such EU initiatives.

Newcomers in a given society are often perceived as the classic "other," who does not belong. Such constructions of the "other" may be based on legal grounds (aliens), physical appearance (race), perceived cultural and religious differences, class characteristics, or on any combination of these elements. These constructions may be used politically, for example by the anti-immigrant movement, or express themselves in discriminatory practices, in deteriorating interethnic relations and through a weakening of social cohesion in communities, cities, and states.

Current immigration into Europe, particularly visible in European metropolitan areas and larger cities, necessitates long-term, consistent integration policies in order for those areas to remain viable as communal entities and livable for all residents. The absence of such policies would be nothing less than a recipe for disaster. Integration policies should go hand in hand with and simultaneously enhance proactive immigration policies.

In this chapter, I will outline in three steps the form such integration policies should take. First, I will address the basic features of the processes of integration and exclusion. Any integration policy should be based on a thorough, science-based knowledge of the processes of integration and exclusion, since a policy can only steer the process of integration if it is clear which instruments can be used to intervene in this process and at what point and in which part of the process such intervention can be most effectively employed. Second, I will turn to some basic notions of the logic of policymaking. Knowledge of the processes of integration and exclusion is a solid starting point, but it is not enough. The process of policymaking and implementation has its own logic, of which we should also be aware. Finally, I will attempt to draw conclusions and offer some recommendations, particularly for policies at the EU level.

THE LOGIC OF INTEGRATION PROCESSES AND EXCLUSION

At the moment immigrants settle in a country, they must acquire a place in that new society, both in the physical sense (a house, a job and income, access to educational and health facilities, etc.) and in the social and cultural sense. This is particularly necessary for societal acceptance when newcomers are perceived as physically, culturally, and/or religiously different by the receiving society. Integration is the process of becoming an accepted part of society.

This elementary definition of integration is, by design, open: it does not state the particular requirements for acceptance by the receiving society. Such requirements may differ markedly, both along ideological lines (integration by assimilation versus integration in societies that define themselves as multicultural or even plural) and along practice-based, empirical lines.

There are two parties involved in integration processes: the immigrants themselves—their characteristics, efforts, and adaptation—and the receiving society, with its reactions to these newcomers. It is the interaction between the two that determines the direction and the ultimate outcome of the integration process. These two parties, however, are unequal partners. The receiving society, its institutional structure, and the way it reacts to newcomers is much more decisive in the outcome of the process.

Integration policies are part of the institutional arrangements in a society. Since these are defined politically by majorities in the receiving society, there is the inherent danger of their being lopsided, representing the expectations and demands of the society rather than being based on negotiation and agreement with immigrant groups themselves.

This process of integration of immigrants is thus not—as often supposed—only taking place at the level of the individual immigrant, whose integration is measured in terms of his or her housing, job, education, and social and cultural adaptation to the new society. It also takes place at the collective level of the immigrant group. Organizations of immigrants are the expression of mobilized resources and ambitions. Mechanisms of the integration process apply at this level as well: immigrant organizations may become an accepted part of civil society (and a potential partner for integration policies), or they may isolate themselves or be excluded.

Integration also occurs at the level of institutions, which can be divided into two types. The first type consists of general public institutions of the receiving societies or cities, such as the educational system or institutional arrangements in the labor market. Laws, regulations, and executive organizations, as well as unwritten rules and practices, are part of such institutions. These, however, may hinder access or equal outcomes for newcomers, or even completely exclude them. The functioning of these general public institutions (and their possible adjustment in view of growing diversity) is thus of paramount importance: it is on this level that integration and exclusion are mirrored concepts.[1]

The second category of institutions includes those that are specific to the immigrant groups themselves, such as religious or cultural institutions. These institutions and their possible integration can be viewed in the same way as immigrant organizations: they may become an accepted part of society on the same level as comparable institutions of native groups, or they may isolate themselves or remain unrecognized and excluded.

The mechanisms working at the individual level, the group level, and the institutional level are different, but the results at each of these levels are clearly interrelated. Institutional arrangements determine the opportunities and scope for action of organizations. Institutions and organizations together create the structure of opportunities and/or limitations for individuals. Conversely, individuals may mobilize and change the landscape of organizations, and ultimately even contribute to significant changes in institutional arrangements.

The interconnectedness of integration on different levels[2] can be illustrated by comparing the development of the position of Turkish Muslims in the Netherlands and in the Federal Republic of Germany, for immigrants who came in the same period, for the same reasons, and with roughly the same characteristics. Policy reactions to Islam and to the Turkish group have differed markedly in the two countries. The Netherlands introduced an ethnic minorities policy in the early 1980s, which implied among other things an official recognition of Islam on the same footing as other religions, thus opening opportunities for its public expression. The policy also brought about recognition of Islamic organizations as potential partners in integration policies. This implied ongoing negotiations between these organizations and public authorities on different levels. In contrast, Germany (although pursuing different policies in its various states and cities) has in general been much less accommodating.

The interesting result of these policies at the institutional level and organizational level is that on the individual level attitudes towards the receiving country and integration, in particular as measured among young and second-generation Turks in the Netherlands and the Federal Republic of Germany, seem to differ markedly. The results of Heitmeyer's research in the Federal Republic of Germany and a comparable survey done by Sunier in the Netherlands illustrate this point (see note 3). While Heitmeyer's study registers inward-oriented and even fundamentalist attitudes on an alarming scale, Sunier's study signals a much more positive attitude towards integration and involvement, particularly in local society. This corroborates more critical and independent views of established Islamic umbrella organizations, like Milli Görü_, the Süleymancı movement, and Metin Kaplan's Union of Islamic Communities and Societies (ICCB), all headquartered in the Federal Republic of Germany.[3]

Since the outcome of the integration process is the result of the interaction between two different parties, immigrants and the receiving society, at various levels, this outcome cannot be expected to be uniform. Studies that compare the integration process of different immigrant groups in the same institutional and policy context show that immigrant groups follow different patterns of integration. The integration process of immigrants of the same origin in different national contexts also leads to very diverse patterns.

There are numerous examples to illustrate different patterns of incorporation of immigrant groups in one country. In the Dutch case, for example, Vermeulen and Penninx have shown that Moluccan, Surinamese, Antillean, southern European, Turkish, and Moroccan immigrants differ in the speed of their integration and in the tracks they tend to follow.[4] A consequence of the design of such studies, however, is that explanations for such differences are found primarily in the characteristics of the immigrant groups, simply because the national context in which they are being integrated is the same.

Cross-national, comparative studies looking at the integration of the same group in different national contexts do exactly the opposite: major differences in outcome are ascribed to the differential functioning of the context in which the group is integrated. These differences are significant, as is illustrated in two studies of the Institute for Migration and Ethnic Studies of the University of Amsterdam. The first compares the institutionalization of Islam in the Netherlands, Belgium, and the United Kingdom in the postwar period—resulting in markedly different outcomes as a consequence of institutional arrangements and traditions of public acceptance of religions in these societies—and the subsequent difference in interaction.[5] The second study concerns the attitudes and actions of trade unions in relation to immigration and the position of immigrants in society in seven European countries.[6] Here, too, remarkable differences become evident. For example, the high degree of union membership by Turkish immigrants in Sweden (above 90%) and the low degree of union membership among the same group in France (around 15%) turns out to be basically the consequence of how trade unions are organized and are incorporated (or not) in socioeconomic decision making at the national level.

THE LOGIC OF POLICY AND POLICYMAKING

Policies intend to steer processes in society, in this case the immigration and integration processes of immigrants. As mentioned in the beginning of this chapter, European immigration policies have been until now largely defensive and reactive in nature or simply nonexistent, the two reinforcing each other. In view of the expected need for immigrants and the anticipated increase in immigration to Europe in the future, comprehensive integration policies that are consistent and coordinated with immigration policies are required. These integration policies must be able to manage processes of settlement by influencing the behavior of both the immigrants and the receiving society on all relevant levels and by mobilizing resources on both sides in order to implement policies. Such explicit policies do matter, because they offer a framework for thinking about common goals aimed at guaranteeing viable and livable communities, and they provide guidelines and instruments to all concerned parties on how to contribute.

Processes of integration are long-term in nature. At the individual level, an adult immigrant may significantly adapt the cognitive dimension of his behavior, but he is in general much less likely to alter the aesthetic and normative dimensions of his behavior: knowledge may change, but feelings, preferences, and evaluations of good and evil remain fairly persistent over a lifetime. At the group level, this means that the litmus test for integration, and for the success or failure of policies in this area, lies with the second generation.

In contrast, political processes in democratic societies demand that policies bear fruit within a much shorter period (for example, within an election cycle). Unrealistic promises and demands resulting from this democratic impatience often lead to backlashes.

The latter part of this thesis refers to a basic logic of policymaking. Formulating a knowledge-based, scientifically solid policy is one thing, but having it politically approved and supported is another, often more problematic, question. The latter is part of the functioning of the political system and has several implications. Democratic impatience—that is, the political desire to have quick solutions for problems and processes of a long-term character—is perhaps a relatively innocent problem. More difficult is the situation in which a political climate of anti-immigration and anti-immigrant sentiments, translated into political movements and resulting in the politicization of questions relating to immigration and integration, prevents well-argued policy proposals from being politically accepted. Unfortunately, this has become the case in many northwest

European countries. Consequently, much more attention should be given to the question of how to frame immigration and integration policies in such a way that they become politically acceptable.

Integration policies are—as argued in the previous section—by necessity context bound. This is implied in the answer to the question, *into what* should immigrants integrate? In the socioeconomic sphere, for example, integration mechanisms in societies with a strong liberal market orientation (and limited welfare and social facilities) differ from those with extensive welfare states that are based more on principles of social solidarity and which redistribute a much greater part of the national income. Historical peculiarities of institutional arrangements in the cultural and religious domain also create significant differences in the feasibility of policies, as has been illustrated earlier. As a consequence, the scope, actors, and instruments of policy action differ accordingly.

Two studies by the Institute for Migration and Ethnic Studies at the University of Amsterdam may illustrate this. The first study compares immigrant policies in five European countries since the 1960s, in particular in relation to integration and labor market policies, policies relating to immigrant languages, and policies concerning religious systems introduced by immigrants.[7] The study shows, basically, that the actual content of integration policies is to a great extent dependent on or inspired by the preexistent institutional arrangements in these domains within the different countries. For a country that tradition-

ally had different recognized languages within its territory (or religions, for that matter), it is in principle easier to make additional provisions for newcomers in this domain.

In the second study, Vermeulen and Slijper (2003) analyze the practice of multicultural policies in Canada, Australia, and the United States. Multiculturalism differs not only in terms of its historical development in each of these countries; its practice also turns out to be clearly context bound.

Such differences also exist at lower levels, for example between cities and municipalities within one national context. Differences in context thus lead to divergence and to a plurality of integration policies.

Interestingly, the settlement process itself acts as a force encouraging a convergence of policies, particularly as it presents itself at the local level. Whatever the institutional arrangements, local authorities face similar questions, such as how to provide immigrants with adequate housing and jobs and how to react to immigrants' demands to fulfill religious obligations or to provide facilities to use and teach their mother tongues. Local authorities also have to deal with reactions to immigrants on the part of the native population and with processes of discrimination and social exclusion.

CONCLUSIONS AND RECOMMENDATIONS

What conclusions and recommendations can be drawn from the foregoing observations? I will first draw some conclusions on integration policies in general, and then turn to the possible significance and form of EU policies in particular.

The first conclusion is that a proactive, consistent, and transparent immigration policy is a prerequisite for a comprehensive integration policy. A key element of such a policy is transparency in the admission of immigrants: what is expected from immigrants and what they can expect. Any opportunity for long-term residence should be expressed through legal status, through provision of the tools necessary for newcomers to function adequately in society, and through access to public facilities on an equal footing with nationals. Long periods of uncertainty about future residence (and dependency, in the case of asylum seekers) should be avoided, both because of the negative implications for the migrants concerned and because of the negative image and endangered legitimacy of admission policies which such circumstances engender.

It is at the local level (in municipalities and cities) that tensions between national and local governments become visible and the need for coordination between immigration and integration policies becomes urgent. Large cities, in particular, are confronted with rapid changes in population. Admission of newcomers, however, is controlled by national and European policies. Furthermore, these newcomers are migrants of all sorts and have different origins, bringing with them different cultures, religions, and lifestyles. Their integration into the social fabric of the city is not a natural process: social segregation, social exclusion, and margin-alization of certain of these immigrant groups threaten the social cohesion in these cities.

While local authorities face special difficulties and unique responsibilities as compared to national authorities, they also face special opportunities. The local level is where important things happen that affect the daily life of all residents, including immigrants. It is also the level where understanding between newcomers and old residents can be gained, or for that matter, lost.

Since, from the point of view of the immigrants themselves, integration processes take place at a local level and since circumstances there may vary significantly, local integration policies that build on an active interaction between immigrants and local society should have the highest priority. Such local policies should be provided with more instruments and sufficient room to act in ways suitable to the local community. National policies, and by implication European integration policies, should set general frameworks, rules, and instruments aimed primarily at facilitating the work of local actors.

Local integration policies should follow strategies and tactics that engage partners in the integration process at different levels. They should combine top-down elements with bottom-up mobilization. They should create an open process of integration within the rules of liberal democratic societies, leaving room for the development of a more diverse, but cohesive society. The diversity achieved in this way is neither predetermined nor static, but negotiated, shared, and ever changing.

Local, national, and EU governmental agencies are all potentially important actors, but they are not the only actors. Numerous nongovernmental entities have great influence (positive or negative) on the integration of immigrants. Institutional actors, such as churches, trade unions, employers' organizations, political parties, and the media, just to name a few, may be equally important. Also involved is the conglomerate of various organizations and institutions commonly referred to as "civil society," a term closely related to social cohesion. It seems self-evident that government policies that aim to shape the processes of settlement and integration should actively involve not only the immigrants themselves, but important players in civil society as well.

Such nongovernmental partners are important in two ways: as direct partners in the implementation of policies and, perhaps more significantly, as political actors. They may influence the political climate and contribute to framing policy questions in such a way that the passage of adequate policies becomes more acceptable. Nongovernmental entities can also serve as important agents in combating exclusion, discrimination, and xenophobia. In the Swiss case, for example, institutional agents like churches, trade unions, and employers' organizations have often helped to avert the danger of anti-immigrant referenda being accepted.

Integration policies should define clear priorities for action in a number of societal sectors with direct bearing on integration. For long-term immigrants, priority should be given to those sectors in which authorities have effective and generally accepted instruments for promoting integration (and preventing exclusion)- namely, the economic sector (employment) and the social sector (particularly education and housing). Policies in the political and cultural sectors (including religion) are indispensable over the long term in order to bring about the full integration of immigrants. The initial forms that policies directed toward the latter sectors may take depend to a great extent on the existing institutional arrangements in the receiving societies. In the long run, however, gradual changes towards more inclusive policies are indispensable.

In view of the division of tasks outlined in this section, what could or should be the responsibilities of EU policies? In my view these can be listed briefly as follows:

First of all, it is at the EU level where a norm-setting framework for comprehensive, future-oriented, and proactive migration and integration policies can and should be established. The immigration and integration policy fields should be seen as linked from the beginning. The European Union has in principle already opened political debate about such developments through the Treaty of Amsterdam and the Tampere Summit. After a period in which future-oriented and proactive approaches to migration and integration ceased to be a priority at the highest level, yielding to short-term, defensive, and control-oriented approaches, the 2003 summit in Thessaloniki seems to have brought the political discussion back to the more future-oriented Tampere concept. This new momentum should be used as much as possible to establish a norm-setting framework. A number of documents have been produced at the EC level (particularly the June 2003 European Commission communication on immigration, integration, and employment) that can serve as a good starting point.

The importance of such a norm-setting framework can be phrased in at least two different ways. Negatively formulated, it will help us escape from the negative spiral that—through the competitive model—tends to lead to the lowest common denominator and defensive national policies. Positively formulated, it will help bring about a common effort to optimize the possible gains to be had from migration and integration and minimize the costs and problems.

On a more concrete, policymaking level, the European Union can develop norm-setting regulations and actions, particularly in those areas in which the European Community has concrete opportunities and instruments for doing so. One area where action can be taken is in promoting residence security and access by long-term immigrants to the political system of their country of residence. Here, first steps have already been taken through new directives.

A second area, combating discrimination and social exclusion, is to a certain extent a counterpart of the first area. The establishment and work of the European Monitoring Centre on Racism and Xenophobia serves as a good starting point. But the theoretical underpinning and the scope of the work of the center could be extended significantly, by, for example, addressing much more systematically the phenomenon of institutional and institutionalized forms of discrimination.

A third area of action has to do with labor market policies and policies related to entrepreneurship. This is a field in which the European Union has developed significant general instruments. The approach here could be, mutatis mutandis, similar to that taken on gender issues at the EU level, studying and monitoring (and where possible amending) the often unintended consequences of general laws, regulations, and rules for specific groups or categories of persons (like women, disabled persons, and ethnic minorities).

A fourth area where action can be taken is that of education, an institution crucial to the social mobility of second and later generations. The approach here could parallel that outlined for the labor market.

The development of coherent and proactive migration and integration policies will imply the establishment of strong and sound horizontal coordination between several EU directorates-general, including Justice and Home Affairs as well as Employment and Social Affairs. Mainstreaming new comprehensive policies should also involve directorates-general that deal with areas such as political relations with immigrant countries of origin, development cooperation, and trade along with directorates-general that are concerned with specific sectors relating to integration.

Canada currently offers what is perhaps the most sophisticated model in terms of policy content, the integration of immigration and integration, policy organization (through the department of Citizenship and Immigration Canada), and efforts to base policies on relevant empirical data and research and systematic evaluation in Centres of Excellence.

ENDNOTES

1 See Rinus Penninx, "Immigrants and the Dynamics of Social Exclusion: Lessons for Anti-discrimination Policies," in *Dedication and Detachment: Essays in Honour of Hans Vermeulen*, eds. Flip Lindo and Mies van Niekerk (Amsterdam: Het Spinhuis, 2001), 193-211.

2 See Rinus Penninx, "Het dramatische misverstand," in *Bij nader inzien: Het integratiedebat op afstand bekeken*, Infoplus minderheden, eds. J.E. Overdijk-Francis and H.M.A.G. Smeets (Houten and Lelystad: Bohn, Stafleu & Van Loghum and koninklijke Vermande, 2000), 27-49.

3 For the Federal Republic of Germany, see Y. Karakasoglu, *Türkische Muslime in Nordrhein Westfalen* (Duisburg: Ministerium für Arbeit, Gesundheit und Soziales NRW, 1997); Y. Karakasoglu and S. Koray, *Islam and Islamic Organizations in the Federal Republic of Germany: A Short Summary of Study of the Zentrum für Türkeistudien on Islamic Organizations in Germany* (Birmingham: Centre for the Study of Islam and Christian-Muslim Relations, 1996); Y. Oezbek and S. Koray, section on Germany, pts. 1 and 2 in *Muslim Voices: A Stranger Within?* (Essen: Zentrum für Türkeistudien, 1998); W. Heitmeyer, J. Müller, and H. Schröder, *Verlockender Fundamentalismus: Türkische Jugendliche in Deutschland* (Frankfurt am Main: Suhrkamp, 1997).

For the Netherlands, see J. Doomernik, *Turkse moskeeën en maatschappelijke participatie: De institutionalisering van de Turkse islam in Nederland en de Duitse Bondsrepubliek* (Amsterdam: Instituut voor Sociale Geografie, 1991); N. Landman, *Van mat tot minaret: De institutionalisering van de islam in Nederland* (Amsterdam: VU-uitgeverij, 1992); J. Rath et al., *Western Europe and Its Islam* (Leiden, Boston, and Koeln: Brill, 2001); T. Sunier, *Islam in beweging: Turkse jongeren en islamitische organisaties* (Amsterdam: Het Spinhuis, 1996); T. Sunier, "Niederländisch-Islamische Staatsbürgerschaft? Ansichten über Islam, Bürgerschaft und Bürgerrechte unter türkische Jugendlichen in den Niederlanden," in *Der Fundamentalismus-verdacht: Plädoyer für eine Neuorientierung der Forschung im Umgang mit allochtonen Jugendlichen*, eds. W.D. Bukow and M. Ottersbach (Opladen: Leske und Budrich, 1999), 85-97.

4 See H. Vermeulen and R. Penninx, *Immigrant Integration: The Dutch Case* (Amsterdam: Het Spinhuis, 2000).

5 See Rath et al. (note 3).

6 R. Penninx and J. Roosblad, eds., *Trade Unions, Immigration, and Immigrants in Europe, 1960-1993: A Comparative Study of the Attitudes and Actions of Trade Unions in Seven West European Countries* (New York and Oxford: Berghahn Books, 2000).

7 H. Vermeulen, ed., *Immigrant Policy for a Multicultural Society: A Comparative Study of Integration, Language, and Religious Policy in Five Western European Countries* (Brussels and Amsterdam: MPG (Migration Policy Group) and IMES (Institute for Migration and Ethnic Studies), 1997).

Identification of a Framework for Common Principles, Guidelines, and Objectives for Integration

Rinus Penninx

This chapter is intended as a mental exercise, presenting proposals and arguments that could possibly lead to concrete elements for a program of action on integration in the European Union, either now or in the future. Discussions both within the European Community and between the European Community and external advisors have led to a number of interesting documents on the contours of an EU integration policy for the near future, documents that serve as the starting point for this chapter.[1] In order to move from this starting point and bring the discussion from an abstract to a more concrete level, one has to deal with various practical and strategic questions. What could or should be the functions of an EU integration policy in relation to national and local policies? What would be the role of actors involved in such policies? How could EU policies realize these functions? What instruments are available to the European Community for concrete action? Which strategies should the European Community follow?

The following considerations (which are clarified in the documents mentioned in note 1) provide useful background in trying to answer these questions:

First, integration processes take place primarily at the local level. Policies at the national and EU level should be of a facilitating nature, creating and promoting conditions and regulations (general basic minimum norms, delegation of power, provision of financial resources and instruments, accumulation and dissemination of knowledge, expertise, and best practices, etc.) that assist policymakers and implementers at the lowest levels.

Second, integration processes are essentially context bound (related to the institutional arrangements locally, the specific characteristics of immigrants, and the interaction between these two). Processes and modes of incorporation vary significantly, and thus the policies that aim to steer such processes are by necessity diverse in practice.

Third, the logic of policymaking is essentially dependent on mechanisms of a political nature, at least involving majority-minority relations (if immigrants have access to the political system) and, in most cases, the absence of direct political influence among immigrants (no voting rights). In addition, issues of immigration, immigrants, and their perceived nonintegration are often politically sensitive topics that lend themselves to political exploitation.

Fourth, as explained in the EC communication on immigration, integration, and employment of June 2003 and made explicit by Bernd Schulte's chapter in this book, the only way the European Community can operate in the area of integration is through the open method of coordination, seeking consensus by persuasion: counting on (and pressing for) implementation through the principle of subsidiarity. These form the basic mechanisms at hand.

Fifth, the concept of integration is interpreted in diverse ways, with its definition varying in scientific debates, in popular use, and in policy creation. Interpretations and connotations of policies differ markedly cross-nationally, and sometimes also locally within a single nation-state. These differences are strongly related to normative and political concepts of how local and national communities are organized and institutionalized, and, as a consequence, how newcomers acquire, individually and/or collectively, an accepted and recognized place in society.

Keeping these five basic points in mind, I see the following fundamental possible functions of EU policies in the field of integration:

A first function or task of the European Union is frame setting. One of the most important tasks of the European Community is to frame both immigration and integration, and the nexus between the two, in a way different from that practiced (predominantly at the national level) in most EU countries thus far. This includes moving from a defensive and mainly control-centered approach to a proactive, future-oriented, and more comprehensive approach; providing a balance between realistic problem

orientation and direct and possibly future gains, thus furthering acceptance of immigration not only as an unavoidable phenomenon (as illustrated by the recent past and indicated by prognostic models of both population and workforce) but also as a source of opportunities; and accentuating the necessity of common action in both the immigration and integration domain.

The European Community is in principle in a position to bend negative competition and burden shifting into an approach that focuses on common interests. This has worked in the past. When Italy was still essentially an emigration country, the Italians consistently pleaded for free circulation of labor within the European Economic Community (EEC). The topic was, for a long time, a very sensitive one but has more recently achieved greater acceptance through consistent frame setting and agenda setting.

The frame-setting task should be approached first within the political and bureaucratic setting of the European Union as well as between Brussels and the national and local authorities and policymakers. This will involve tough and long negotiations. But the European Union should also, as Sarah Spencer has pointed out, take "active responsibility for leading a balanced, informed, public debate about the reasons migrants are in Europe by putting into the public domain information about the contribution they make and barriers they experience, acknowledging public fears, and correcting misinformation."[2] This wider task relates to Werner Weidenfeld's remarks in the introduction to this book: how does the

European Community sell its present and future framework and ideas? This is an important task, particularly since, as mentioned earlier, the logic of policy-making is essentially dependent on mechanisms of a political nature. Engaging the public is vital in order to prepare the population at large, and civil society in general, for the creation of appropriate policy measures and to mobilize a counterforce against populist anti-immigrant political exploitation.

A second function or task that follows from frame setting is norm setting. The previously mentioned general frame-work should be worked out in a number of norm-setting regulations, directives, or even laws that pinpoint basic starting points for integration policies. Such norms pertain to the following:

1) Determination of which immigrants should be regarded as residents for whom comprehensive integration poli-cies are applicable and at what point in time this should apply: Here again, immigration/admission policies and integration policies should be carefully coordinated. In principle, admission policies should be able to distinguish between temporary migrants and long-terms residents. At the same time, how-ever, it should be made clear (to both migrants and the receiving community), what temporariness means with regard to those migrants initially admitted on a temporary basis. The norm-setting function here could involve procedures by which immigrants who have lived continuously in their new country of residence for three, four, or at most five years should be treated as permanent residents and should have, in principle, safe and guaranteed residence rights.

Those immigrants who may arrive at a later time—including family members and marriage partners of established immigrants—may be given preferential treatment and offered the same measure of certainty at an earlier point in time.

2) Full access, in principle, of long-term residents to all public institutions and facilities in the society of settlement: This idea is far-reaching and differs markedly from the practice in EU Member States today. Nevertheless, any serious concept of integration policy for long-term residents of immigrant origin cannot allow the current situation, involving different classes of citizens with differing rights, to continue. In the course of time, a system of norms should be developed, through political negotiation, for the three basic dimen-sions of citizenship: socioeconomic, legal-political, and cultural-religious. This system should be developed by focusing on the three dimensions of citi-zenship in the following order, reflecting the measure of consensus that exists within each dimension:

Economic and social rights and access to social security
Economic and, in particular, work-related rights are the easiest to tackle, since a considerable measure of norm setting (equal rights and full equal access to work-related institutions) has already taken place. But this work has not yet been completed. Social security is a heavily controlled sector within the welfare state, and substantial work must still be done to reach equality of access. Since social security systems differ, norm setting will not take place in terms of content, but rather in terms of granting access equal to that enjoyed by

natives or national citizens. The same applies for social rights.

Legal-political rights

Norm setting in this field is more complicated, because there are different strategies to attain the norm of full access to the relevant institutions. One strategy is to promote and ease access to citizenship of the country of residence. Work has been done here, and there seems to be some convergence of national regimes. But this work is only beginning. Much can be learned from traditional immigrant societies (like Canada) that perceive citizenship for long-term immigrants as the natural way of laying a solid foundation for integration. If this first option is not realized, there are other more partial and provisional ways to set norms for access to political decision making. Granting voting rights and enabling other forms of political participation at the local level is one step now practiced in some EU countries. A still weaker form of political integration is achieved through the formation of alternative, consultative structures, both locally and nationally, for those who are long-term residents but who are excluded from the formal political system.

Cultural-religious rights

This is the most difficult and controversial area for norm setting, since normative political assumptions and practices differ significantly (compare, for example, language, culture, and religion policies in France, the United Kingdom, the Netherlands, and Sweden). In view of these differences, I see two ways of norm setting. The first is to work on content norms derived from human rights in general in the fields of language, culture, and religion. This is a long-term goal. The second is more practical: relative norm setting, demanding equal treatment of immigrants with comparable native groups.

3) Antidiscrimination norm setting: This is the negative corollary of the positive norm setting of the previously mentioned option, full access. Antidiscrimination norm setting is a necessary element of policy creation, but it also has severe limitations. Any antidiscrimination norm setting requires positive norm setting to counter that which is causing discrimination in the first place. Since positive norm setting differs from one national context to another, the practical application of antidiscrimination norms will differ accordingly. Unequal treatment and discrimination may take place on completely different grounds: unintended or intended, institutional, and so forth. Applying the same negative, accusative label to all of these causes may hinder the actual work of undoing unequal treatment. Agents like the European Monitoring Centre on Racism and Xenophobia, along with similar national and local organizations, could do more efficient work if their mandates could be widened and their names changed in such a way that they are freed of negative associations.

Apart from frame setting and norm setting, the European Community has other instruments to promote activities related to the development of integration policies. Specific budget lines available to those European Commission directorates-general responsible for certain policy domains can be used to mobilize forces, both governmental and nongovernmental. Already operating in this area are the European Refugee Fund and the newer and still small Integration of Third Country Nationals (INTI) Programme. Again, the question here is, "What functions could be promoted by financing such activities?"

Monitoring could be used as a device for developing awareness, empirically based diagnosis, and policy steering. The basic assumption is that the position of newcomers in a society is determined to a large extent by the mostly unintended differential impact of general public institutions and unequal outcomes for immigrants. Because of immigrants' socioeconomic status, their immigration-related characteristics, and sometimes their cultural-religious characteristics, outcomes for immigrants are unequal (for example, overrepresentation in social welfare or disabled benefit programs in the Netherlands or concentration or segregation through housing policies and regulations). Turning this reasoning around means establishing a monitoring regime that produces results that lead to a clear diagnosis and awareness of the functioning of general public institutions available to immigrants. The Annual Report on Migration and Integration (decided on at the European Council Meeting in Thessaloniki) can be used in the future as one monitoring instrument. Apart from that, the European Community could encourage this method more broadly, including among private companies, always important players in civil society.

An approach related to establishing monitoring institutions would be to stimulate measures and policies that provide a toolkit for immigrants and thus empower them: language education, civic training, and so forth. The basic idea behind this, and the lesson provided by earlier policies related to temporary migrants and guest workers, is that immigrants should be given the necessary tools to find a place in the new society and to prepare for full participation. Several countries are already developing policies in this area; financing experiments, evaluations, and the development of models can further stimulate this process. It is important to look at such efforts as a precondition for facilitating integration processes and avoid normative claims (turning immigrants into natives). Such activities should preferably take place in connection with, and be applicable to, trajectories for entering the labor market or for further education.

An important task is to encourage measures and experiments that mobilize resources within immigrant groups for integration policies. Too much of current policy thinking and conception is top-down, addressing immigrants on an individual level. Successful policy implementation must rely instead on mobilizing forces within immigrant groups. A number of measures that put the potential available within immigrant groups to good use have already been developed while others are still in the offing. Examples include mentor projects involving immigrant students who assist younger coethnics during their secondary education and immigrant organizations mobilizing their rank and file for training and language courses or for labor market projects. Further examples remain scarce, however, and a full-fledged strategy should be developed.

Of course, systematic research—preferably cross—national and comparative-is an important source for policy development. European Commission directorates-general have special budgets to commission studies relevant to their policy domains. Moreover, the Research Directorate-General and its Framework Programmes (involving large sums of money) can be used to build a solid foundation, both for a balanced public discussion and for solid policymaking. As argued by Entzinger and Biezeveld (see note 1), the contexts in which integration is studied and measured are still too different to rely on direct unweighted comparisons and benchmarking. Benchmarking should take place primarily by comparing outcomes for natives and immigrants within a single local or national context. Nevertheless, on a different level, international comparison teaches much about the selective functioning of general public institutions in different countries.

Best practices in one context, however, should be translated first in terms of the particular new context in which one would apply such practices.

Strategically it would be interesting—as an example for the outside world—if the European Community and its organizations would look at their own internal practices and structures. Two sets of relevant questions come to mind. The first pertains to personnel policies of the European Community: Should citizenship in one EU Member State remain a requirement for all jobs within the EC organization? Is there any good reason to exclude long-term third country nationals or residents from all jobs? Second, should the European Community monitor the outcomes of its major programs in a number of different areas with regard to the specific effects they have on the integration of immigrants?

ENDNOTES

1 The EC communication on immigration, integration, and employment of 3 June 2003 (and minutes of the Thessaloniki Summit); Han Entzinger and Renske Biezeveld, "Benchmarking in Immigrant Integration" (report prepared for the European Commission by the European Centre on Migration and Ethnic Relations, Rotterdam, August 2003);

Rinus Penninx et al., "Managing Integration: The European Union's Responsibilities towards Immigrants, Building a Framework for a Common Policy Approach" (discussion paper presented at the roundtable, 15 July 2003).

2 Migration Information Source, Migration Policy Institute, http://www.migrationinformation.org/ and the Platform for International Cooperation on Undocumented Migrants, http://www.picum.org/.

INTEGRATION AS AN INTEGRAL PART OF THE EUROPEAN SOCIETAL MODEL

DIETRICH THRÄNHARDT

INTEGRATION PROGRAMS

Over the last few years, eight of fifteen EU states have introduced integration programs for newly arrived immigrants or announced plans with that aim in mind. These programs exist in the Netherlands, Sweden, Finland, Denmark, and Austria and are planned in France, Germany, and Belgium. Conceptually, they converge around the Dutch model, developed in the 1990s and first introduced in 1998. This model comprises six hundred hours of language training, thirty hours of civic and social education, and a contract between the immigrant and the state (signed by the city mayor). The program is supported by positive and negative sanctions, such as easier access to naturalization and financial fines, respectively. The Dutch model serves as a best practice of integration.[1] It is supposed to offer a rational and pragmatic solution to problems that governments and the public fear all over Europe, problems such as disintegration, ghettos, segregation, riots, and a cultural gap between the indigenous population and newcomers.

The Europe-wide appeal of the Dutch model is puzzling since it contrasts to the current self-criticism in the Netherlands about the failure of integration. In this context, the Dutch government has shifted its position from multiculturalism towards a philosophy of Dutch norms and values. On the other hand, France has moved away from its long established and cherished tradition of assimilation and towards a concept of organized integration.[2] Germany no longer relies on its fifty-year-old tradition of *Aussiedler* integration programs, which went on for decades, were probably the largest integration programs ever, and can be considered successful.[3] These programs do not function as well as in the past since language training has been reduced from one year to only half a year—ironically the same amount of time as in the Dutch model. Nor does Germany rely on its thirteen-year tradition of integrating Russian Jews, a policy which in 2002 attracted more Russian Jews to Germany than to Israel.[4]

A European consensus around the state's responsibility for integration, the inclusion of all legal immigrants into society, and the fight against the fragmentation of society is evolving. These positive measures are accompanied by some restrictive measures, such as a minimum age requirement for inmarriages from foreign countries in Denmark and the Netherlands, minimum income clauses for the marriage partner in the host country, and language tests before entering the country for family migrants in the Netherlands and for *Aussiedler* in Germany.

This European consensus is in stark contrast to the dominant trends in other relevant immigration centers of the world. Policies in the Middle East and in Southeast Asia can be characterized as rotating exploitation—the state deliberately relegating immigrants, particularly female immigrants, to a lesser status in society, with lower income and fewer rights; disallowing entry to family members; giving indigenous agents or employers full control over immigrants; and ending immigrants' stays in the country when they are no longer needed. The European model also differs from the US model, which stresses the economic role of immigrants, denies any social assistance to immigrants in the first five years, and makes sponsors financially responsible for some categories of immigrants.

The US model can be considered a market model of immigration, putting immigrants to an economic test in the first five years after arrival and admitting successful individuals for the benefit of the economy. In contrast, the new convergence around the Dutch model continues the traditions of the regulated European welfare state, even if it is pursued by a government that took office with the intention of bringing about fewer rules in the Netherlands.[5] However, the tendency to have immigrants carry the cost of the programs instead of the welfare state may indicate a new trend, one that can be observed in Denmark, Austria, and the Netherlands.

THE IMPORTANCE OF THE EUROPEAN CHARTER

The insistence on the inclusion of all persons and the fear of a fracture in society has been enshrined in the Charter of Fundamental Rights of the European Union, which is far-reaching. Going beyond the older declarations of the rights of men and citizens, the preamble stresses the "universal values of human dignity, freedom, equality and solidarity" for everybody, not only for citizens. Like the German basic law, Article 1 of the charter proclaims that "Human dignity is inviolable. It must be respected and protected." Moreover, it entitles "everyone . . . the right to freedom of expression," to "peaceful assembly and to freedom of association at all levels, in particular in political trade union and civic matters," the right to education and the right to engage in work (Articles 11, 12, 14, and 15). In particular, the charter stresses that "Nationals of third countries who are authorised to work in the territories of the Member States are entitled to working conditions equivalent to those of the citizens of the Union" (Article 15).[6] In 2004, the charter is likely to become part of the revised EU treaty and consequently become a basis for the rulings of the European Court in Luxembourg. It is clear that the principle of equal pay, which is explicitly mentioned in the charter, will play an important role in future rulings.

ANTIDISCRIMINATION POLICIES OR UNIVERSALISTIC INTEGRATION?

How are equality and integration best pursued, and who are the best agents to do this? In the past, Britain and the Netherlands have developed a network of advocacy bodies to regulate conflicts and to do away with discrimination. In Britain, the official term for these agencies still includes the term "race relations." And in the Netherlands during 2002 (the most successful year for the Pim Fortuyn movement), references to black and white schools, streets, or quarters began to develop. Germany and other continental countries do not have such traditions and rely on general principles about equal rights that are written into the constitution and incorporated into specific laws like the Betriebsverfassungsgesetz (company constitution law), the taxi license regulations, or the restaurant and bar regulations. Moreover, public housing companies are bound to nondiscriminatory practices and compelled to rely on criteria like the number of children or the need for housing.

It is difficult to measure or compare integration and discrimination among countries. A comparison of police statistics puts Britain first with respect to the number of racist crimes. There may, however, be a systematic bias in the statistics as they rely on police categorizations and the public's reports to the police. To look into the problem of discrimination, the International Labour Organization has undertaken an experiment in several countries whose labor organizations were prepared to cooperate. Persons with the same qualifications, one group of indigenous origin and the other of immigrant origin, were sent to companies that were about to hire personnel. The process was followed through various steps, and the performance of both groups was compared. The authors calculated a discrimination rate of 33% in Germany, compared to 55% in the Netherlands.[7]

Discussing such results, US specialist Thomas Pettigrew points to the fact that European antidiscrimination policy lacks "teeth," because there is no class action system like in the United States.[8] Thus, antidiscrimination policies and systems, particularly if they are widely propagated in public, may convey an impression of special care for or even a level of privilege for immigrants, while at the same time providing them with little real help. Symbolically, they seem to set the indigenous population against the newcomers, while at the same time they do not solve their core problems. This is an ideal situation for political opportunists to seek political gain by employing backlash politics, as evident in all European countries with antidiscrimination systems. Universalistic institutions like the works councils in Germany, which integrate both immigrants and indigenous workers and are obligated to work for their common interests, are better suited to improve the situation of immigrants. Comparative evaluations of policy outcomes seem to support this thesis. Comparing the Netherlands and Germany, it has been demonstrated that in Germany in 2000 the rates of unemployment and of education success favored the indigenous population by about one to two, whereas in the Netherlands the ratio was one to four.[9]

CONCLUSION

The policy of the European Union should focus on general principles of equality and openness that apply to everybody irrespective of gender, background, birthplace, religion, and so forth. At the same time, there should be more efforts to monitor policy outcomes. An independent agency or foundation should look after discrepancies.

ENDNOTES

1   Ines Michalowski, "Integration for Newcomers: A Dutch Model for Europe?" (paper presented at the Dutch-German Research Conference on Migration and Integration, Netherlands Institute for Advanced Study, May 2003).

2   Haut Conseil à l'Integration, *Les parcours d'intégration à la francaise* (Paris: Haut Conseil à l'Integration, 2002).

3   Unabhängigen Kommission "Zuwanderung," *Zuwanderung gestalten, Integration fördern.* (Berlin: Bundesministerium des Innern, 2001).

4   Eliahu Salpeter, "Jews from the CIS Prefer Germany to the Jewish State," *Haaretz*, 28 May 2003.

5   *Meedoen, meer werk, minder regels,* Hoofdlijnenakkoord voor het kabinet CDA, VVD, D66, 16 May 2003.

6   Charter of Fundamental Rights of the European Union, *Official Journal of the European Communities*, C 364/1 (18 December 2000).

7   Roger Zegers de Beijl, ed., *Documenting Discrimination against Migrants in the Labor Market: A Comparative Study of Four Countries* (Geneva: International Labour Office, 2000).

8   Thomas Pettigrew, "Reactions to the New Minorities in Western Europe," *Annual Review of Sociology* (1998): 77-103.

9   Heinz Werner, *Integration ausländischer Arbeitnehmer in den Arbeitsmarkt: Deutschland, Frankreich, Niederlande, Schweden* (Nürnberg: Institut für Arbeitsmarkt- und Berufsforschung, 1993); Anita Böcker and Dietrich Thränhardt, "Erfolge und Misserfolge der Integration: Deutschland und die Niederlande im Vergleich," *Aus Politik und Zeitgeschichte* (June 2003).

PART 4

A Concept for a Competitive Integration Policy

A Concept for a Competitive Integration Policy

The Bertelsmann Foundation

Facing the Challenge

After years of limited progress in the area of immigration and integration, the issue has now been infused with a new dynamism. The positive reception of the 2003 communication from the European Commission on immigration, integration, and employment and the Presidency Conclusions of the European Council in Thessaloniki are indicators of this trend. The Thessaloniki agreement provides a comprehensive framework for further action, especially in the field of integration. The Thessaloniki European Council came to the following conclusions on the topic of integration (paragraph 31 of the Presidency Conclusions):

"Integration policies should be understood as a continuous, two-way process based on mutual rights and corresponding obligations of legally residing third-country nationals and the host societies. While primary responsibility for their elaboration and implementation remains with the Member States, such policies should be developed within a coherent European Union framework, taking into account the legal, political, economic, social and cultural diversity of Member States. In order to identify the development of such framework, the definition of common basic principles should be envisaged."

However, how to translate such written intentions into political reality and how to find a way of establishing cooperation between the European Union and its Member States in the sensitive area of integration continue to be major challenges.

On the basis of their individual political and cultural traditions, each EU Member State has developed its own way of dealing with the challenges of integration. Thus the European response must be the development of a common and coherent framework for immigration and integration policy. Though legal measures for steering immigration policy may well be necessary, they will nevertheless be doomed to failure unless they are underpinned by a comprehensive integration policy. For this reason immigration and integration policies are inseparable.

However, the elements needed to form a coherent framework for integration policy are lacking both at the European level and at the level of the nation-states. A bewildering profusion of uncoordinated rules and regulations is predominant instead.

Furthermore, integration policy needs to become competitive on the European and national levels. It should have a clear structure and objectives capable of competing with other policy areas. The issue should be linked with other policy areas in such a way that prompts greater attention on the part of political and economic decision makers.

DEFINING THE OBJECTIVE, PRINCIPLES, AND ELEMENTS

The ultimate objective at the European level is to adapt European and national policies more effectively in order to promote the development of integration policies for both the host society and immigrants.

Common European principles can be used in the development of national integration policies. The three basic principles on which national policies should be based are structural transparency, equitable regulations, and sustainability. The three basic principles for the engagement of various actors are engagement of those directly affected (who benefit economically); engagement of those who may have to face the negative impacts in the case of a lack of an integration policy (at the local, regional, and national levels); and engagement of those who feel responsible for society (nongovernmental organizations and foundations).

Four different dimensions with ten core elements are capable of determining an integration package. First, the private dimension includes family and housing. Second, the cultural dimension encompasses education, language, and religion. Third, the economic dimension includes the labor market and health and social security. Fourth, the political dimension consists of citizenship, civic citizenship, and voting rights.

DEFINING THE ACTORS

European Union
The European Union can and should only set the framework—with the help of generally accepted principles for a common integration policy—in order not to restrict unduly the scope of action available to the Member States. Attempting to do more would be contrary to the community spirit. At the same time, formulating an integration policy at the European Union level would also necessitate committing an appropriate level of budgetary resources in order to make action in this area possible.

Member States
Unlike the European Union, the Member States have clear-cut competencies and responsibilities in the field of integration. For this reason, they are the major interface between the European Union and the regional and local levels. A comprehensive exchange of information, policy objectives, and intended measures between Member States and between Member States and the European Union should be established.

Economic Entrepreneurs
Economic integration is one of the key means of facilitating successful integration into a host society. Economic entrepreneurs must be seen as major partners of both the European Union and the Member States. They are in a position to contribute innovative ideas to liven up directives and communications. As a consequence, different EU policy areas (first and foremost employment and social affairs) should be linked more effectively to the integration issue.

Civil Society

Integration must be built on much more than mere directives, regulations, and laws. The integration process must of course be based on both legal regulations and broad social support. Integration can be understood as an interdependent process between the population of the host country and immigrants, meaning that it relies heavily on a dialogue between various actors within civil society. Nongovernmental organizations, social networks within the immigrant communities, associations, and individuals can, in their various spheres, make significant contributions to integration. Such engagement must be underpinned by programs and competitions, which should also be given financial support.

Science and Research

Comprehensive and reliable information relating to the field of immigration is essential to the formulation of a successful integration policy. However, it will be necessary to conduct an up-to-date Europe-wide survey of the status quo in this field and to intensify the flow of information between the key players. For this reason, an institution-alized dialogue between academics and political decision makers at the European and national levels should be established and conducted on a regular basis. A consistent European integration policy must promote the creation of national and international networks and provide active support for close cooperation between them.

MAKING THE APPROACH OPERATIONAL

The following steps are essential in order to make EU integration policy operational:

■ Defining priorities for the different political levels, policy areas or dimensions of integration, and different categories of migrants (new-comers, second and third generation, women).

■ Defining a well-balanced policy mix. A policy mix is essential with regard to related policy areas and within the integration field. Integration policy needs to be linked with several other policy areas at both the European and national levels. Related policy areas are external relations and security issues (antiterrorism measures), economic policy, social policy, health policy, and education and cultural policy.

■ Providing a clear overview of actions and actors.

■ Defining the instruments: creating a system of incentives, in particular at the national level, for participation in best practice exchanges and providing a financial basis for integration measures. Directives could be supplemented by the open method of coordination. This instrument should initially be used for a specified period, after which, on the basis of an evaluation of the open coordination process, other instruments could be proposed in order to ensure harmonization of common integration policies.

■ Defining the overall objective. The enlarged European Union needs a common European code of conduct for integration. For this reason it is also essential to agree on specific measures relating to the development of an integration infrastructure. Such an integration infrastructure can only become operational if the objectives of equality and inclusion of migrants become part of the mainstream in policymaking and programming of the European Commission.

INTEGRATING THE COMPETITIVE FACTOR

The competitive factor is a central feature of all policy, including integration policy. There is a need for a strategy that describes and benchmarks the national and regional policies and instruments for the integration of immigrants. This will help Member States and regions assess their policies and identify best practices on the basis of national experience. It should also help to identify the role the European Union can play in supporting national and regional efforts.

The benchmarking process must be part of a broader policy approach. As a precondition, national and European policymakers must display a readiness to review existing integration policies, and to define, wherever possible, quantitative and qualitative targets for their implementation.

Furthermore, the aim of the benchmarking process is not to rank the participating countries, but to analyze policies with a view to stimulating new ideas by political decision makers. The benchmarking process is based on the ability to differentiate: what may be an appropriate policy for a specific country or region may not be appropriate in another environment with a different set of challenges and needs.

BENCHMARK INDICATORS

The identification of the benchmark indicators is based on three basic selection criteria:

- Political relevance. Indicators should be suitable for the discussion of integration policies and should provide an overview of current and potential problems; furthermore, the indicators should support the quality of integration policies and map out the role and influence of policymakers.
- Validity. Indicators should be as simple as possible in order to make them easy to interpret; it is important to use indicators that have been tested within the national context of the Member States and are based on national evaluations.
- Comparability. Indicators should make it possible to compare specific measures that differ in the Member States.

Benchmarking national and regional integration policies should be based on four indicators: qualitative indicators, quantitative indicators, curriculum indicators, and financial indicators.

Road Map for Integration

Integration is a long-term process. It is impossible to provide theoretical answers to the questions of which and how many immigrants should be integrated and what kind of measures might be appropriate. The subjective assumptions of the different European societies are the real yardstick. For this reason integration implies that, in the development of pluralistic societies, social concerns must be taken seriously. As a result, Europeans must conduct an open debate about the probable developments and the associated long-term perspectives of immigration and integration. An open dialogue of this kind should be construed as the kind of cultural progress that can lay the foundations for peaceful coexistence in a Europe based on diversity. This debate must include principles, objectives, competitiveness, and a consistent timetable for examining the efficacy of and emendating the various kinds of action on which agreement has been reached. The debate must lead to a road map for integration in the twenty-first century.

Such a road map should include a burden-sharing agreement between the European Union and the Member States and be based on the following guidelines: as much regulation as necessary; as much support as possible; and as much flexibility as is opportune.

The road map will connect integration with other policy areas; dispose of taboos (for instance, the taboo of linking the fight against terrorism with integration issues); and attract attention (try to engage large sections of the public and the media by addressing the issue in a positive way and prevent its exploitation by populists).

BENCHMARKING IN IMMIGRANT INTEGRATION[1]

HAN ENTZINGER AND RENSKE BIEZEVELD

INTEGRATION INDICATORS

This section will explore some of the major indicators of integration and will discuss their usefulness for measuring integration.

SOCIOECONOMIC INTEGRATION INDICATORS

Employment
Employment is widely seen as a major road towards integration. But what exactly should we measure in this category? If we wish to account for the distribution between economically active and nonactive members of migrant communities, do we look at registered unemployment or at labor force participation rates? If we wish to compare these rates with the population as a whole, do we account for differences in skill levels? Migrants tend to be overrepresented at lower skill levels, where unemployment tends to be higher. However, this may blur the problem of deskilling of migrants, many of whom work below their actual skill level.

Income Level
An indicator related to employment is income level. Here two problems arise. First, it is unclear whether income should be measured at an individual level or at the level of a family. This is particularly relevant, as migrants often

tend to be either single or part of a large family. A second problem is that in many cultures income is seen as a private affair, and any survey data gathered on this issue are likely to be unreliable.

Social Security
Regarding social security use, we should first be aware that migrants do not always have the same entitlements as nonmigrants. It is also important to know which types of social security one is studying. If we measure use of social welfare and unemployment benefits, we measure dependency. Not all forms of social security, however, are considered to be signs of dependency. Use of child benefits or pension schemes, for example, may be a sign that migrants are well integrated and able to find their way in the host society. As in many other cases, we should also be aware of differential age structures and skill levels when comparing migrant and nonmigrant communities.

Level of Education
The level of education is of crucial importance for migrants when finding a position in the labor market and for success in later life. It is also relatively easy to measure. The most obvious way to proceed is to compare the level of education achieved by migrants with that of the rest of the population (or the population as a whole). As the gap

gets smaller, integration may be rated as more successful. It should be noted here that several examples exist of immigrant communities whose school achievements are above average, for example people of Indian descent in the United Kingdom.

Housing and Segregation

With regard to housing, we may look both at the quality of housing and at patterns of segregation, given the inter-relation between these two factors. Concerning the quality of housing, it is relevant to know how free a person has been in the choice of his or her accommodation and whether that person is a tenant or an owner. It is also necessary to keep in mind the overall characteristics of the housing market in a particular city or country. Whereas certain Member States have an elaborate system of social housing, others have one that is much more limited, which means that more people will be inclined to buy a house. Concerning concentration and segregation, it is very important to decide at which level these are to be measured. If a certain group were spread over a neighborhood, a town, or an entire country proportionately to the population as a whole, the index for this group would be one hundred. Values superior to one hundred indicate concentration. In the case of comparisons, the unit of measurement very much matters.

CULTURAL INTEGRATION INDICATORS

Attitude towards Basic Rules and Norms of the Host Country

Acceptance of basic rules and norms of the host society is often seen as an indicator of acculturation, but it is also very difficult to measure. Determining what the basic rules and norms of a society are is also challenging. Should the constitution be used as the defining source? The vast majority of people will have no problem accepting constitutional norms and rules. But, the constitution likely does not encompass all of society's basic rules and norms. Furthermore, is acceptance enough, or should we also expect some degree of identification with the basic norms? Should migrants' willingness to behave in accordance with these rules be measured? There is little doubt that attitude towards basic norms is an important indicator of integration, but it is extremely difficult to put it into operation.

Language Skills

Language skills also constitute an important indicator of integration and are easier to measure than some other indicators. Language skills determine whether or not a migrant is able to communicate with members of the host society, and they may also affect attitudes towards migrants in the host society (and vice versa). In some Member States, mandatory programs have now been set up for new migrants to learn the language. Monitoring migrants' language skills through these programs would not be difficult. Measuring the language proficiency of migrants who settled longer ago is more challenging. In the past, little attention was given to the need to acquire language skills, partly because the migrant's stay was seen as temporary. Perhaps most feasible is the monitoring of language skills of children of school age. To a certain extent, their language skills may also be an indication of the language skills of their parents.

Frequency of Contacts with Host Country and Country of Origin

It is often thought that migrants who maintain close ties with their country of origin are not well integrated into the recipient society. At first glance, therefore, the number of contacts in the recipient country may be a useful indicator of integration. But, what is a contact and how does one measure it? Moreover, do we differentiate between contacts within the migrant's own community and those outside that community? Do we take the latter to be a better indicator of integration than the former, and, if so, on what grounds? In the private sphere most people tend to seek the company of people who are like themselves. Finally, the number of contacts also depends on the availability of opportunities for contacts. In an immigrant neighborhood or at an immigrant school, fewer of such opportunities exist than in mixed environments.

Choice of Spouse

Among certain migrant groups, the number of people who marry someone from the country of origin is high, even in the second generation. This is often interpreted as a sign of deficient cultural integration. Recently some Member States have taken measures, or are discussing possibilities of doing so, to curtail such practices by imposing stricter conditions regarding age, income, and language proficiency.

Delinquency

High delinquency rates within certain migrant communities are often seen as an indication of weak integration, not only in the socioeconomic sphere but also in cultural terms. Of course, one has to be extremely careful in the comparative use of crime statistics. When comparing immigrants and nonimmigrants in this respect, class and age differences provide a substantial part of the explanation for higher crime rates among immigrants. Furthermore, some offences are specific to migrants, such as working without the required permits. Under all circumstances, it is useful to remember that people are more likely to resort to unlawful acts when formal rules or discriminatory practices make access and participation difficult or impossible.

LEGAL AND POLITICAL INTEGRATION INDICATORS

Annual Number of Migrants Naturalized or with Secure Residence Status

The number of naturalizations and the number of migrants with a secure residence status can be taken as indicators of the willingness of the host country to grant rights and of the migrants to make use of these rights. Naturalization, in particular, can be seen as an expression of loyalty of the migrant toward his or her new country. In this respect, considerable differences exist not only between migrant communities but also between Member States. To a certain extent, differential naturalization rules and practices, rather than divergence in loyalties, account for such dissimilarities. Legislation not only varies among EU Member States, but also among countries of origin. Such differences make benchmarking in the field of immigration and naturalization law very complicated.

Number of Migrants with Dual Citizenship

What has just been said about the difficulties in using naturalization as a benchmark for integration also applies to dual citizenship. Some Member States are much more open towards dual citizenship than others. For citizens of certain states (for example, Morocco), it is impossible to give up their citizenship. Furthermore, as discussed earlier, a continued attachment to the country of origin does not necessarily imply that a migrant is less integrated in the new society.

Participation in Politics
Political participation is usually understood as participation in elections. However, immigrants who are foreign residents do not have the right to vote or to be elected, except at the local level, and only in certain Member States. Still, it is useful to compare turnout and voting patterns of migrants who are entitled to vote with those of the electorate as a whole. Also, the number of councillors and members of parliament with an immigrant background may be a helpful indicator of political involvement among immigrant communities.

Participation in Civil Society
An interesting question when using participation in civil society as an indicator is whether membership in mainstream organizations should be accounted for in the same way as membership in specific ethnic or immigrant organizations. In the case of ethnic or immigrant organizations, some people argue that they foster segregation, while others claim that a truly multiethnic society must offer space to people associating on the basis of a shared cultural identity or a common national origin.

ATTITUDES OF RECIPIENT COUNTRIES AS INTEGRATION INDICATORS

Reported Cases of Discrimination
It is a well-known fact that measuring discrimination is difficult. This holds true for discrimination by individuals and for discrimination at the institutional level, for example by the police. Relevant data from the various Member States are hard to compare because not every country uses the same monitoring system or the same definitions. The European Monitoring Centre on Racism and Xenophobia in Vienna keeps records, but these still do not tell the full story, since the information provided by the Member States has not been standardized. An additional problem is that a high incidence of observed discriminatory practices does not necessarily indicate the existence of more discrimination. It may also be a result of better monitoring systems, which may reflect a strong awareness of the harmful impact of discriminatory and racist practices.

Perceptions of Migrants by the Host Society
A useful tool for comparing attitudes of the population in the Member States is the Eurobarometer Survey Series. As of 2003, it had carried out two surveys of attitudes towards migrants. Dimensions taken into account were multicultural optimism, support for policies that aim at improving migrants' social conditions, attitudes related to repatriation and immigration restriction, and questions concerning the blaming of migrants and the need for assimilation. The problem with this type of survey is that it measures attitudes, not actual behavior. Another disadvantage is that, in terms

of sensitive issues like attitudes towards immigration and integration, there is always a risk that people will give socially and politically desirable answers and not their actual views.

Incidence and Effects of Diversity Policies

Some Member States have actively encouraged diversity management practices both in public institutions and in private organizations. This includes antidiscrimination legislation and measures meant to increase awareness of the need to diversify recruitment practices. The scope of such measures and their effectiveness can be analyzed and compared.

Role of the Media

In all Member States, the media plays a predominant role in the formation of attitudes towards immigration and integration. It is useful to examine this role, for example by analyzing ways in which the media reports on immigration and integration issues. It would be equally interesting to count the number of people of immigrant origin who appear in the media, taking note of the capacity in which they appear. Of course, the media, like many other civil society institutions and organizations, does not really lend itself to government influence. Therefore, any benchmarking studies undertaken in these areas should take place with the full consent of media organizations. Nevertheless, well-designed research concerning the role of the media is strongly recommended in order to acquire a fuller insight into attitudes of recipient societies towards immigration.

IS BENCHMARKING POSSIBLE AND USEFUL?

Now that we have considered a large number of potential indicators for integration and reviewed their strong and weak points, it is time to turn in a more systematic manner to the subject of benchmarking. In this section we will try to answer, at a more general level than in the previous section, whether benchmarking in integration is possible, whether it is useful, and what major pitfalls we may encounter. Can we develop indicators that are sufficiently reliable to inform us about the degree of integration of immigrants in each of the EU Member States, or at least in a number of them? The idea behind these indicators, of course, is that they can be used for comparisons, the main objective of benchmarking. Three types of comparisons seem to be most useful in this field: those between immigrant groups, those between Member States, and those over time.

Assuming that we are able to compare levels of integration with the help of indicators, does this also imply that we can measure and compare the effectiveness of policy instruments aimed at promoting integration? Even if we can find reasonably reliable indicators for integration, the answer to this possibly crucial question is not necessarily affirmative. Measuring the effectiveness of integration policies presupposes a reasonable consensus on how their instruments actually affect the course of the integration process. It is a very difficult question to answer, not only in the area of immigrant integration, but also in many other areas of public policy.

We have defined three major problem areas that must be tackled before we can answer the main question of whether benchmarking is possible and useful: differences in definitions and registration, ambiguity of certain indicators, and differences in policy approaches.

DIFFERENCES IN DEFINITIONS AND REGISTRATION

It is a well-known fact that the Member States differ considerably in defining who is an immigrant. Achieving some form of consensus on this seems imperative for a comparison of immigrant integration. For obvious reasons, differences in definitions also lead to differences in registration. In common international practice, the number of foreign citizens legally residing in a country is usually taken as a proxy for the number of migrants. Immigrants who posses or obtain the citizenship of their country of residence at the moment of their arrival are not counted as immigrants, although they may still be subject to some forms of integration policy. This has been the case, for example, for many migrants originating in former colonies and overseas territories of several Member States and also for migrants with an ethnic background in the country of settlement (for example, Aussiedler in Germany and Pontians in Greece). Migrants who have become naturalized in the recipient country are also no longer included. By contrast, in Member States where the jus soli system prevails, children of foreign migrants born in one of these Member States are counted as immigrants, even though they have never immigrated to that Member State. After a certain number of years, the effects of differences in naturalization policies become clearly visible in the statistics on foreign residents. As one can assume that more integrated migrants tend to be overrepresented among those naturalized, this trend will affect the comparability of the social situation of migrants in different Member States in the long run.

This is why some Member States (e.g., Denmark and the Netherlands) not only register their foreign citizens, but also their foreign born and the children of these foreign born. Doing so makes it possible to monitor the social integration process of immigrants and their communities over a long period of time. Other Member States, however, strongly object to keeping special records of their citizens once they have become naturalized, as this is perceived as discriminatory. Furthermore, by definition, undocumented immigrants are not registered and therefore cannot be included in any form of benchmarking. Yet, in public perception they are still seen as immigrants. The fact that, on a per capita basis, their numbers vary considerably from one Member State to another also has a negative impact on comparative efforts.

The question of who shall be defined as an immigrant may be the most crucial one in any comparative assessment of immigrant integration; it certainly is not the only definition problem we encounter. Many of the potential indicators mentioned in the previous sections are not defined in the same way throughout the European Union. It is well known that indicators such as educational achievement, delinquency, quality of housing, and income levels are defined and registered in different ways in the various Member States. This is not to say that data in these and related fields are always incomparable, but one certainly needs to be aware of such differences before drawing premature conclusions on levels of integration and effectiveness of integration policies. For some indicators, notably those related to the labor market and to unemployment, common European definitions have been developed. For many other indicators, such definitions do not yet exist.

An additional problem is that although Eurostat keeps records on a wide variety of issues, there are few issues where citizenship, nationality, residential status, or migrant origin are used as variables. Apart from data on the number of migrants entering the European Union, records are kept on the labor market position of third country nationals in the different Member States and on naturalizations of foreign citizens. Along with the country reports on these data, Eurostat does provide an overview of these figures, making explicit how they are being measured and what the related policies in the Member States are. To overcome the lack of comparable data on the social and economic integration of immigrants and their descendants in Europe, the Comparing National Data Sources in the Field of Migration and Integration (COMPSTAT) project has been initiated.[2] The objective of COMPSTAT is to collect essential technical information on various sorts of regularly produced microdata sets and statistics that could be used for the analysis of integration of immigrant minorities in Europe. An additional goal is to contribute to increased comparability of these data. COMPSTAT

provides information on where to look for data at the national level, as well as on the quality of the data.

Most of the problems of definition and registration discussed so far in this section relate to the socioeconomic and the legal-political situation of immigrants. Indicators in the cultural domain as well as indicators that reflect attitudes of the recipient population are even more difficult to define and to measure. Apart from statistics derived from censuses, the Eurobarometer could be a useful tool for this type of data. Since 1973, the European Commission has been monitoring the evolution of public opinion in the Member States, thus aiding the preparation of texts, decision making, and the evaluation of its work. Eurobarometer surveys and studies address major topics concerning European citizenship: enlargement, social conditions, health, culture, information technology, environment, the euro, defense, and so forth. Special Eurobarometer reports are based on in-depth thematic studies carried out for various services of the European Commission or other EU institutions and are integrated in standard Eurobarometer polling efforts. The qualitative studies provide in-depth assessments of motives, feelings, and reactions of selected social groups towards a given subject or concept. Data are partly collected through listening and analyzing how respondents express themselves in discussion groups or in nondirective interviews. In 1988 and 1997, special Eurobarometer reports were written concerning attitudes towards minority groups. Another special Eurobarometer report is on employment and discrimination.

AMBIGUITY OF CERTAIN INDICATORS

As discussed in previous sections, several of the indicators are not as clear-cut as they may seem and therefore should be used with care in any benchmarking exercise. For example, segregation indices in housing constitute a commonly accepted indicator of integration. But what does this indicator actually show? What one observer may call segregation, others may see as migrants' understandable preference for living close to one another, perfectly acceptable in a free society. Moreover, immigrant concentrations in certain neighborhoods may serve as a basis for an ethnic infrastructure (shops, places of worship, associations), which ought to be valued positively in a multicultural society.

A similar dilemma may arise in education. Throughout Europe immigrant children tend to become concentrated in specific schools. However, there is ample evidence that the level of achievement of children at schools with high numbers of immigrants does not necessarily differ from that of children at schools with low immigrant concentrations. One possible explanation for this is that over a period of years high-concentration schools have been in a better position to acquire the expertise required for coping with immigrant children than schools with only a few of these pupils.

More ambiguities can be seen in other potential indicators. In fact, such ambiguities reflect differences in policy objectives and contradictions between the course of integration processes in different domains. An integration policy that aims implicitly or even explicitly to assimilate immigrants will define its objectives in terms that are quite different from those of a policy that aims to recognize and facilitate migrant cultures. The same indicators may be used to evaluate these divergent policies, but when it comes to interpreting the effects of these policies, the conclusions that are drawn may be opposite.

Another indicator of integration that is not as obvious as it may seem at first glance is the number of contacts an immigrant has in the country of residence. The usual assumption is that a growing number of such contacts is a sign of integration, as is a diminishing number of contacts with the country of origin. The two trends are assumed to go hand in hand, and that is indeed the case—sometimes. But what if migrants with many contacts in the country of residence also turn out to be the ones with the most contacts in the country of origin? Recent Dutch research has revealed that this is common in many cases.[3] Thus, whereas a distinction is generally made between migrants oriented towards the country of residence and those oriented towards the country of origin, in practice, the distinction should be made between migrants who are well connected and those who are ill connected or marginalized in either society.

In all efforts that aim at measuring integration, we have to be very careful in our choice of indicators. We should ask whether the indicator really indicates what we believe it to indicate and whether our assumptions are based on common wisdom or on facts.

A final problem that arises in any comparative exercise is related to the basis of comparison. To give an example: currently a dispute is going on between German and Dutch scholars about the effectiveness of integration policies in their respective countries.[4] From the German side it has been claimed that unemployment among immigrants of Turkish descent in that country is twice as high as among the population as a whole. By contrast, unemployment among Turks in the Netherlands is three to four times higher than the national average in that country. According to absolute numbers, 18% of all Turks in Germany are unemployed as compared to 10% of all Dutch Turks. The question, of course, is which country has been faring better? The one with the lowest unemployment rate for Turks (the Netherlands) or the one with the narrowest gap in unemployment between natives and immigrants (Germany)? Benchmarking in integration is likely to produce many such dilemmas.

DIFFERENCES IN POLICY APPROACHES

A third obstacle in defining indicators of integration and, more particularly, in benchmarking is the fact that there are substantial differences in integration policies between the Member States. Leaving aside once more the very important question of under what circumstances policy effects can be measured, we must conclude that there are other significant differences.

First, not all Member States have developed integration policies in the same domains. As we have seen earlier, some Member States, particularly those faced with immigration more recently, emphasize the need to improve

migrants' legal situation, but they do not specifically concern themselves with promoting migrants' social integration. They assume that general policies that address legal status will also improve the living conditions of migrants. This policy approach is generally known as mainstreaming. Any form of special treatment is considered either discriminatory or counterproductive, as it may mobilize anti-immigrant feelings. Other Member States, by contrast, have no problems with the development of specific measures aimed at immigrant integration. They argue that the existing instruments may not always account sufficiently for the specific situations in which many migrants find themselves. Therefore, some extra measures are justified, either to recognize migrants' uniqueness (e.g., their religious or cultural identity) or to promote their integration (e.g., through language classes or interpreter services). As a consequence of these very different views of the role of public authorities in promoting integration, a comparative analysis will also produce very different policy instruments. How can we compare the effectiveness of instruments if the objectives of these instruments are totally different, largely because the definitions of integration on which they are based are also quite different?

Second, differences between Member States exist not only in the objectives they define for their integration policies, but also in the policy domains that they are are likely to choose for the implementation of these objectives. If, for example, a country or city has a small public social housing sector, that country or city is not very likely to choose housing as an area for immigrant integration. The obvious reason is that the country's or city's limited involvement in that sector makes it less likely that the objectives can actually be achieved. Likewise, a country with a large public school system is more likely to choose education as a major domain for integration than a country where public influence on education is more limited. Similarly, Member States with an elaborate social welfare system are more likely to give that system a role in their integration policies than Member States with restricted welfare provisions.

In this context, it is also relevant to note that significant differences exist between Member States in their policies of decentralization. In certain situations (e.g., in social security matters) major responsibilities for specific policy areas are situated at the national level, whereas in other cases the same responsibilities lie at the local level. Also, policies that in some cases are developed and implemented by the state are in other cases left to independent agencies or private organizations (e.g., in education or in broadcasting).

The various factors discussed in this chapter will seriously affect any effort in benchmarking of integration and, to an even greater degree, benchmarking of integration policies. However, this does not imply that benchmarking is impossible.

CONCLUDING REMARKS AND RECOMMENDATIONS

Although this chapter is titled "Benchmarking in Immigrant Integration," its ambition is not to set a standard for an ideal integration process of immigrants nor for the possible role of public authorities in that process. This is simply impossible, given the wide variety of factors that influence immigration and integration, the immense heterogeneity of migrant populations throughout the European Union, and the substantial differences in approach of these matters across the Member States.

Nevertheless, awareness is growing that there are not only differences among Member States, but also similarities. First, there is a growing consensus that immigration and integration are interrelated. A well-managed immigration policy should include provisions to facilitate the integration process of newcomers. Second, it is increasingly acknowledged that integration processes are long-term processes. They affect not only the immigrants themselves, but also their children and the receiving populations. Third, immigrant integration is a fairly autonomous process. It can be affected by and supported by public policies, but in our liberal democratic societies it is impossible for the authorities to steer integration completely.

Analysis of developments in the different Member States shows a certain convergence in the assessment of the major issues related to immigration and integration. It is generally understood now that there are institutional as well as cultural aspects to integration. Institutional integration involves immigrant participation in the major institutions of a society, whereas cultural integration has to do with attitudes and identification. The two aspects are interrelated, but in a very complex manner. Moreover, integration occurs in a variety of spheres, where the pace of the process is not always the same. In this chapter we have distinguished between the socioeconomic, the cultural, and the legal and political spheres.

To a certain extent, the various approaches to integration by the different Member States reflect their degrees of experience with immigration. Member States that have been faced with large-scale immigration only recently tend to concentrate their efforts on improving the legal status of immigrants and on combating racism and discrimination. States with a somewhat longer immigration tradition are inclined to incorporate more socioeconomic elements into their policies, such as facilitating integration in the labor market and in the educational system. More recently there has also been a growing attention to the cultural aspect of integration in many of these Member States. They are faced with the dilemma between respect for immigrant cultures in a multicultural environment on the one hand and the perceived need for a core of commonly shared values and identifications on the other. The trend in many Member States recently has been to strive for acculturation through their integration policies. This trend is reflected inter alia in the large-scale introduction of language classes for immigrants, often of a mandatory nature.

In light of the many similarities and differences among the Member States, can benchmarking be a useful exercise? Indeed, divergent immigration traditions and integration patterns as well as variations in legislation and policy instruments make benchmarking a difficult process. Differences in the naturalization policies of Member States, for example, affect the overall number of foreign residents in a country, particularly when viewed over a period of many years. Benchmarking requires indicators that are sufficiently comparable, and these can only be developed if there is a basic consensus on definitions, for example, on seemingly simple questions such as who is an immigrant.

Our assessment of possible indicators in this chapter brings us to the conclusion that benchmarking in integration is possible, but only in a modest way. Currently, no uniform indicators are available that enable us to make relevant and reliable comparisons between all Member States on the process of immigrant integration and the effectiveness of policies. The wide diversity of immigrant populations, policy instruments, definitions, and statistics precludes this. However, on a more modest scale and in specific cases it is possible to draw fruitful and methodologically justifiable comparisons between situations that are relatively similar.

Certain indicators lend themselves much better than others to comparisons across Member States. Especially in the field of labor market participation, the available indicators appear to be sufficiently comparable, although differences in the definition of immigrant still have to be accounted for. We may think here of indicators relating to employment by skill level and by sector, to registered unemployment, and to entrepreneurship. Likewise, in the field of education, available data allow comparisons to be made with relatively little effort. Potential indicators in this field include participation rates for different immigrant communities by school level, school results, and dropout rates.

In virtually all other areas, comparisons between Member States tend to be more difficult, because of differences in indicators (if indicators are even available) and differences in definitions and evaluation. Nonetheless, benchmarking in these areas can be effective if it is limited to a smaller number of Member States, which employ similar definitions and indicators or which pursue similar policies. Much can be learned from the vast body of academic and policy-oriented studies already available that compare aspects of immigrant integration in a limited number of countries.

Benchmarking need not always imply comparisons between countries. It is equally possible to draw comparisons within a single Member State, for example between different immigrant groups, different regions, or over time. This approach enables us to compare patterns of integration within a single Member State under differing conditions. Methodologically, this is somewhat easier than comparisons across Member States, given the greater similarity in definitions, statistics, and policy instruments. Another promising approach would be to compare immigrant communities of the same national origin who live in different Member States. This approach is relatively rare in academic research, but it may help us to understand how differing conditions and differing policies may affect the integration process of a specific national community.

As a general rule, benchmarking tends to be more fruitful the more similar the situations being studied. This facilitates comparisons, not only of trends and developments in integration, but of policy measures and their effectiveness. Under such conditions, benchmarking may help to identify best practices, which may then be discussed and shared among the responsible authorities at the state level and at the local level. After all, it is at the local level where integration often takes shape and where many policy measures are being developed.

In situations where benchmarking has achieved such a level of sophistication, it may be sensible to define policy targets that can be measured on a truly comparative basis. Of course, policy targets can be set any time and under practically all conditions. However, as long as insufficient opportunities exist for comparison, particularly across Member States, it makes little sense to do this in the context of benchmarking.

Benchmarking can be a very useful and effective instrument in the promotion of immigrant integration. However, in this highly diverse and very complex policy field, many obstacles need to be overcome before benchmarking can be implemented on a reasonably large scale. A very useful and slightly less ambitious step towards this would be to develop a monitoring system through which relevant data concerning immigrant integration could be collected from the Member States. Several Member States (e.g., the United Kingdom, Germany, the Netherlands, and Denmark) already have monitoring systems. These systems could be made more comparable, and other Member States could be encouraged to develop similar arrangements. This could be a very useful step on the road towards more sophisticated forms of benchmarking, which, eventually, would benefit immigrant integration throughout the European Union.

ENDNOTES

1 This chapter contains sections 4, 5, and 6 of the authors' report "Benchmarking in Immigrant Integration" (prepared for the European Commission under contract no. DG JAI-A-2/2002/006 by the European Centre on Migration and Ethnic Relations, Rotterdam, August 2003). The full report may be consulted at http://europa.eu.int/comm/justice_home/doc_c entre/immigration/studies/docs/benchmarking_f inal_en.pdf.

2 COMPSTAT was funded by the European Commission in the Fifth Framework Programme. The main product of COMPSTAT is a freely accessible online database containing detailed information on 346 data sets usable for research on migration and integration of immigrant minorities in ten European countries. The database can be found at http://www.compstat.org/.

3 G. Engbersen, et al., *Over landsgrenzen: Transnationale betrokkenheid en integratie* (Rotterdam: Risbo and Erasmus Universiteit, 2003).

4 Ruud Koopmans, "Zachte heelmeesters: Een vergelijking van de resultaten van het Nederlandse en Duitse integratiebeleid en wat de WRR daaruit niet concludeert," *Migrantenstudies* 18, no. 2 (2002): 87-92; Anita Böcker and Dietrich Thränhardt, "Is het Duitse integratiebeleid succesvoller, en zo ja, waarom? Reactie op Koopmans," *Migrantenstudies* 19, no. 1 (2003): 33-44.

The Open Method of Coordination as a Political Strategy in the Field of Immigrant Integration Policy

Bernd Schulte

The Lisbon European Council of 23-24 March 2000 introduced the open method of coordination (OMC) as a new means of coordinating the national policies of EU Member States in policy areas aimed at combating social exclusion and promoting social protection, in particular old-age pensions. This approach followed the model laid down for coordinating fiscal and employment policies at the national level contained in the EC Treaty, though it has not yet been incorporated into the treaty. The OMC is designed to help Member States progressively develop their own national policies. It involves

- creating guidelines for the European Union combined with specific timetables for achieving short, medium, and long-term objectives;
- establishing, where appropriate, quantitative and qualitative indicators or benchmarks for "the best in the EU," tailored to the specific needs of Member States and as a means of comparing good or best practices;
- translating these guidelines into national and regional policies by setting specific targets and by adopting specific measures, taking into account national, regional, and local differences;
- putting in place periodic monitoring, evaluation, and peer review

organized as mutual learning processes in relation to the respective national contexts.

The OMC is, above all, a cross-national learning process, which not only respects but is built on national diversity (e.g., different immigration policies and procedures, different demographic challenges, different traditions and integration policies).

At the same time, the OMC exemplifies a dynamic process of self-transformation of the European social model. It may also function as a key tool for safeguarding and/or developing this model. All European welfare states share certain distinctive characteristics that embody the European social model: normatively, there is a common commitment to social security and social justice. Full employment, universal access to health care, education, and adequate social protection for sickness, maternity, invalidity, old age, unemployment, and social assistance to prevent poverty and social exclusion are widely accepted by all EU Member States and deeply entrenched in law, policies, and institutions. The European social model is based on the conviction that social security and social justice can contribute both to economic efficiency and social progress. As a rule, European governments agree that there is no fundamental conflict between economic competitiveness and social cohesion. In the event of a market failure, the welfare state is able to ensure against specific social risks, including unemployment, sickness, and disability, which the market is unable to provide at an adequate level. Social policy measures can reduce economic uncertainties, enhance the capacity of the individual to adjust, and increase his or her readiness to accept technological, economic, and social change, bear more risks, acquire specialized skills, and pursue opportunities.

Finally, the European social model is marked by a high degree of organization around common interests and by comprehensive negotiations between governments, the social partners, and civil society over conflicts of interests in matters of economic and social policy.

The OMC is a rather pragmatic political strategy that supplements the other European Community instruments, such as legislative procedures, financial means (e.g., the structural funds), and intergovernmental cooperation. The OMC is only one instrument among many. Due to the limitations of EC competencies in the area of immigration, the OMC can be an appropriate way to support national integration policies and thus contribute to the development of an overall EC immigration policy. With regard to the other EC instruments mentioned previously, it must be borne in mind that the OMC as a political strategy must not circumvent the legislative procedures established in the EC Treaty. That means that the OMC must not be overstretched to the detriment of the traditional and "hard" forms of lawmaking,

where these provide a suitable alternative. This will not happen with regard to policies on immigrant integration, however, as this area has not yet been Europeanized, but is instead generally determined by salient national differences in policy legacies and interests, which rule out common European solutions. Instead, the OMC grants opportunities to act in a policy area of common concern where EC competencies are weak and where traditional regulation, as in most Member States, remains inadequate. The core advantage of the OMC lies in its potential for reconciling both national diversity and democratic accountability at the Member State level with common policy ambitions and measures aimed at greater policy effectiveness through indicators, benchmarking, and monitoring.

The OMC must be adapted to the special characteristics of each field of action. This means that it must be applied differently to cater to each specific area of application and that an appropriate procedure must be developed in each case. The experiences drawn from other OMCs are therefore of relevance, but only of limited importance as far as the implementation of this strategy in the field of integration policy is concerned.

Exclusion is multidimensional in nature. As a result, measures to combat social exclusion must be developed in a wide range of policy areas, such as education and vocational training, employment, housing, health, and social protection.

It should be borne in mind that the fight against social exclusion is one of the highest objectives on the agenda of the European Union, and that effort is now oriented around the OMC. Immigrants are one of the main target groups of this policy, because their share in the number of socially excluded persons is, as a rule, very high.

Inclusion means encompassing the entire population in the operations and services of the individual function systems (Luhmann). This signifies that every person must have access to every function system if and to the extent that his or her mode of living requires the use of these respective functions of society. The social welfare system is the manifestation of inclusion, wherein everyone not only enjoys legal status and protection of the law, but must be educated and vocationally trained, must acquire and spend money, and so forth. Against this background, inequality of opportunity is a common problem of all Member States confronting the need to integrate immigrants.

Experience has furthermore demonstrated the need for ensuring active participation of all stakeholders, especially those excluded or exposed to social exclusion, organizations working for their interests, and civil society actors.

The Member States will have to agree on common indicators, the quality of which depends to a great degree on the availability of relevant statistical data. The quality of the entire OMC process is thus strongly influenced by the quality of technical work, because the availability of indicators is an essential prerequisite for the comparability of immigration processes and integration policies in the EU Member States. This is of particular importance with regard to the eight Central and Eastern European Countries (CEEC), as well as Cyprus and Malta, that are set to become EU Member States on 1 May 2004, who must become involved in the OMC process as well. This fact must be borne in mind in the design of appropriate indicators.

The trio of citizenship rights—political rights, civil rights, and social rights—as embodied in Member States' constitutions and in international legal instruments, rests on the assumption that specific rights are essential for members of society to be full citizens. For instance, the fundamental social rights to basic health care and to sufficient resources in order to live in a manner compatible with human dignity[1] are an essential part of a policy to combat social exclusion.

Employment is rightly seen as one—if not *the*—main road towards integration. Access to employment depends, however, on the legal and political status of the immigrant. The same applies to access to the social welfare system, another major path towards integration. Legal and political integration must therefore be considered as the gateway to socioeconomic integration and cultural integration. The impact of legal status on integration policies can be illustrated by reference to socioeconomic integration and, in particular, the social welfare system. The range of persons covered by social protection schemes means exactly that group of individuals included under the provisions afforded by such schemes. The criteria according to which individuals are included depend on various fundamental determinants, in particular the social precepts governing a state's policies.

Social protection schemes based on a universal principle of coverage define the group of protected persons primarily by reference to membership in society as a whole, because they presuppose that all individuals are in need of protection and concern themselves with the social problem situations in which protection is to be afforded. With this approach, the target population for social protection is primarily the entire domestic population, the decisive feature thus being membership in domestic society as a whole.

This membership can be determined according to different inclusion features, namely, (1) national status (i.e., nationality principle); (2) geographical link with the nation's territory (i.e., territorial principle); or variations and combinations of (1) and (2). In the European Union the nationality principle is supplemented by the union citizenship principle.

Inclusion features in social protection can be arranged in different ways. They can include, for example, all persons with a particular national status (e.g., all Germans, whether at home or abroad); all nationals living in the country concerned (e.g., all Germans resident in the Federal Republic of Germany); all individuals, irrespective of nationality, actually resident in the country concerned (e.g., in Germany); all citizens of European Union Member States (nationals, e.g., Germans) resident in the country concerned (e.g., Germany); or EU citizens and those non-EU nationals (i.e., third country nationals resident in the country) who benefit from the specific legal status owing to bilateral or multilateral agreements or to international conventions (e.g., the Geneva Convention). These different designs can vary further by adding a requirement that one of the characteristics mentioned needs to have existed for a certain period of time—for example, a claimant must have been a citizen of the country for a specified minimum period or must be resident in the country. The duration of residence can thus be decisive for inclusion in the social protection scheme.

Accordingly, as far as a person's inclusion in such schemes is concerned, different approaches are feasible. The exact scope of such schemes may embrace

- all nationals of the country concerned at home and abroad (delimitation according to a pure nationality principle);
- all nationals resident in the domestic territory (delimitation according to the nationality principle, restricted by the territoriality principle);
- all nationals of an EU Member State-that is, all European Union citizens or, since 1 January 1994, all nationals of a European Economic Area (EEA) who are resident in the domestic territory concerned (extension of the nationality principle to include all EU or EEA nationalities in connection with the pure territoriality principle);
- all persons resident in the territory concerned (delimitation according to the pure territoriality principle);
- all persons who resided in the territory of the country concerned for a certain period of time and for a definite purpose during their work-

ing lives (delimitation according to the territoriality principle with reference to life history), supplemented by

a) definite period of residence (a time factor);

b) definite period of residence (a time factor) supplemented by other prerequisites such as contribution payments, marriage, child rearing, and social care for elderly or handicapped persons;

c) definite period of residence (a time factor) along with other prerequisites such as EU or EEA nationality.

The eligibility requirements of social protection schemes define the circle of persons to be included in the coverage of such schemes. In this way, they also indirectly regulate the equal or unequal treatment of nationals and non-nationals. It goes without saying that social security schemes linked to residence and not to occupation are best geared toward including not only non-nationals but also nonworkers (either national or non-national).

Existing laws concerning foreigners provide a more or less uniform legal basis regulating the legal status of non-nationals with respect to residence, employment, and other activities and confer upon non-nationals—depending, inter alia, on their origin and the reason for their stay—different titles of residence, stay, and employment. By contrast, however, at the national level there is no specific social law, forming a branch of overall social law, whose purpose it is to confer upon immigrants legal entitlement to benefits and services needed for integration in the host coun-

try. Rather, the status of non-nationals in terms of social law is determined by a sum of different individual regulations of national, international, and supranational (that is, European Union or European Community) origin. In most cases, provisions of social law pertaining specifically to non-nationals take the form of restrictions applied through general social legislation with respect to the non-national status of the person concerned or with respect to extrinsic criteria affecting his or her legal status.

The extent of inequalities in terms of education, vocational training, income from work and other sources, assets, housing, health, company benefits, private insurance, or living conditions affects a variety of different groups, such as the elderly, children, women, the unemployed, and persons with disabilities, but also immigrants. The effective reduction of such inequalities through the legal system, the social welfare system, and other policies and programs is a criterion for the success of integration policies (outcome).

The antidiscrimination rules contained in primary (i.e., the EC Treaty) and secondary EC law have much significance for tax and transfer or benefit systems, as they are directly applicable provisions of higher-ranking (i.e., supranational) legal instruments that take precedence over the municipal law of the Member States and, accordingly, have the power to break national regulations impeding or hampering equal treatment of EU migrant workers and national workers. The antidiscrimination clause was used by the European Court of Justice in order to allow EU citizens to enjoy tax and social advantages in their host countries and to strengthen the statutory legal position of third country nationals in agreements of association or cooperation concluded between the European Union and its Member States or between the European Union and third or non-EU countries. According to the principle established by the case law of the European Court of Justice, a Member State in which specific facts or events take legal effect shall take into consideration, as required, the same facts or events occurring in another Member State as if they had occurred within its own jurisdiction. This principle is of considerable importance as it forbids indirect, or concealed, discrimination and greatly promotes equality of treatment.

We cannot measure progress without comparable indicators. Finalizing a set of commonly defined and accepted indicators relating to immigrant integration must be a top priority. Such indicators should not be a vehicle for defining a pecking order among Member States, but should instead be a tool for preserving and strengthening the quality of integration policies for the benefit not only of immigrants but of Member State nationals as well. Integration must be not a one-way but rather a two-way process.

The EU Member States possess diverse immigration policy traditions and legal and institutional arrangements. They face diverging demographic challenges and immigration processes. Accordingly, their objectives and the instruments they employ to meet the integration challenge will vary widely. At this very early stage, therefore, the objectives of the OMC in the field of migrant inte-

gration cannot be aimed at achieving a common policy but rather at institutionalizing processes for sharing policy experiences and the diffusion of best practices.

Consequently, the following list of indicators to be defined and commonly agreed to by the Member States is very tentative. Debate on these proposed indicators should result in a proposal for a definitive set of indicators, which will serve as a basis for further discussion with both Member States and the European Commission representatives. The number of indicators needed to reflect the different national integration policies of EU Member States must be numerous. Three categories of indicators—(1) legal and political, (2) economic and social, and (3) cultural—are proposed, with several indicators attributed to each of these categories along with subindicators intended to highlight the relevance of the individual indicators.

LIST OF POTENTIAL INDICATORS

I. LEGAL AND POLITICAL INTEGRATION

1.1. Legal Status
- Citizenship (naturalization, dual citizenship)
- EU citizen (citizen of an EU Member State)
- Third country national (status depending on national law of the host country or on bilateral and multilateral agreements, etc.)
- Refugee, asylum seeker
- Foreigners' law

1.2. Political Status
- Right to vote

- Membership or function in a political party or a similar organization

1.3. Immigration Policy
- Objective of immigration policy (e.g., permanent residence, guest worker status)
- Categories of immigrants (e.g., green cards for specific professions)
- Specific integration measures (e.g., language courses, specific forms of education, vocational training)
- Antidiscrimination policies

2. SOCIOECONOMIC INTEGRATION

2.1. Employment (as compared to nationals)
- Education
- Vocational training
- Employee or self-employed
- Profession (e.g., unskilled worker, blue-collar worker, white-collar worker, academic)
- Type of work (standard employment relationship or atypical work such as wage work, part-time, flexible working hours, and new self-employed)
- Formal or informal employment

2.2. Incomes and Income Levels (as compared to nationals)
- Sources of income (e.g., income from work)
- Assets (in the home country or in the host country)

2.3. Tax and Benefit System (as compared to nationals)
- Taxation (e.g., income tax)
- Promotion of savings
- Social welfare or social protection (social security and social systems and related benefits, social services, rehabilitation services, educational assistance, vocational training, etc.)

2.4. Housing (as compared to nationals)
- Ownership or tenancy
- Quality of housing

2.5. Health (as compared to nationals)
- Health status (physical, psychological)

2.6. Family Policy
- Family benefits
- Parent-friendly policies (e.g., in the field of employment)
- Child-care facilities
- Health insurance
- Tax allowances

2.7. Occupational Benefit Schemes (e.g., occupational pensions, fringe benefits)

2.8. Private Insurance Schemes (health care, disability, old-age, etc.)

3. CULTURAL INTEGRATION

- Age
- Sex or gender (equality of men and women)
- Family situation (spouse or partner, children or nationality, origin)
- Length of residence in the host country
- Language skills
- Other learning skills
- Knowledge of the host country (legal and political system, social welfare system, culture, etc.)
- Frequency of personal contacts with nationals of the host country
- Respect by nationals of the host country (e.g., civil servants, fellow workers, neighbors)

- Depiction of immigrants in the media
- Membership in trade unions, employers' associations, other economic, professional, and social organizations
- Participation in elections
- Participation in cultural activities
- Delinquency

- Access to modern technology (e.g., the Internet)
- Access to the legal system (courts or tribunals, legal advice, lawyers, etc.)
- Use of consumer goods (e.g., private car, television set)
- Holidays (home country, host country, third country)

ENDNOTES

1   See in this respect Article 1 of the German Basic Law and Article 1 of the Charter of Fundamental Rights of the European Union.

CIVIC CITIZENSHIP: A NEW CONCEPT FOR THE NEW EUROPE

RAINER BAUBÖCK

CIVIC CITIZENSHIP

The basic idea of civic citizenship has been outlined in the Presidency Conclusions of the Tampere meeting of the European Council on 15-16 October 1999: "The legal status of third-country nationals should be approximated to that of Member States' nationals. A person who has resided in a Member State for a period of time to be determined and who holds a long-term resident permit, should be granted in that Member State a set of uniform rights which are as near as possible to those enjoyed by EU citizens." The council meeting in Thessaloniki on 19-20 June 2003 reaffirmed and broadened this target by calling for "the elaboration of a comprehensive and multidimensional policy on the integration of legally residing third-country nationals."

In its 22 November 2000 communication on a community immigration policy and its 3 June 2003 communication on immigration, integration, and employment, the European Commission has further elaborated on this idea and has introduced the new term "civic citizenship." The main elements of this concept that emerge from the Tampere conclusions and these communications are as follows:

■ The intended beneficiaries of civic citizenship are long-term resident third country nationals residing legally in a Member State.

■ The area within which the status applies is the whole territory of the European Union.

■ Civic citizenship is a legal status with attached rights and responsibilities.

■ Rights and responsibilities of third country nationals should be provided on a basis of equality with those of nationals but need to be differentiated according to length of stay with a progression towards permanent status.

■ The rights and responsibilities of civic citizenship should be based on the EC Treaty and inspired by the Charter of Fundamental Rights.

■ These include the right to reside, receive education, work as an employee or self-employed person, as well as the principle of nondiscrimination vis-à-vis the citizens of the state of residence (Presidency Conclusions of Tampere European Council).

■ A specific right of civic citizenship that the European Commission wanted to include in the new treaty is participation in political life at the local level, such as the extension of local voting rights to third country nationals.

- The opportunity for long-term legally resident third country nationals to obtain the nationality of the state where they reside is mentioned as an objective endorsed by the council (Presidency Conclusions of the Tampere European Council). Civic citizenship could also be regarded as a first step in the process of acquiring the nationality of a Member State (European Commission communication of 3 June 2003).
- Civic citizenship is part of a general policy of coordinating Member States' integration policies towards immigrants from third countries. The commission wants to promote the exchange of information and best practices in this area, including the implementation of nationality laws.

THE NEED FOR CIVIC CITIZENSHIP

The European Union has become one of the main immigrant-receiving global regions. In 2000 about 5% of EU residents did not possess the nationality of the state where they lived; more than two-thirds of these (3.4%) were third country nationals, and only 1.6% were EU citizens living in a second Member State. International migration in the European Union is therefore primarily coming from outside the region, while internal migration remains at a very low level compared to large federal states such as the United States. In some of the major immigrant-receiving countries, the percentages of third country nationals are much higher. In Germany, for example, the share of third country nationals in the total population is 7%, and in Austria 8%.[1]

In contrast to the United States, Canada, Australia, and New Zealand, most Member States of the European Union have until recently not regarded themselves as countries of immigration, and traditional conceptions of nationhood have everywhere been in tension with ethnic diversity resulting from immigration. As a consequence, immigrants are rarely regarded as future citizens, and there is wide divergence between Member States with regard to integration policies towards new minorities emerging from immigration. At the same time, the democratic constitutions of Member States and the common European human rights regime have guaranteed migrants a certain range of basic rights.

Acting on the basis of Article 13 of the EC Treaty as amended by the Amsterdam Treaty of 1997, the European Commission enhanced this common framework in 2000 by proposing two directives on antidiscrimination policies that have since been adopted by the Council of Ministers (Council Directive 2000/43/EC and 2000/78/EC). This is a very important step, although compliance is so far disappointing apart from those Member States that had already developed their own comprehensive national antidiscrimination legislation prior to the directives (Belgium, the Netherlands, Ireland, the United Kingdom, and Sweden). Harmonized antidiscrimination policies are an essential element of creating a common area of freedom, justice, and security in a Europe that has become an immigration continent. Yet they are not sufficient. First, the directives do not cover all grounds of discrimination. While employment-related protection is defined extensively, prohibited grounds of discrimination in access to goods and services are limited to racial and ethnic origin. Second, protection against discrimination in private economic relations cannot overcome those disadvantages and inequalities that emerge from public policies themselves. These disadvantages derive, on the one hand, from an inferior legal status of third country nationals compared to EU citizens and nationals of the state and, on the other hand, from a dominant public culture that creates obstacles for immigrants who do not speak a national language or who practice a minority religion. The idea of civic citizenship responds to the first of these two concerns that are not covered by antidiscrimination legislation.

Three reasons support the need for civic citizenship in the European Union: social cohesion, economic competitiveness, and political equality.

SOCIAL COHESION

An insecure legal status and unequal rights for long-term resident third country nationals contribute to ethnic and racial segregation in labor markets and urban residential areas. For first-generation immigrants these factors reinforce immigrants' reluctance to invest their income into a long-term future in the receiving country and to learn the dominant language. The lack of equal rights specifically affects a second and third generation born in Europe with immigrant ancestry who have inherited their parents' nationalities. Low educational

achievements and blocked social mobility for youths with migrant backgrounds have become severe problems in many European states. In some countries legal disadvantages for long-term resident third country nationals include restricted access to employment and to social welfare benefits, which may directly contribute to higher rates of unemployment and poverty compared to the native population.

ECONOMIC COMPETITIVENESS

Most of the present fifteen and future twenty-five Member States of the European Union face a severe demographic problem resulting from low rates of fertility and increasing life expectancy. This demographic deficit already has a dramatic impact on public health care and retirement pension systems and is expected to create labor supply shortages within the next decade. Although the amount of immigration that would be needed to stabilize the dependency ratio between retired and working-age populations is socially and economically unfeasible, most experts agree that additional immigration will be needed to alleviate the problems of demographic transition. Moreover, in the 1990s a global labor market has emerged for certain skills, especially in information technology, but also to a certain extent in personal services such as health care. Traditional immigration countries, which are confronted much less with demographic problems, have reacted to this by stepping up their efforts to recruit skilled immigrants. Europe is going to face an increasingly tough competition with the United States, Canada, and Australia for the most wanted migrants. In this context, national legislation that does not offer legal immigrants secure long-term residence and rights to family reunification will become an obstacle.[2]

POLITICAL EQUALITY

All Member States of the European Union are democracies whose governments are representative of, and accountable to, their citizens. In modern understanding, the legitimacy of democratic governments rests on principles of equality and inclusion so that those who are permanently subjected to the law are treated as equals before the law and are also represented equally in the making of these laws. The status of permanent resident foreigners is the major exception to these two principles. European states where a significant percentage of the population does not enjoy rights comparable with those of citizens and cannot participate in democratic elections face, therefore, a democratic deficit.

This deficit can be overcome by two complementary means: extending rights that have historically been privileges of nationals to all permanent residents and facilitating access to formal citizenship through naturalization and at birth. The idea of civic citizenship combines both avenues but puts a special emphasis on the equalization of rights for residents independent of their nationality.

The introduction of European Union citizenship by the Maastricht Treaty has highlighted and exacerbated the problem of political inequality. Citizens of the European Union residing in another Member State enjoy special privileges compared to immigrants from third

countries; among these is the right to vote and run as candidates in local elections. European Union citizenship is essentially a bundle of rights for migrants who are nationals of Member States. It provides, therefore, a reference point (which is absent in overseas immigration countries) for determining the rights that can be extended to foreign nationals and a yardstick for measuring the legal discrimination to which third country nationals are subjected.

ALTERNATIVE CONCEPTS AND TERMINOLOGIES

There are some difficulties with interpreting the concept of civic citizenship that are basically of a terminological nature. Since the concept has not been used widely in the context of migration and with the meaning given to it by the European Commission, it is important to clarify how the concept of civic citizenship overlaps with related concepts used in political and academic discourses.

The first difficulty concerns the term "citizenship" itself. In some contexts it is used as a synonym for nationality, which is itself an ambiguous term that may relate either to a legal status of persons as nationals of a state or to membership in a historical community with aspirations for self-government. In a broader sense, citizenship is also used to characterize a bundle of rights and obligations attached to the status of nationality. The widest meaning of citizenship, finally, refers to a collective identity shared by the members of a democratic polity and to virtues (of good or active citizenship) that help to sustain such a polity.

The term "civic" has been frequently used, especially in the US literature, in the last of these three senses. Civic republicanism is a body of ideas that emphasize political obligations and the virtues of political engagement. "Civic" in this sense is often distinguished from "civil," which refers to the public but nonpolitical spheres of society: civil liberties are those that individuals enjoy as private persons; civil society is the realm of voluntary associations and market relations.

The description of civic citizenship provided by the European Commission seems to put more emphasis on the first and second meanings of citizenship as a legal status and bundle of rights and duties. The qualifier "civic" does not refer to ideas of civic republicanism but instead serves to describe a legal status that is more inclusive than citizenship as nationality. In fact, civic citizenship appears to relate to the notion of civil society by suggesting that all long-term residents in European societies should enjoy a common citizenship that is independent of their nationality. This interpretation is confirmed by the German version of the commission's communications, which uses the term "Zivilbürgerschaft."

"Civil citizenship" would, however, not necessarily be a less ambiguous term. In 1949 the English sociologist T.H. Marshall introduced a widely used distinction between civil, political, and social citizenship as three stages of development and bundles of rights that refer to equality before the law, democratic representation, and social welfare provisions, respectively.[3] The content of civic citizenship as outlined by the

commission would clearly cover all three elements, although voting rights for third country nationals would remain less extensive.

Alternative concepts that cover the same ground have been suggested by political scientists since the early 1990s. Tomas Hammar has derived the notion of denizenship from the legal status of denizen, which in English law since the fifteenth century applied to aliens to whom the sovereign granted the status of a British subject but who could not hold public office, inherit property, or obtain a grant of land from the Crown.[4] Hammar has reintroduced this concept to describe the contemporary tendency in democratic states to disconnect citizenship rights from formal nationality and to base them instead on residence. I have in previous works suggested that the same phenomenon could also be described as residential citizenship (or *Wohnbürgerschaft* in the German translation) and that it should be seen as one element in a broader phenomenon of transnational citizenship that also includes naturalization entitlements, a growing toleration for multiple nationality as well as external citizenship that relates immigrants to their countries of origin.[5]

Although the concept of civic citizenship may be regarded as too ambiguous by the standards of academic analysis, it can serve well in political discourses where attributed meanings do not so much depend on initial definitions as on connotations that derive from contexts within which a term is used. A proper and more precise interpretation of civic citizenship will thus prevail if, and only if, the policies behind the idea carry sufficient weight and support. From a political perspective the importance of the concept is that it can now serve as a shorthand reference to a set of policies associated with the Tampere process and might at a later stage become transformed into a formal legal term that could even be included in a European constitution. It would be unwise to change or abandon the terminology at a stage when this process may have lost momentum but has not been irreversibly derailed.

THREE MODELS OF LEGAL AND POLITICAL INTEGRATION OF IMMIGRANTS IN EUROPE

As mentioned above, legal and political integration of immigrants in receiving countries may be achieved along two paths: by promoting the acquisition of the host state's nationality or by extending equal rights to all permanent residents. In the European context, EU citizenship provides for a more complex structure with three possible avenues: acquisition of Member State nationality, direct acquisition of EU citizenship, and civic citizenship.

ACQUISITION OF MEMBER STATE NATIONALITY

In traditional overseas countries of immigration, newcomers have been generally perceived as future citizens.[6] Jus soli acquisition of citizenship by the second generation and easy-to-meet conditions for naturalization have led to the view that there is no need for a special status of civic citizenship. Although the extension of equal protection of the law and various social welfare benefits

to resident aliens has contributed to significantly lower naturalization rates among some groups of immigrants, the acquisition of nationality is strongly encouraged and is still regarded as the main remedy against the insecurity attached to the status of foreign residents. Moreover, the immigration quota and point systems in the United States, Canada, and Australia have meant that large numbers of newcomers receive permanent status as landed immigrants or green card holders right from the start. This is different in Europe, where the normal path of legal integration involves a gradual consolidation of status and extension of rights in several stages over a number of years.

On both sides of the Atlantic, access to nationality is interpreted not only as a change of legal status but also as involving a significant change of national identity in the sense of belonging to a political community. However, in those nations that had been built by European settlers, newcomers have been seen as joining the nation as it already defines itself, whereas in Europe dominant conceptions of nationhood have at best been neutral and at worst hostile towards ethnic diversity resulting from immigration. Although there are significant trends towards more liberal nationality laws in Europe,[7] divergence in this respect is still wider than with regard to the legal status of permanent residents.

Establishing EU citizenship could have provided a reason for adopting a policy goal of harmonizing nationality laws. It appears problematic that access to a common status of citizenship in the European Union is regulated by the

Member States in such very different ways. One could also have assumed that governments have a reason to adopt common standards in order to prevent migrants choosing to settle first in Member States where they can easily naturalize and then moving on to other destinations where they then enjoy access as EU citizens. However, such considerations have prompted neither governments nor the European Commission to put nationality laws on the European agenda. This is still regarded as a remaining core of national sovereignty where Member States want to exercise exclusive control.

DIRECT ACQUISITION OF EU CITIZENSHIP

In response to this peculiar situation, the European Union Migrants' Forum and some other organizations in 1995 suggested bypassing nationality laws by giving third country nationals direct and automatic access to European Union citizenship after five years of residence.[8] This proposal has, however, not gained significant political support. It may also be regarded as problematic on several grounds. First, the proposal would remove internal and external reform pressure from those Member States whose nationality laws are currently very restrictive and still based on an outdated notion of ethnic homogeneity. Second, it could also further devalue EU citizenship in the eyes of native majority citizens for whom it already has little relevance unless they are themselves migrants within Europe. Third, one can argue from a federalist perspective that in a multilevel system of democratic representation every individual who is a member of the encompassing polity must also be a member of one constituent polity. In EU decision making, European citizens are mainly represented by their national governments in the Council of Ministers and secondarily by the members of the European Parliament. EU citizenship for third country nationals would therefore still mean unequal representation in Europe, and it would probably not increase the democratic legitimacy of European institutions.

CIVIC CITIZENSHIP

In the European context, introducing civic citizenship as a distinct status would retain the present differentiation between national citizens residing in their Member States, EU citizens residing in another Member State, and long-term resident third country nationals. Yet it would considerably reduce the difference between the rights and duties associated with these three positions. Moreover, just as EU citizenship is a common status for the first and second group, so civic citizenship should be understood not as a separate set of rights for third country nationals, but as a common baseline shared by all residents in the European Union irrespective of their nationality.

Some observers have interpreted this tendency of disconnecting rights from nationality as a devaluation of citizenship[9] and as opposed to the first strategy of promoting the acquisition of citizenship.[10] In response to these objections, one can point out, firstly, that a strict dichotomy between citizens and aliens has become an anachronism in democratic societies of immigration. Secondly, if naturalization is meant to express a change of political identity and voluntary commitment towards the political community, then a strong discrepancy between the rights of aliens and citizens is itself a devaluation of citizenship because it creates a purely instrumental incentive to naturalize in order to escape legal insecurity and disadvantages. Of course, removing such incentives through civic citizenship may lead to lower rates of naturalization just as the extension of rights for EU citizens has done. It would, however, turn naturalization from an escape route into a personal choice, and this is consistent with asserting the specific value of national and EU citizenship as consensual membership in a democratic community.

This argument presupposes, however, that Member States grant immigrants access to their nationality via naturalization or jus soli acquisition at birth. Ideally, civic citizenship must therefore include common standards for access to the nationality of Member States and thereby also to EU citizenship. In the absence of European Community competence for harmonization in this area, the European Commission can promote comparison and mutual exchange of experiences between Member States and thereby foster convergence towards liberal standards.

So far, this chapter has interpreted and defended the general idea of civic citizenship as outlined by the European Commission. The following sections attempt to go beyond this by making specific suggestions concerning the regulation of access to civic citizenship and its contents in terms of rights and obligations.

ACCESS TO AND LOSS OF CIVIC CITIZENSHIP

On 25 November 2003, the Council of Ministers adopted the European Commission's proposal for a directive concerning the status of third country nationals who are long-term residents. In response to reservations by some Member States, the draft version of the directive (COM (2001) 127 final) has been watered down substantially with regard to conditions of access and the level of protection provided by long-term residence status and accommodates policies of Member States that are irreconcilable with the idea of civic citizenship. Although this may be politically difficult to achieve, a new initiative for civic citizenship should therefore attempt to reopen the debate on some of the provisions in this directive and to define more uniform conditions and entitlements for long-term resident third country nationals. The European Commission might use its prerogative to propose amendments to the directive to this effect. Since the directive has not yet been officially published at the time this chapter was written, the following brief remarks are based on an informal document.

AUTOMATIC ACCESS

In contrast with naturalization, which requires an application and generally allows for an exercise of discretion by public authorities, acquisition of civic citizenship should be automatic after a certain time of residence. Article 7 of the directive mandates access when the criteria are met, but also requires individual application for both first acquisition and renewal and no longer contains the original provision that the issuing of the permit must be free of charge. The notion of automatic access contained in the draft version has been dropped. This mode of access may create obstacles due to financial reasons, lack of information, or bureaucratic procedures. Instead of relying on individual applications, public authorities should have a positive obligation to inform registered immigrants when they have reached the required time of residence (in addition to spreading general public information that encourages immigrants to apply).

CONTINUOUS LEGAL RESIDENCE

A period of five years of residence as a condition for first acquisition seems adequate since this is a frequent standard in Europe for permanent residence status. The directive requires that residence must also be continuous. Continuity is defined as an absence of no more than six consecutive months and a total absence within the five years of no more than ten months. This condition will exclude large numbers of migrants who have settled permanently in a Member State but have spent longer periods in their country of origin (mostly for family reasons). The directive allows for taking into account longer absences for important reasons, but leaves it to the Member States to define these reasons. Generally, only periods of legal residence will count.

REFUGEES AND ASYLUM SEEKERS

The final version of the directive does not apply to refugees or asylum seekers whose applications are still pending (Article 3(2)d). Presumably their status is to be regulated elsewhere. It would,

however, be contrary to the Geneva Convention to give refugees a status less privileged than that of other third country nationals. It should also be clarified that for recognized refugees the period of examination of their asylum claims will count retrospectively (as was suggested in the 2001 draft version of the directive). A difficulty arises for rejected but nondeportable asylum seekers who may stay in Member States for long periods in a semilegal status. In order not to create a class of foreign nationals permanently excluded from civic citizenship, it would be advisable to clarify that their presence in the territory counts as legal residence so that they, too, can be given access after five years.

SUBSISTENCE

The directive requires that permanent residents must provide evidence that they are covered by sickness insurance and have sufficient means of subsistence for themselves and their dependents without recourse to the social assistance system of the Member State concerned (Article 5(1)).[11] Yet once immigrants have acquired an EU long-term residence status they can no longer be expelled on these grounds. Moreover, current national legislation in many Member States already recognizes a principle of consolidation of residence and does not allow the expulsion of immigrants who have stayed legally in the country for a long time for reasons of unemployment or need for social assistance. Permanent exclusion from civic citizenship on these grounds appears therefore unjustifiable. A compromise would be to define a second threshold (of no more than eight years) after which evidence of subsistence is no longer required for access to civic citizenship.

Civic citizenship must be obtained under conditions that are uniform throughout the EU territory. Article 14 of the directive allows Member States to introduce more favorable conditions for the acquisition of a permanent residence permit (e.g., a shorter residence period), but this status does not confer the right of residence in other Member States. For the same reason, the list of conditions for access to civic citizenship must be exhaustive so that Member States cannot introduce additional criteria that bar immigrants from access to this status. According to Article 5(2) of the directive, Member States may, however, require third country nationals to comply with integration conditions, in accordance with national law. This opens the door wide for unequal conditions of access in different Member States. For example, this provision would permit Austria to retain its recent legislation that introduced a mandatory language test as a requirement for permanent residence and threatens those with expulsion who fail to meet this test within four years after arrival. The acquisition of a dominant language by new immigrants should be strongly promoted, and a certain level of proficiency may be required for naturalization. However, permanent residence and access to civic citizenship should not be made conditional on proof of language skills.

RETAINING AND LOSING CIVIC CITIZENSHIP

According to Article 8(2) of the directive, a status of long-term residence in the European Union is granted for a period of at least five years with automatic renewal on expiry if this is required at application.[12] This makes the European Union permit less attractive for highly skilled migrants than the US green card or landed immigrant status in Canada. The permit can be withdrawn by the authorities only under specified conditions such as fraudulent acquisition or expulsion on grounds of serious threats to public policy or public security (Article 12(1)). The notion of threats to public policy appears to be much wider and less well-defined than public security and could permit Member States to exercise broad discretion with regard to expulsions.

When a person holding this status exercises his or her right of residence in another Member State, he or she may retain his or her status in the first state for a transitional period of up to five years until acquiring civic citizenship in the second state. Outside the territory of the European Community, the status can be retained during an absence of twelve consecutive months (with a possibility for states to allow for a maximum of six years of absence in case of special circumstances (Articles 9(1)c and 9(4)).[13] This very short period fails to take into account patterns of transnational migration that often involve longer periods of return to the country of origin for family reasons. The probably unintended effect of this provision is to create a significant disincentive for return migration. The directive does not spell out whether retaining the status during a stay outside the European Community territory will also give its holder a claim to new admission in any other Member State of the European Union under the same conditions as for those who exercise their right of free movement within the European Union.

RENUNCIATION OF CIVIC CITIZENSHIP

The directive does not provide for voluntary renunciation of civic citizenship. In the case of national citizenship, renunciation is constrained by the desire to avoid statelessness and is often only permitted after leaving the country permanently. This also restricts possibilities to opt out of citizenship duties such as military or jury service while staying in the country. At the same time, liberal democracies must grant renunciation to persons who want to acquire another nationality after having settled abroad.

None of these reasons apply to civic citizenship. Normally, holding civic citizenship in the European Union should not create disadvantages with regard to third country nationality, such as deprivation of rights to own real estate property or to inherit. Nor should it be an obstacle for acquiring the nationality of another third country. However, third country practices in these areas cannot be determined by the European Union, and individuals may have special reasons for wanting to waive their rights as civic citizens. There should, therefore, be a simple procedure of voluntary renunciation. Since civic citizenship carries hardly any specific legally enforceable duties that would not also be imposed on temporary residents,

there is no obvious reason to refuse such renunciation for persons while they continue to reside in the European Union's territory.

RIGHTS INCLUDED IN CIVIC CITIZENSHIP

RIGHTS INCLUDED IN THE DIRECTIVE ON LONG-TERM RESIDENT THIRD COUNTRY NATIONALS

The directive on long-term resident third country nationals covers the following core rights that must be included in civic citizenship, but in its final version fails to provide for full equality of treatment and nondiscrimination vis-à-vis EU citizens and nationals of the state of residence:

- right of residence (right to settle in another Member State, protection against expulsion)[14]
- right to work (employment or self-employment anywhere in the European Union)[15]
- right to education, vocational training, and recognition of qualifications
- family reunification (when establishing residence in a second Member State)
- freedom of association (including membership in organizations representing workers and employers)
- right to social security, social assistance, and social protection[16]
- access to goods and services available to the public (including procedures for obtaining housing)

Rights in the Charter of Fundamental Rights

The European Commission's communications suggest that additional rights should be eventually included in a status of civic citizenship and refer in this regard to the Charter of Fundamental Rights. The charter's rights can generally be subdivided into three categories: universal human rights, rights regulated under national and/or European Community law, and specific rights of EU citizens. Civic citizenship will obviously cover the first group of rights and ought to include those from the second group that are specifically relevant for migrants (such as respect for cultural diversity in Article 22). The most important question is which among the rights currently attached to EU citizenship should be extended to civic citizenship.

In this category are rights to mobility—the freedom to work and to reside in any Member State (Article 15(2), Article 45) and to nondiscrimination on grounds of nationality (Article 21(2)). In these matters, civic citizenship ought to remove restrictions and inequalities that the directive on long-term resident third country nationals still allows for.

A second kind of right involves accountability and transparency of the European Union's administration towards its citizens. They are covered in Article 41 (good administration), Article 42 (access to documents), Article 43 (access to ombudsman), and Article 44 (right to petition). These rights are granted not only to EU citizens but to any natural or legal person residing or having its registered office in a Member State.

The final group consists of rights to diplomatic protection (Article 46) and political participation—that is, the right to vote and to be elected in European Parliament elections (Article 39) and municipal elections (Article 40).

EU citizens have a subsidiary right to diplomatic protection by other Member States in countries where their own state of nationality cannot provide such protection. It is probably difficult to extend this right to third country nationals, since this could be seen as illegitimate interference under international law unless their state of nationality agrees. Diplomatic representatives of Member States should, however, offer assistance to third country civic citizens in matters where this is acceptable to the state of present abode and to the state of nationality.

Political Participation Rights

The arguments raised against the proposal to give third country nationals direct access to EU citizenship apply also to the right to participate in European Parliament elections. The main reason why granting this right to third country nationals may appear relatively unproblematic today is that participation rates and general interest among European citizens in the debates and decisions of the European Parliament are shockingly low. If the European Parliament gains additional powers and elects the European Commission president and if EU citizens would eventually regard the Parliament as their direct and individual representation in the European Union, then the reasons for reserving European voting rights for EU citizens who are also citizens of Member States would become more obvious. As pointed out in the previous section, in a federal system the constituent units are themselves also represented in the governance of the wider polity. Equality of representation requires therefore that voting rights in constituent units and a federal legislature be connected with each other. Within a federal democracy it would be quite unthinkable to give the franchise at the federal level to a group of persons who do not also possess it in provincial elections.

This argument does, however, not apply to the local level. Municipalities are neither constituent units for the Member States nor for the European Union. From a perspective of democratic theory there is no clear argument why local voting rights have become an exclusive right of EU citizens. This privilege is especially hard to justify since it creates an inequality within the municipality between third country nationals who must in some countries wait ten years before they can naturalize and vote in their local community and EU citizens who can vote shortly after taking up residence. The extension of freedom of settlement throughout the European Union to long-term third country nationals will make this unequal treatment even more obviously illegitimate.

The main objection against including local voting rights in civic citizenship refers to constitutional obstacles in several Member States that want to preserve homogeneous conditions for participating in local, regional, and national elections. However, this objection is rather weak since these countries already had to amend their constitutions as a result of the Maastricht Treaty provisions on the local franchise for EU citizens. The experience in countries that already have extended the local franchise to all long-term resident third country nationals (i.e., all Scandinavian states, the Netherlands, and Ireland) shows that this contributes importantly to the political integration of immigrants by creating incentives for political parties to compete for their votes.

One additional right that is currently curtailed for third country nationals in several present and future Member States is the freedom to join political parties and to be a member of their governing boards. This political liberty ought to be included in civic citizenship as well. Even if voting rights in national elections remain attached to the nationality of the state in question, participation of third country nationals in political parties can serve for the individual as an important step towards naturalization and for immigrant groups as a vehicle for articulating their interests that are otherwise ignored as long as they cannot vote.

OBLIGATIONS OF CIVIC CITIZENSHIP

The two communications of the European Commission emphasize that civic citizenship should encompass rights as well as responsibilities or obligations. However, the relevant legal documents such as the EC Treaty and the Charter of Fundamental Rights provide hardly any cues as to which specific responsibilities and obligations might be attached to this status.

Quite obviously, individual rights of EU citizens and third country nationals imply corresponding obligations of government institutions at national and European levels. If responsibilities and obligations are, however, understood as those of individuals, their relation to rights and their specific content is far from clear. A strong asymmetry between rights and obligations is a general feature of modern democratic citizenship. There is a "changing balance between rights and duties. Rights have been multiplied, and they are precise. Each individual knows just what he is entitled to claim."[17] Citizenship duties include paying taxes and social insurance contributions, compulsory education, and military service. "The other duties are vague, and are included in the general obligation to live the life of a good citizen." [18]

Since the 1980s, a communitarian current in Western and East Asian political thought has claimed that rights-based liberalism might be corrosive for social cohesion and has suggested redrawing the balance by emphasizing civic responsibilities and duties. The policy implications of these ideas focus, however, more on widening the scope of government powers to promote specific values, ways of life, and cultural identities but remain often vague with regard to legal and political obligations of individuals.[19]

For native European populations, adding responsibilities and obligations to rights when introducing civic citizenship may help to increase the political acceptability of the idea that third country nationals need more rights. However, if the connection between rights and obligations remains only a public relations exercise, then the idea itself may come under attack for lacking clarity and consistency. A discussion of which general and specific duties are included in civic citizenship should therefore not be avoided.

GENERAL DUTIES: OBEYING THE LAW AND SUPPORTING CONSTITUTIONAL VALUES

There is no difference between third country nationals, EU citizens in other Member States, and nationals of those states with regard to the general obligation to obey the law of the Member State and of the European Union. Whether citizens of all three kinds also have an individual obligation to support the basic values and principles listed in the European treaties and the draft European constitution is a more controversial question, since this is a nonenforceable duty that might be invoked rhetorically to justify intolerant attitudes towards religious and ethnic communities that are not regarded as sharing European traditions. One important difference between naturalization and the acquisition of civic citizenship is that in the former case foreign nationals are in some countries actually tested for basic knowledge of the constitution or asked to take an oath to support it. Making similar requirements for civic citizenship would be entirely inappropriate. It would undermine automatic acquisition of this status and could serve as a pretext for discretionary denial.

SPECIFIC DUTIES OF LOYALTY

Similar considerations apply to the question of whether civic citizens have the same duties to be loyal towards their state of residence as naturalized and native-born citizens of that state. Growing up as a citizen creates a presumption that the state can demand proofs of loyalty in cases where its vital interests are at stake, especially in the case of international conflict. In the process of naturalization immigrants consent explicitly to this obligation. However, no such consent can be implied from applying for a status of permanent residence and civic citizenship.

Generally, countries of origin expect some loyalty from their citizens abroad who have chosen not to naturalize in their country of residence. This holds for European citizens living abroad just as it does for third country nationals in Europe. Attaching an obligation of loyalty to civic citizenship would therefore provide a ready excuse for regarding this status as incompatible with holding or newly acquiring the nationality of a third country and could in extreme cases even generate statelessness.

EU citizenship does not include specific duties of loyalty towards the European Union itself, so the question of whether such duties should be extended to civic citizenship is currently a moot one. This might change if and when the Common Foreign and Security Policy will have been fully integrated. Even then, however, the special relations of third country nationals to their countries of origin ought to be taken into account.

Taxes and Other Financial Contributions

The duty to pay taxes and compulsory contributions for social insurance or fees for public services is included in the general duty to obey the law and is the same for all residents. On a European level, direct individual taxation as a contribution to the budget of the European Union should also apply in a uniform way to all residents. This would strengthen the public perception that third country nationals contribute to financing European integration and should therefore also enjoy rights within an integrated European Union and not merely within their states of residence.

Third country nationals may, however, be in a special position in certain regards that require specific exemptions. For example, the US government taxes its citizens' income earned abroad, and European states responded by concluding bilateral agreements to avoid double taxation. Third country nationals also enjoy specific protection against certain government policies, such as expropriation without compensation. In the realm of fiscal policies this is again a moot question since such policies are prohibited under European law.

Compulsory Military and National Service

This is very different with the right of states to draft their citizens for military service. Under international law, this obligation must not be imposed on foreign nationals. The US view of immigrants as presumptive citizens has, however, served to justify the rule that foreign nationals can be drafted too.

Military service has historically been the core obligation of (male) citizenship. In nineteenth century France, it also provided a reason for facilitating the acquisition of citizenship in order to redraw the balance between the obligations of nationals and foreign residents.[20] The contemporary trend towards professional armies and voluntary service has made this a less important and controversial asymmetry. No military obligations of this kind are included in European Union citizenship, nor is it likely that they will ever be, even if eventually integrated European defense forces are created.

In some countries where compulsory military service has been abandoned, there have been suggestions to replace it with an equally compulsory national service that would oblige young people to perform unpaid work for charitable organizations, public emergency services, and so forth. As far as I know, no such policy has yet been adopted by a Member State. If it were implemented, one could argue that such a duty does not involve a commitment of loyalty that is incompatible with holding a foreign citizenship and may therefore also be imposed on long-term resident third country nationals under the condition that their states of origin agree to accept this as a substitute for military service in the state of their nationality.

Conclusions

Civic citizenship for third country nationals is an idea that has great relevance and potential in contemporary Europe. It can be regarded as responding to the specific context of immigration in the European Union, which is different from traditional approaches towards immigrant integration in overseas countries as well as in many of the EU Member States. The basic elements of civic citizenship as outlined in the Presidency Conclusions of the 1999 Tampere European Council and the communications of the European Commission on harmonizing immigration policy provide a useful starting point for fleshing out the idea and for including it in a future constitutional treaty or revision of the EC Treaty. The European Commission's draft directive concerning the status of third country nationals who are long-term residents would have provided a good starting line for this endeavor, but the final version adopted by the Council of Ministers takes several steps backwards. What is currently needed is a vigorous public campaign in order to give some political life to the idea of civic citizenship as a status of equality for all long-term residents in Europe irrespective of nationality. If such a campaign is successful it could lead to a fresh start and a more detailed consideration of the rights and obligations that should be attached to this status.

ENDNOTES

1 European Commission, *European Social Statistics: Migration* (Luxembourg: Office for Official Publications of the European Communities, 2002), 17.

2 In August 2000, Germany introduced a green card program with residence permits limited to five years. With only 15,000 applications as of mid-2003, the attractiveness of this package has been weaker than expected.

3 Thomas H. Marshall, "Citizenship and Social Class," in *Class, Citizenship, and Social Development: Essays by T. H. Marshall* (New York: Anchor Books, 1965).

4 Tomas Hammar, *Democracy and the Nation-State: Aliens, Denizens, and Citizens in a World of International Migration* (Aldershot: Avebury, 1990), 14; Tomas Hammar, "Denizen and Denizenship," in *New Concepts of Citizenship*, CEIFO Publications, no. 93, eds. Atsushi Kondo and Charles Westin (Stockholm: Centrum för forskning om internationell migration och etniska relationer, 2003), 39.

5 Rainer Bauböck, *Transnational Citizenship: Membership and Rights in International Migration* (Aldershot: Edward Elgar, 1994); Heinz Kleger, ed., *Transnationale Staatsbürgerschaft* (Frankfurt am Main: Campus, 1997).

6 There have been certain exceptions to this rule, such as the exclusion of Chinese immigrants from US citizenship between 1882 and 1943.

7 Randall Hansen and Patrick Weil, eds., *Towards a European Nationality: Citizenship, Immigration, and Nationality Law in the EU*, (Basingstoke: Palgrave Macmillan, 2001).

8 Migrants' Forum, "Proposals for the Revision of the Treaty on European Union at the Intergovernmental Conference of 1996," *The Forum Series* 2 (1996).

9 Yasemin N. Soysal, *Limits of Citizenship: Migrants and Postnational Membership in Europe* (Chicago: University of Chicago Press, 1994); David Jacobson, *Rights Across Borders: Immigration and the Decline of Citizenship* (Baltimore: Johns Hopkins University Press, 1996).

10 Noah Pickus, ed., *Immigration and Citizenship in the Twenty-First Century*, Lanham: Rowman & Littlefield, 1998).

11 In its opinion on the 2001 draft directive, the Economic and Social Committee has urged reconsideration of this provision, as long-term resident status should be granted solely on the basis of the period of legal residence (CES 1321/2001).

12 The initial version of the draft directive had defined the status as permanent with no need for periodic renewal.

13 The draft directive had suggested a period of two years of permissible absence.

14 Article 14 allows for a derogation that permits Member States to retain existing legislation that limits the total number of persons that may be granted right of residence. Immigration quotas for third country nationals exist in Austria and Italy.

15 Article 11(3)a of the directive permits Member States, however, to "retain restrictions to access to employment or self-employed activities in cases where, in accordance with existing national or Community legislation, these activities are reserved to nationals, EU or EEA citizens." This could, for example, allow Member States to deny long-term resident third country nationals access to certain segments of their labor markets or to restrict the overall numbers of third country nationals employed through a quota regime. This provision is incompatible with the core intention of the directive that long-term resident third country nationals should enjoy the same access to a European labor market as EU citizens.

16 Article 11(1)d of the directive has watered down the right to equal social protection by allowing Member States to limit equal treatment as regards social assistance and social protection to core benefits that cover at least minimum income support, assistance in case of illness, pregnancy, parental assistance, and long-term care.

17 Marshall, 129.

18 Ibid.

19 Will Kymlicka and Wayne Norman, "Return of the Citizen: A Survey of Recent Work on Citizenship Theory," Ethics 104, no. 2 (1994): 352-81.

20 Patrick Weil, *Qu'est-ce qu'un Français ? Histoire de la nationalité française de la Révolution à nos jours* (Paris: Grasset, 2002).

PART 5

BEST PRACTICES

INTRODUCTION

The previous sections dealt with the conceptual aspects of integration and developed common European indicators for successful integration.

The aim of this section is to bridge the gap between conceptual knowledge and practical experience by providing concrete examples of integration activities in European Member States. In European countries a great variety of formal and informal integration practices exist on the local, regional, and national levels that foster social, cultural, and/or economic integration.

The following chapters analyze current integration programs and examine original projects across the European Union that approach immigrant integration in an innovative, proactive, and sustainable way. In so doing, we want to offer ideas, insights, inspiration, and instructive success stories of integration strategies that have been proven to work.

In order to develop comparable and transferable models of best practices, a questionnaire was prepared to identify the effects, results, resources, and sustainability, as well as the expertise and networks, that are involved in best practices. The authors were invited to address these guiding questions in their chapters. While the first sections of this book focus on the integration of immigrants, this section includes practices that emphasize the integration of refugees and asylum seekers. Although the methods of integration do not essentially differ, refugees pose a wholly different challenge to the European Union. As the 1990s showed, regional wars increasingly lead to often unexpected and rapid waves of refugees entering the European Union. This trend demonstrates a need for the European Union to meet the challenge of adequately receiving and integrating refugees. The examples included in this section intend to contribute to this increasingly pressing issue.

The chapters focus on Member States that are experienced with integration as well as those that are less experienced with integration. Some countries have long-standing practices in the area of integration, while others have only just started to develop national policies and regional and/or local practices. Thus, the following chapters demonstrate once more that Member States vary considerably in the ways they conceive of and approach the integration of third country nationals and in the extent to which they have developed and implemented integration strategies.

Belgium

Thierry Timmermans

The King Baudouin Foundation project presented here is only one of many initiatives that have been successfully developed in Belgium to foster admission, reception, and integration of new migrants. By no means should this project be perceived of as superior to others; rather, it is a modest contribution toward developing migrants' abilities that deserves recognition.

Description of the Project

The project, Mutual Support for Newcomers, was launched in April 2003 as part of a King Baudouin Foundation initiative focusing on "migration and new forms of hospitality." The initiative will be run over a three-year period, until 2005, as part of a wider social justice program. The program's mission is to enhance the ability of vulnerable or discriminated people to realize their aspirations to well-being.

With Mutual Support for Newcomers, the King Baudouin Foundation seeks to support, as a grant maker, projects that groups or associations of new migrants are keen to develop for their own benefit or for the benefit of other new migrants. The projects should provide for concrete solutions to real precarious and vulnerable situations that new migrants face while starting a new life

or seeking to develop new perspectives in Belgium. No field of activity is excluded: improving housing conditions, facilitating access to information on services developed for new migrants, encouraging participation in these services, offering aid or support for various administrative functions, bringing people out of their isolation, facilitating access to medical and mental-health care, and so forth.

For the purpose of this campaign, all foreigners having arrived in Belgium after 1992 and living in the country as an asylum seeker, as a refugee, as a regularized foreigner, or as a newcomer having applied for family reunification are considered to be new migrants. The supported projects could even benefit undocumented migrants by helping them gain access to fundamental rights in the fields of emergency medical care, education, and labor.

In 2003, project proposals were solicited via a call for proposals in three languages: Dutch, French, and English, so as to ensure that the target groups of potential initiators and beneficiaries were reached. Information was distributed through specific channels (associations, magazines, churches, etc.) that were primarily identified through consultations with key observers of newcomer communities.

Supported projects had to be completed within one year. Grants were limited to five thousand euro. An independent jury selected the grantees. Members of the jury were representatives of regional or local authorities, academics, experts in migration-specific mental-health care, journalists, new migrants, and staff members of associations defending the rights of or working for the benefit of foreigners. An advisory committee helped the King Baudouin Foundation shape and evaluate the Mutual Support for Newcomers project as a whole.

THE PROJECT'S APPROACH

The Mutual Support for Newcomers project is part of a larger migration initiative at the King Baudouin Foundation, based on analysis that divides migration and postmigration processes into three successive phases: admission, hosting, and integration of migrants. Mutual Support for Newcomers focuses on the first two stages, admission and hosting facilities, by recognizing the abilities that new migrants develop through what are usually called newcomer communities but which might be described more accurately as informal and mobile networks of strategic alliances that often help vulnerable newcomers to cope with difficulties. The project aims to empower these networks of shared resources so that they can better match the private and public services offered by the host communities or authorities. As a result, service providers and designers of reception policies can learn from the projects in order to tailor their services to the needs and abilities of new migrants.

Since not all newcomers are accustomed to applying for project support or conducting project implementation, they were allowed to seek support from voluntary project partners (for example, public assistance services and Belgian associations).

THE PROJECT'S RESULTS

In the first year of the project, the King Baudouin Foundation received 240 submissions, out of which the jury selected twenty-nine projects for funding. The projects covered the following main areas:

- spreading information about refugee rights and procedures, as well as social services, for the benefit of newcomers via community-linked communication tools (the *Gazetka* paper for Polish communities; the Iranian online community http://www.iranian.be/; a local Russian community journal; and a newly created leaflet for Roma refugees from Kosovo);
- creating helpdesks for information sharing, services orientation, and mediation in problem situations (among English-speaking African communities in Brussels, mixed groups of refugees in different localities, etc.);
- helping newcomers escape social isolation (through workshops, musical events, discussion groups, etc.);
- helping groups of refugees obtain access to mental-health care;
- easing refugees' access to basic goods (for example, creating shops in the vicinity of integration centers with food items from the home country);

helping people gain access to housing (for example, assisting members of an African church choir to mediate between tenants and owners in Antwerp for the benefit of their community).

Almost all supported projects depended upon the assistance of active and devoted volunteers; the grants were mostly used to equip volunteer networks.

FUTURE CHALLENGES

After having examined the first round of submissions and selections, the jury and the advisory committee came to the following conclusions:

- The overwhelming response demonstrates a strong demand for recognition of newcomers' abilities.
- While highlighting their communities' capabilities, project organizers sometimes overlooked real problems that their beneficiaries face in daily life.
- There seem to be strong signals that some refugees are caught in situations of isolation.
- While the Mutual Support for Newcomers project has drawn a wide response, it still has not reached many potential project initiators or promoters.

- Newcomers need opportunities to help Belgian institutions become more accessible to others in the newcomer community.

The King Baudouin Foundation initially planned to launch a separate campaign that would specifically target welcomers —that is, people who live or work with new migrants and who are eager to remedy the difficulties they may encounter while living or working together with newcomers. The distinction between newcomers and welcomers proved to be less than clear-cut. The first newcomers campaign revealed that sometimes welcomers were the undeclared project initiators.

The King Baudouin Foundation has since decided to merge both initially separate campaigns into one single call for projects. Projects can now be set up by groups of new migrants or by established immigrant aid groups who want to cooperate with them to create synergies. Projects will still be aimed at remedying difficult situations faced by newcomers and their hosts. The merger increases available budgets; so, an increased impact can be expected. The consequences of this will be assessed after completion of the first supported projects.

ENGLAND

AUDREY ADAMS AND HAVEN LUTAAYA

THE 1990 TRUST

The 1990 Trust is a national black[1]
-led nongovernmental organization. Established in 1990 to
influence policy decisions, the work of
the 1990 Trust involves analyzing policy
from a black perspective and empowering
and enabling local communities to self-
organize around issues that affect their
daily lives. This chapter outlines how
the 1990 Trust worked with these
groups of women to develop and deliver
a capacity-building project aimed at
empowering and reducing the barriers
to engagement with civic society.

BACKGROUND

The United Kingdom has experienced a
significant change to its population
since the 1950s. The late 1950s, 1960s,
and 1970s saw the migration of immigrants from the Caribbean, sub-Saharan
Africa, and Southeast Asia. However,
more recently with legal restrictions on
immigration from these regions and the
increase in civil wars and insurgencies
around the world, the United Kingdom
has seen a shift in migration from the
old empire to people from war-torn
states seeking asylum and refuge.

Black and other minority groups still
experience hostilities and racial dis-

crimination in the form of social exclusion, manifested in the criminal justice
system, housing, education, and
employment. However, the aftermath of
September 11 and the war on Iraq has
increased religious discrimination, in
particular anti-Muslim feelings leading
to a significant rise in hostility and
attacks on Muslims. Coupled with this
has been an increase in the antagonism
directed at asylum seekers. The anti-
asylum rhetoric from some sections of
the media and some politicians has
inflamed the situation further by implying that terrorists are now entering the
United Kingdom under the guise of
seeking asylum. Far-right parties have
seized the opportunities of the inflamed
race debate to field more candidates in
local and European elections.

Misinformation from sections of the
media has led to a general view that
many more members of black and other
minority groups live in the United
Kingdom than actually do. For example,
a Market and Opinion Research
International (MORI) poll in 2001
found that most people estimated the
number of black people and other
minorities to be about 22% of the population.[2] In fact, the 2001 Census
showed that only 8% of the population
classified themselves as nonwhite.[3]
These small numbers, however, are not
reflected in the proportion of black and

other minority people in public life. Structural inequalities within the United Kingdom reinforce this general lack of representation and, in particular, the lack of representation of black women in the political process at all levels.

There is, therefore, a climate of increasing disenfranchisement of black people in Britain, and it is this element that is driving the current work program of the 1990 Trust. The program's aim is to ensure that more black people have a voice in the social and political policy debates that are currently being led by government, the media, and academia.

Policies and Strategies

The principal legislative means of tackling race discrimination in the United Kingdom is through the Race Relations Act 1976, as amended by the Race Relations (Amendment) Act 2000. The act provides protection in employment, education, planning, and access to goods and services. In 2003, two new directives from the European Commission were adopted in the United Kingdom-the Race Directive, which makes it unlawful to discriminate in employment, training, education, health, security, cultural beliefs, and goods and services, and the Employment Directive, which makes it unlawful to discriminate in employment on the grounds of religion, sexual orientation, or age. In addition, the Human Rights Act 1998 adopted the European Convention on Human Rights into domestic law and, for the first time, allowed individuals to take any complaints deemed to be in breech of the convention rights to domestic courts.

The Human Rights Act is particularly important in regard to the right to practice one's own religion and culture.

The implementation of such schemes, however, is meaningless if communities are unaware of their existence and of their entitlements under the schemes. It is important that people are empowered with the skills, knowledge, and information to make effective use of the legislation. The 1990 Trust Capacity-Building Project with black women was developed within this context. The aims were to ensure that participants played a role in determining the content of the project, to familiarize groups with political systems, and to inform participants of recent changes to legislation that would protect against inequalities and improve standards of living.

Capacity-Building Project with Black and Other Minority Women

Recent changes to legislation and social policy have meant that black communities have an array of new information to consider. The 1990 Trust, with the strategic objective of developing community leadership, initially worked with local community leaders in Bedford, Hillingdon, and Lambeth on the issue of social housing. Through this exercise, some of the women expressed a need to gain a more in-depth understanding of local structures, since a lack of knowledge and information on the workings of local government was preventing them from accessing some local services. The women wanted assistance in acquiring these skills, and, consequently, the capacity-building programs[4] were developed to enable knowledge of the political system that would provide the means to effective engagement in local issues. Three groups of women—representing a cross section of Caribbean, African, and Asian women—were targeted by these programs. The participants were drawn from a Bangladeshi Asian women's group in Bedford; an Asian women's group in Hillingdon consisting of Punjabi, Sikh, Gujarati, and Hindu women; and African and Caribbean women connected to Single Parent Aid in the London Borough of Lambeth.

AN OUTLINE OF THE PROJECT

The 1990 Trust Capacity-Building Project was participant led, and, as such, the women were involved in developing the content of the programs in each area and in identifying their own learning and development needs. The programs included a course composed of ten monthly sessions that focused on key public services, authorities, and agencies that would be important to the participants' everyday experiences. Women with local knowledge were employed to run the programs, with the assistance of volunteers. The areas of study chosen by the women included central and local government and their relationship to the European Parliament; key services, such as education, housing, and health departments; race legislation; and the police department and criminal justice system. Policymakers and decision makers, including local members of Parliament and department heads, were invited to speak to and with participants throughout the programs.

Programs also included visits to the houses of Parliament and a trip to Brussels for thirty women drawn from the three groups mentioned previously. This enabled women from the different areas to meet up and to share program experiences. The trip itself was a first for many women who had not traveled out of the country for many years and who had never been to anywhere else in Europe.

The project provided an innovative and creative way of learning for the women. This included the development of learning portfolios, which were either written in English or the participant's mother tongue-for example, Bengali for the Bangladeshi women's program in Bedford. Individual reviews of the women's personal development plans with the program coordinators and the 1990 Trust ensured that learning objectives were met and that any additional support needs were identified and tackled. For example, the Lambeth group discovered that one of the participants had literacy needs. The coordinator, a qualified teacher, was able to provide additional resources to help to improve her literacy skills, thus ensuring the continuation and completion of the course by the individual. To provide additional literacy support, photographic records of each session were developed and kept.

EFFECTS AND RESULTS OF THE PROJECT

"While attending to all the sessions which were run at the centre, I gained lots of skills and had an opportunity to go to the parliament with our local MP. Had a chance to go to Brussels also. The speakers from all various departments came and explained to us how the council and other departments are run."
(Lambeth participant)

"It was the first time I had the opportunity to work with honourable MP John McDonnell, Chief Inspector Mr. Mick Morris, Director Social Services, Housing, Education, Primary Care Trust and Leader of Council. I'm very pleased with their kind support and assistance learnt to educate me. Despite the fact of being a housewife, I believe there's a lot to learn and achieve as the scope is vast."
(Hillingdon participant)

Black and other minority communities are often in the position of implementing policies and decisions that affect their daily lives without having had a role in the decision-making process. The Capacity-Building Project begins to address this deficit. The project concentrated on delivering the following outcomes: strategic and analytical thinking; problem solving; interpersonal skills, including influencing, persuading, and communication; managing relationships; and decision making and planning.

The training course provided a means of linking community groups with local members of Parliament and other statutory agencies. The subjects covered in the course were based on the learning outcomes that the women themselves had identified as development needs. Following the course, the women's increased knowledge of the political system has permitted informed engagement with local agencies and leaders and has provided a platform for the groups to become involved in the decision-making process from an earlier stage.

For example, the introduction of Bengali language education at the General Certificate of Secondary Education (GCSE) level in Bedford

schools is now being debated. The Bengali women in Bedford have asked to work in partnership with the local education authority to ensure that the introduction of the new language to the curriculum will go hand in hand with a rise in educational achievement. The discussions around the issue have enabled the local education authority to gain a greater understanding of why Bengali families want to retain aspects of their cultural heritage and have allowed the women to express what they believe to be essential in recognizing their right to determine their own way of life. Through partnerships with local colleges, accreditation for the course is being sought with the National Open College Network (NOCN). The NOCN is important for courses such as these as it allows individuals to obtain educational credits that can be accumulated towards a recognized qualification, thus enhancing employment and education routes into further or higher education. Already two members of the Bangladeshi women's group will start English for Speakers of Other Languages (ESOL) teacher training courses.

The Capacity-Building Project also addressed some of the cultural barriers experienced by Asian and Bangladeshi women and, to a lesser extent, women from African and Caribbean communities. For example, funding for child care and transportation was offered to ensure access to the training courses and to motivate the women to attend the sessions outside of their homes. In addition, employing local facilitators who were known for their community development work and who were bilingual gave the training course credibility, minimized the cost of employing translators, and allowed the participation of women for whom English was not their first language. Advice and support from all partners were made available to the trainers, volunteers, and course participants. The 1990 Trust also offered both administrative and financial support to the trainers and volunteers as required.

Finally, the project played a positive role in facilitating a dialogue between leaders of local government, members of Parliament, and the women themselves. The project also enabled networking. The women's groups in Bedford, Hillingdon, and Lambeth have now become part of local networks which include local colleges, private enterprises, and other statutory agencies that have provided invaluable knowledge about their respective areas.

SUSTAINABILITY

The groups continue to pursue additional funds to sustain the individual programs. The three groups have come up with various ways of raising funds. The Hillingdon group is targeting heads of services from the local government to contribute at least 2,500 pounds from their individual budgets. The Bedford group has asked their member of Parliament and local government officers to look at the possibility of providing rent-free accommodations, which will address a major part of the budget needed to run the program in that area. The Lambeth group has applied to the local government for a grant and is also looking for affordable accommodations that they can share with other organizations.

Steering groups in all three localities have been formed and include representatives from the local education authorities, private businesses, and other statutory agencies. In Hillingdon, there has been local support from the London Borough of Hillingdon Connecting Communities Initiative, the Hillingdon Association for Voluntary Services, and Uxbridge College. In Lambeth, support has come from the independent advisory group that is involved with the Safer Communities Initiative; the Greater London Authority; the Detainees Support Group, an organization that assists refugees and asylum seekers; and Blackliners, an organization dealing with teenage sexual health issues. Belgrave Baheno Women's Organisation in Leicester, local housing associations, and the local government are supporting the Bedford group.

KEY AREAS OF BEST PRACTICE

- Ensuring women identify and prioritize their own learning and development needs and have a key role in setting the agenda and learning processes
- Removing barriers to empowerment and supporting learning (translation, child care, local one-to-one support)
- Employing and engendering trust through the use of facilitators and program administrators who are representative of communities
- Enabling direct contact between policymakers and politicians and smaller organizations and individuals
- Enabling firsthand experience of how civic society works so that participants can become self-advocates rather than relying on professionals or filter organizations

- Incorporating a variety of learning methods (trips, speakers, question and answer sessions, preparation and practice sessions to build confidence, debriefing sessions to evaluate learning)

CONCLUSION

In conclusion, the 1990 Trust Capacity-Building Project attempted to address the lack of representation of black women at a local level from a rights-based perspective. The right of self-determination was central to the learning objectives of the project. The project emphasized the development of a two-way process of learning between the local women's groups, local governments, and other agencies in the localities. The 1990 Trust's approach to integrating black and other minority groups into the United Kingdom is to enable the individual to challenge structural inequalities in the United Kingdom through the legislative processes that exist to protect against discrimination.

ENDNOTES

1   "Black" refers to the political term and includes persons of African, Asian, and Caribbean descent.
2   Commission for Racial Equality, Press Release, 13 February 2003.
3   See Census 2001 at http://www.statistics.gov.uk/.
4   The term "capacity-building programs" refers to the activities in specific localities that were part of the 1990 Trust Capacity-Building Project.

France

Catherine de Wenden

Background

Though the word "integration" remains largely undefined, integration policies have been in place in France since 1974. These thirty years can be divided into three periods, which correspond to various philosophies of immigration.

The first period (1974-1984) was characterized by a functional policy linked to the migrant worker approach. Immigrants were viewed as birds of passage, who aimed to eventually return to their countries of origin. Consequently, integration policies only dealt with social questions, not with matters relating to political expression. Most of the social policy, administered by the Fonds d'Action Sociale (the FAS, created in 1959), focused on collective housing of foreign male workers in foyers and on literacy programs, in order to enable minimum integration in the welcoming country while incurring minimum costs (Le Pors Report, 1977). In order to facilitate return, migrants were taught the language and culture of origin, and return policies were implemented starting in 1977, inspired by the German model in place since 1972. The idea was that unemployed French workers would progressively replace foreign workers during these years of economic crisis. However, this approach failed: returns were scarce, and family reunifications led to changes in public policies affecting integration.

The second period (1984-1990) is the *beur* period. Public policies were aimed at offering political answers to the problems of integration. In the early 1980s, the emergence of a second generation in the inner cities, the political pressure exerted by the National Front, and the threat posed by Islam as a socialization factor led to more priority being placed on citizenship. The freedom of association, granted in 1981, gave way to a new definition and practice of citizenship in cities and at the local level. New civic values were expressed—such as antiracism, multiple allegiances, and participation in local life—while new actors appeared, such as cultural mediators, leaders of civic associations, and ethnic or political entrepreneurs. Some of these actors, working with the support of political parties, tried to become electoral machines, facilitating *beurs'* voter registration as well as their presence on local lists. These actors capitalized on the contradictions inherent in the French political system, engaging in republican discourse while cultivating a sense of ethnic separatism. But most of these civic associations were dependent on public funding, and many of their leaders were disappointed that the French political system failed to give their claims proper attention (opposition to *double peine* or double jeopardy, the policy of sending foreign convicts back to their countries of origin once they have completed their punishment in France; local political voting for parents; fighting against discrimination) and did not provide the opportunity for them to participate in politics at the national level (for example, there is no member of Parliament of Maghrebi origin).

This period was also characterized by a growing inclusion of the beurs into French citizenship, not only on a philosophical level (through the introduction of the ideas of citizenship of residence and the new citizenship into general political discourse), but also with respect to the debates about access to French nationality. The French nationality code is a product of an equilibrium between the right of blood, as established by Napoleon I, and the right of the soil, progressively introduced to counter the demographic decrease that began at the end of the nineteenth century. Following a long debate over reform (from 1987 to 1998), the nationality code finally became more open to persons born in France, persons having lived in France for five years prior to the age of majority, children of Algerians (double right of the soil) born in France, persons married to French citizens, persons asking for reintegration in French citizenship (Algerians), and persons applying for naturalization (the criteria have hardly changed for twenty years). Access to citizenship is one of the most important tools of integration in France, coupled since 2003 with a contractual definition of belonging,

aimed mainly at recent newcomers of foreign citizenship (and based primarily on French language proficiency).

The third period (1990-2000) focused on the locality as the hub of integration. In the early 1990s, immigration continued to be a central political issue and a focus of political pressure from the extreme right. Its emergence as a political force, however, began declining due to a lack of support by political parties for the beur movement and because of the rise of other forms of expression available to foreigners, including the undocumented (*sans papiers*). Exclusion is a central issue in the inner cities, and many association leaders have turned their attention to social concerns: fighting against the *galère*, unemployment, delinquency, drugs, urban violence, discrimination, radical Islamism. Policies directed at localities were implemented to answer problems arising from social disenfranchisement and were aimed at the prevention of violence, bringing about affirmative action based on local and social criteria, the renovation of public housing, the development of sociocultural activities for families at the local level, and the creation of incentives to attract new businesses. The results so far have been mixed, but, due to the magnitude of the inner cities phenomenon, this particular French policy of integration is one of the most voluntary in Europe.

Three best practices can be identified from France's policies over the past thirty years: freedom of association and civic participation, access to nationality, and localized policies. Any consideration of these three best practices, however, would be incomplete if it failed to take into account existing negative practices. An antidiscrimination policy was implemented only recently, and only under pressure from the European Union. Antidiscrimination remains an important issue. Local voting rights, promised since 1981, have not yet been granted. The undocumented population, in part a consequence of the crisis in asylum rights, is still waiting for legalization. The policy of *double peine* was not cancelled until 2003. The headscarf affair continues to provoke awkward debates and public reactions. French society has been slow to accept multiculturalism as part of French identity.

Integration, however, is on the way, and there are many invisible success stories involving the negotiation of multiple identities in spite of discrimination and unemployment. The presence of the "other" in France has seldom been properly recognized. Over 150 years of immigration, the character of immigration has changed. But the sense of otherness remains the same with respect to matters of religion, politics, fears of a demographic invasion, fears about health risks, concerns about a sense of cohesive community identity, and worries about the lack of citizen allegiance—all in contradiction to French values. It is too early to conclude that today's Muslim immigration presents historically unique challenges, but we should stress that poverty and discrimination are the main factors leading to a failure of integration.

PRIORITY EDUCATION ZONES AT SCIENCES PO, PARIS

Among the most successful and original practices in the area of integration is at

Sciences Po. The director of the prestigious university, Richard Descoings, a high-level civil servant, decided to offer a special entrance exam to exceptional youth from the inner city. Noting the handicaps in successfully completing the very selective entrance exams that inner city youth face due to cultural gaps, he encouraged implementation of special tests and provided the participants who performed well with funding and coaching. The program has been in operation since 2001. Seven neighborhoods have been identified as priority education zones (ZEP) for the program.

The program at first was not very welcome among the other students at Sciences Po, who had themselves been subject to stringent selection criteria. They felt that it violated the French notion of equality of rights, and, led by the National Interuniversity Union (UNI), they challenged the new entrance procedure in court. A media-intensive struggle took place during September 2001, after which, on 4 April 2001, the court rejected UNI's demands for the cancellation of the special entrance procedure for the ZEP students. The judge reasserted the value of implementing such a program. Then, on 11 July 2001, the court confirmed that the ZEP measure was valid, provided that it was based on objective criteria of selection aimed at maintaining the equality of treatment between candidates. The lawyer for Sciences Po said that "If human, pedagogic and financial means are applied, there is no social determinant which cannot be overcome by individual struggle, work and the will to perform."

The ZEP program recruits students through agreements with secondary schools in the priority education zones. These agreements, known as Conventions ZEP, are aimed at "reinforcing mobility, giving content to integration." In 2003, eighteen secondary schools were partners of Sciences Po, and thirty-seven students were admitted from these schools. From 2001 to 2003, eighty-seven students were admitted. Half of the students admitted had parents from the working class or employed in low-skill service industries in 2001, 57% in 2002, and 68% in 2003. Of the students admitted in 2003, three-fourths received scholarships (boursiers) while they were in secondary school. In 2002, three-fifths of the admitted students had at least one parent born outside of France, while two-thirds of admitted students in 2003 had foreign-born parents. Girls made up 70% of applicants in 2001 and 2002 and slightly more than 56% of applicants in 2003.[1] In 2003, 18% of applicants to the ZEP program were admitted. Students are selected according to criteria of excellence (i.e., merit and prospects).

Admitted ZEP students benefit from financial support (6,100 euro each year for five years and eventually 3,000 euro for housing). They have a tutor during their first months at Sciences Po and, prior to that, some training courses in their secondary schools in preparation for the oral entrance examination.[2] Once at Sciences Po, the ZEP students' academic performance is on par with that of the other students: of the students admitted in 2001, roughly nine out of ten were admitted to the second year.[3] The students are generally well integrated, as indicated by involvement in student associations and election as class delegates.[4]

ORIGIN AND NUMBER OF STUDENTS IN THE CONVENTIONS ZEP PROGRAM, 2001

High School	Candidates	Approved	Admitted
L'Essouriau-Les Ulis	11	5	3
Auguste Blanqui-Saint Ouen	11	6	3
Félix Mayer-Creutzwald	17	6	3
Saint-Exupéry-Fameck	17	7	4
Poncelet-Saint Avold	18	6	1
Maupassant-Colombes	10	1	1
Jean Zay-Aulnay-sous-Bois	12	4	3
Total	96	35	18

Socioeconomic Background of Sciences Po Applicants

Occupation Category of Students' Parents	Sciences Po Entrance Examination Candidates	ZEP Program Candidates
Farmers	**	**
Artisans, merchants, managers	15.5%	5.5%
Teachers, lecturers, university staff	64.2%	17%
Employees	4.1%	23%
Workers	1.6%	17%
Middle-class	8.4%	26%
Others (retirees, unemployed, etc.)	6.2%	11.5%
Total	100%	100%

Socioeconomic Background of Students Nationwide and Admitted to Sciences Po

Occupation Category of Students' Parents	All University Students (first cycle)	Students Who Passed Sciences Po Entrance Examination 1998	Students Who Passed ZEP Examination 2001
Farmers	2.6%	**	**
Artisans, merchants, managers	8.5%	12%	11%
Teachers, lecturers, university staff	32.4%	71.5%	5.5%
Employees	14.6%	2.5%	34%
Workers	14.5%	0.5%	16.5%
Middle-class	18.8%	7.5%	16.5%
Others (retirees, unemployed, etc.)	8.6%	5.5%	16.5%
Total	100%	100%	100%

Source: Sciences Po. "Conventions education prioritaire." Press Release. 26 September 2002 (available at http://www.sciences-po.fr/presse/zep/cep.pdf).

Fostering social diversity and democratization at Sciences Po, which is viewed as an elite university aimed at educating France's future political decision makers, is a challenge. For most children in inner cities, the temptations of the street are the strongest competitors to school. The Conventions ZEP program aims to offset the lack of financial resources available to families, the absence of specialized information of such a *filière d'excellence*, the social bias of selection due to cultural gaps, and the self-limitation that comes from students thinking that Sciences Po is not for them. In accordance with the French values of equality and equity, which give no consideration to ethnic origins, no quota of origin or social origin has been introduced. The ZEP program has introduced some competition at the participating secondary schools: although there were no scores at the level of excellent (*très bien*) at the baccalaureate in 2001 and 2002, four applicants obtained scores at this level in 2003. Overall, the ZEP program has led to a Sciences Po that more closely reflects the plural France (*France plurielle*) celebrated in 1998.

Some other Institutes d'Etudes Politiques, such as Lille, Aix-en-Provence, and Rennes, have implemented programs that open their doors to excellent students from excluded areas, while the trade school ESSEC is helping these students gain access to prep schools.

ENDNOTES

1 Sciences Po, "Conventiones education prioritaire," Press Release, September 2003 (available at http://www.sciences-po.fr/presse/zep/bilan_3ans_apres.pdf).

2 Ibid.
3 Sciences Po, "Conventions education prioritaire," Press Release, 26 September 2002 (available at http://www.sciences-po.fr/presse/zep/cep.pdf).
4 Sciences Po, 2003.

GERMANY

KATRIN UHL

I ntegration is a dynamic process that affects both immigrants and the society of the receiving country and requires an equal degree of commitment and will to succeed from both sides. Integration aims at equal participation of immigrants in all aspects of life. The framework for integration is set by the state through its policies. However, it is at the level of the local community where individual integration processes take place.

While there has been a legal framework for immigration in place in Germany for some time, the country's recent history has been marked by the lack of a comprehensive integration policy. In its absence, integration has been shepherded and fostered by a broad range of civil society actors such as community organizations, workers' and employers' groups, schools and kindergartens, sports clubs, religious groups, and immigrant organizations. The success of many of their activities underlines the important role these organizations and groups play in supporting integration. This chapter reports on some of these outstanding initiatives, presenting strategies for integration that have proven to be successful in the German context.

THE ROLE OF IMMIGRANT ORGANIZATIONS

A large variety of self-help organizations, as well as cultural and religious groups, exist within the immigrant community in Germany. While the discussion about the role of immigrant organizations is still partially dominated by the issue of ethnic segregation, these organizations are increasingly recognized for their role in fostering the social and political participation of immigrants, integration, and intercultural dialogue. In recent years many of these organizations have begun broadening their focus, concentrating less exclusively on their country of origin and its culture and more on their role as intermediaries between the ethnic community they represent and the majority population. The organization Diên Hông, based in the city of Rostock and founded by former Vietnamese contract workers in the German Democratic Republic in 1992, is one example of an immigrant organization that has transformed itself from a specialized interest group to an important partner of immigrants of all ethnic backgrounds and the community and administration at large.[1]

Through a variety of activities, the organization, with a staff of both full-time employees and volunteers, works for a better understanding between immigrants and Germans and equal opportunities for immigrants. Its main focuses are integration into the labor market, language training, and social integration. Diên Hông has not only become an officially recognized educational institution but also a well-established partner of the local administration. It often serves as a link between immigrant organizations, local authorities, potential employers, and educational institutions. Especially with regard to integration into the labor market, the organization is a much sought-after authority—more than one thousand immigrants have participated in job training programs offered by the organization in cooperation with the local employment agency.

A key to its success lies in the strategy of using experiences and competencies acquired during the process of integration by one group of immigrants to support the integration of others inside and outside the Vietnamese community. This approach empowers immigrants to act as self-confident actors and become involved in the local community.

With its large staff and a well-established working infrastructure, Diên Hông is a highly professionalized organization and effectively represents the interests of immigrants while acting as a partner of the local government. For the majority of immigrant organizations, however, that depend largely on the voluntary commitment of their members, this type of professionalization proves to be a challenge.

In order to support the professionalization of the work of immigrant associations as interest groups and self-help organizations, the State Center for Immigration Affairs in North-Rhine Westphalia (LzZ) has developed a comprehensive concept for qualification of immigrant organizations, supporting them in their contacts with public administration and public relations activities. The program is disseminated through a network of facilitators.

The state of North-Rhine Westphalia, which is home to more than 2 million of the 7.3 million people living in Germany without a German passport, founded the State Center for Immigration Affairs in 1998 to support the integration of immigrants living in the state. This type of institution is currently unique in Germany. Through a large network of partners, it aims to create new initiatives for better integration policies, educating the public, improving opportunities available to immigrants, and promoting immigrant self-initiative. The center is an example of a successful public-private partnership in the field of integration, a well-working cooperation between a state-run agency and nongovernmental organizations in general and immigrant organizations in particular.

NETWORKS FOR INTEGRATION

Managing integration and social inclusion is a challenge for cities and municipalities. There are a growing number of local networks and alliances that focus on the issue of integration in Germany. Two types of networks have emerged that coordinate local integration initiatives: networks with a bottom-up approach that bring together civil society organizations and networks with a top-down approach initiated by municipal authorities. These networks and alliances build bridges, foster synergies, and help to reduce possible resistance from within the majority population by providing a structure for integration measures at the local level.

Effectiveness and sustainability are increased if the network includes both municipal authorities and civil society organizations. An example of this type of comprehensive integration network can be found in the city of Stendal. The network initiated by the city engages immigrant organizations as equal partners not only in the implementation of local integration policies, but also in its planning stage, thereby supporting the social and political participation of immigrants.

Some cities have taken the issue of integration even further. In line with the realization that integration concerns all aspects of society, they have developed comprehensive strategies to mainstream the issue, transforming it from a specialized task to a topic all branches of local administration take into consideration in their work. Intercultural competencies of administrative staff play an important part in this process. Essen is often cited as an example of a city with a large immigrant population that has not only developed ties with the central actors in the field of integration at the community level, but has successfully developed a comprehensive intercultural strategy as well as an action program on the integration of foreign workers and their families. Initiated in 1986 and revised in 1997, the program was developed by the city in cooperation with public and private organizations, from the very beginning

relying on the expertise of immigrant organizations.[2]

COMMUNITY-ORIENTED APPROACH

At a more grassroots level, a great number of organizations work to improve the situation of immigrants in city districts. Often targeting the inhabitants of a district in general rather than immigrants in particular, these organizations strive to engage the local community in improving their living and housing conditions. The Planerladen in the northern district of the city of Dortmund follows this approach.[3] Since 1982 this area-based nonprofit organization has focused on social-oriented community and neighborhood development processes aimed at improving the living and housing conditions of all inhabitants in the district, with an emphasis on intercultural conflict resolution. An important target group is disadvantaged households often found in immigrant communities. Direct contact with inhabitants and their active participation are crucial elements in developing a holistic notion of the city district and for generating an integrated regeneration strategy.

After more than twenty years in existence, the Planerladen today has a large network of cooperating organizations and several branches in different neighborhoods, providing a platform for communication and cooperation for inhabitants with and without a migration background. The project draws from the expertise of the local community and over the years has helped to form close ties across ethnic boundaries. It has contributed to the local community as a whole and has been effective in supporting the integration of immigrants as part of this holistic strategy. In recognition of its successful work in supporting democratic city planning and local communities, the Planerladen has received several awards.

BUILDING BRIDGES: FOSTERING INTERCULTURAL DIALOGUE

Intercultural competencies are an important component in achieving equal social participation of immigrants and integration, and they help to increase understanding of different values and views among the majority population and immigrants. As in many other countries, there is an expanding market for intercultural training programs in Germany. More often than not, however, these programs take part in a strictly monocultural setting.

As an area of interaction between immigrants and members of the majority population prone to misunderstandings and situations of conflict, intercultural competencies are increasingly called for in public administration. Again, the State Center for Immigration Affairs in North-Rhine Westphalia has taken a different, innovative approach to intercultural training: it has developed strategies to facilitate intercultural communication among public service providers and to create better customer relations with immigrants. A central component of this initiative is certifying key employees and individual immigrants to act as partners of authorities and public institutions. Strategies and curricula for certification are developed

within the project network and provided through classes at adult evening schools in several cities. Developed as a pilot project, the program can serve as a model for similar endeavors elsewhere.

The police of the city of Düsseldorf in cooperation with immigrant organizations have shown how intercultural meetings can help to improve government-immigrant relations, even in situations of conflict. Initiated in 1999, these intercultural meetings have become a regular event and have opened doors to staff of other public administration bodies that regularly work with immigrants. Cooperation between immigrant organizations and the police has intensified through this process and has led to the establishment of a roundtable that includes the head of policy and the leaders of several local immigrant organizations, building ties that last.

CONCLUSION: CRITERIA FOR SUCCESSFUL INTEGRATION

The projects and initiatives presented in this chapter, run by very different organizations and groups, both public and private, reach out to different target groups and address very specific issues aimed at facilitating the integration of immigrants. They show that integration can be supported through a wide variety of activities. Despite their apparent differences, however, the initiatives discussed in this chapter point to three strategies for successful integration-though certainly not the only effective strategies: actively involving immigrants, recognizing the interests and needs of immigrants and the majority population, and facilitating cooperation between the public sector and the private sector.

ACTIVELY INVOLVING IMMIGRANTS AND THEIR RESOURCES

A number of the organizations and projects mentioned previously follow an approach that actively involves immigrants in shaping the integration process. They employ the resources and competencies of immigrants as a starting point in supporting the integration of others, developing ties with the majority population, bringing together people of all nationalities that share a common interest, and initiating processes of change.

RECOGNIZING THE INTERESTS AND NEEDS OF BOTH IMMIGRANTS AND THE MAJORITY POPULATION

Projects like those run by the Planerladen show that integration is most effective and less prone to tension (though certainly never free of conflict) when it recognizes the interests, needs, and resources of both immigrants and members of the majority population and involves them equally as active partners. Such projects underline the fact that integration is not one-sided nor something that happens overnight, but something that has to be achieved by all members of society, be they German or any other nationality.

COOPERATION BETWEEN THE PUBLIC AND PRIVATE SECTOR

As the activities of the State Center for Immigration Affairs in North-Rhine Westphalia or the partnership between immigrant organizations and the police in the city of Düsseldorf show, cooperation between the public and the private or nongovernmental sectors helps to build a comprehensive basis for integration, fostering synergies and contributing to the effectiveness and sustainability of integration activities.

ENDNOTES

1   For further information see http://www.dienhong.de/.

2   See, for example, Stadt Essen, Konzept für die

interkulturelle Arbeit in der Stadt Essen (January 2003).

3   For more information see http://www.planer-laden.de/.

Italy

Giulia Henry

Two main features of Italian integration policies should be taken into consideration in order to better understand the best practices implemented in Italy. First, integration policies in Italy have developed according to a local adaptive model. Second, innovative policies are implemented in a context of wide access to social services for immigrants, including illegal immigrants—which of course does not mean that barriers to their integration have been eliminated. After providing general background on integration policy in Italy, this chapter focuses on best practices in the area of access to housing.

The Centrality of the Local Level

From a general perspective, the state has the task of promoting, monitoring, and financing projects, but it is the local level that is mainly responsible for the implementation of integration policies. This is even more the case after the recent moves toward decentralization and subsidiarity, particularly relevant in the domain of social services.[1]

However, the role of local governments, together with associations, is not only limited to policy implementation. Regions, municipalities, and non-governmental organizations have also played a major role in changing and improving legislation concerning immigrant rights. The Italian decision-making process on immigration issues is bottom-up in nature. Local actors not only put into practice what the law prescribes, they also contribute to changes in immigration policy, by making new rules and by breaking old ones.

For illegal immigrants,[2] services not yet foreseen by the law, or even in violation of the law, were introduced through spontaneous local practices, supported at first by informal and later by formal agreements. These new practices then became administrative directives and were progressively codified, first in some regional laws and finally in the national law.[3]

In order to deal with the real and urgent problems that legislation failed to address, some public hospital doctors began to provide free assistance to illegal immigrants. Some doctors were even prosecuted for their actions. In 1983, the San Gallicano Hospital in Rome was the first public institution to institute a public service that provided preventive care for immigrants, including illegal immigrants. Physicians involved in this activity were penalized and requested to pay compensation for damages to the Audit Office. In response to pressure from physicians, a decree was issued in

1995 that extended to temporary foreign immigrants the opportunity to receive urgent and essential care, as well as the opportunity to access preventive medicine and pregnancy programs anonymously and free of charge. From 1985 to 1999, 34,415 patients who were irregular or illegal immigrants received medical care through the San Gallicano service. Since 1996, cultural and linguistic mediators have also been involved in the program. The San Gallicano service has organized mediation courses and a sociohealth research center, financed by the municipality, which collects a range of statistical data on the health conditions of disadvantaged people.

A similar practice occurred in the field of public education. Schools were not formally open to all children living in Italy until 1998. Before that, illegal immigrant children were accepted in some schools as temporary students, auditing students, or as enrolled students waiting to regularize their status. In Turin, illegal immigrant minors were accepted in schools for the first time in Italy, thanks to an agreement between the juvenile court, the municipality, the schools, and the police. Through this bottom-up approach, Italian social services were opened to immigrants, including illegal immigrants.

This local adaptive model has turned out to be flexible and suitable to different contexts and demands, but it also means a huge variety of practices across diverse geographical areas where initiatives remain dependent on local systems and stem from different experiences in social policies. For this reason, it is difficult to define a single Italian model of integration. It is possible however to identify territorial best practices which could be diffused throughout the whole territory.

WIDE ACCESS TO SOCIAL SERVICES

Since 1998, a national law has codified relevant principles that, as pointed out in the previous section, had already been experimented with at the local level and put into practice in some areas. The center-right government's reforms did not, in general, amend this integration practice.

Primary education is not only a right of every foreign child, it is also compulsory; intercultural activities and Italian-as-a-second-language courses are organized in order to better integrate newcomers into the education system. Legal immigrants have access to secondary education on the same terms as Italian students.

Concerning health services, all immigrants have access to both basic and emergency treatments. Legal immigrants have access to health care on equal terms with Italian citizens. Different social integration and assistance measures are extended to immigrants. The goal of making general public services open to any person resident in the country is pursued through cultural mediation services, which aim to help immigrants negotiate the procedures required to obtain work permits and gain access to the labor market, schools, and hospitals or other health-care institutions.

In Bologna, the CD/Lei (Centro Documentazione/Labratorio per un'educazione interculturale), an expert association in the field of integration, is one of the first organizations to have an agreement with the local education office, the municipality, and provincial sectors to organize innovative courses on immigration and intercultural education.

THE HOUSING PROBLEM

According to recent surveys, access to housing is a more urgent problem for foreign citizens than that of obtaining a legal residence permit or finding a job. Immigrants want the Italian state to provide them with housing. The lack of proper accommodation is perceived as the worst aspect of the migratory experience.

Regions, in collaboration with municipalities and third sector organizations, provide reception centers for newcomers. Immigrants who are legal residents and work for at least two years in Italy have access to public social housing and to any intermediation service implemented by social boards, established at the local level to facilitate the matching of housing demand and supply.

In any event, the housing problem in Italy is structural in nature and, even if immigrants have more difficulties (due to discrimination, a lack of networks, the absence of family bonds, etc.), the Italian poor face similar problems. Subsidized housing is very limited in Italy. Publicly funded houses are very few, and the decentralization process, which devolved these responsibilities to regional and local administrations after 1998, occurred without any provision for additional financial resources.

In some areas, bottom-up solutions have been instituted. Initiatives to deal with the housing problem began at the level of civil society. Addressing housing certainly constitutes a precondition of any integration policy. These initiatives range from changes in the access criteria to public housing, in order to include the immigrant population, to the establishment of different intermediary agencies, which facilitate access to rented accommodations, providing financial resources or local networks that landlords can trust. In some cases, the municipality itself serves as a guaranteed intermediary; in other cases, successful experiences in self-construction or self-restructuring carried out by the immigrants themselves are implemented.

PADUA HOUSING INITIATIVES

In the region of Veneto, immigrant manpower is fundamental to the local economy. Many immigrants work in local enterprises, and employers have an interest in providing their employees with proper accommodation.[4]

Padua has implemented a policy that involves different actors in finding a solution to immigrants' increasingly urgent housing problems. This heterogeneous policy network is made up of private actors such as employers, banks, and foundations; representatives of third sector organizations and volunteer associations; and public sector actors, including municipalities and provincial and regional administrations. Experts and academics are also involved in the development of the policy.

The participation of different actors allows for mediation between the immigrant worker and his or her employer, a relationship which can be exploitative in nature. According to Italian law implemented in 2002, immigrants are dependent on the employer for both work and residency permits. It is therefore crucial that the employer is not the only source of accommodation as well. At the same time, it is important that, in a situation involving a lack of public resources, the employer be involved in finding an appropriate solution.

Participation by entrepreneurs in finding a solution to immigrants' social problems is a relatively recent phenomenon. Collaboration between private and public actors constitutes a turning point for these policies, as initiatives like La Casa Onlus Foundation and the Nuovo Villaggio Cooperative demonstrate.

The Nuovo Villaggio Cooperative is constantly seeking dialogue with public actors and attempting to increase cooperation with these institutions. Projects always originate with the cooperative, but the inclusion of public actors in their implementation is a main goal of the program. Unfortunately, this objective is made difficult by the interest that institutional local actors have in simply delegating the problem to the third sector. Sometimes they allocate financial resources for buying or restoring houses for social welfare purposes.

The innovative mechanism implemented in Padua is supported by the Nuovo Villaggio Cooperative, Acli (a Catholic organization), Banca Etica (an Italian bank specializing in financing the third sector), and the Padua Chamber of Commerce. These actors, together with the province of Padua, promote the nonprofit La Casa Onlus Foundation.

By subscribing to deposit receipts issued by Banca Etica, employers can have at their disposal apartments or beds for their immigrant employees. This fund provides the means for the purchase, management, and restoration of real estate (the cooperative built eight apartments), but also operates as a reliable intermediary in the rental market. Landlords can count on both a solid economic guarantee and on the involvement of a well-known nongovernmental organization. At present, the Nuovo Villaggio Cooperative provides sixty apartments with a total of 250 beds. Almost all the apartments are restored by employing partners of the cooperative.

In 2001, Nuovo Villaggio had 527 partners—162 of whom were Italian individuals, 317 of whom were foreign individuals (immigrants), and 48 of whom were associations. People who work in the cooperative are mostly volunteers (seventy are volunteers and twenty-nine are employees). In the housing area in particular, there are four employees and sixteen volunteers.

In terms of housing, only legal immigrants who have a regular job can benefit from the cooperative's services. Single beds are assigned in the order in which requests are received but can be modified in urgent situations or by special request by the municipality, which has an agreement with the cooperative. For apartments, the cooperative evaluates the reliability of the potential tenant through all of the information available to the cooperative (family and job situation, previous accommodations, etc.). The applicant is often well-known to the cooperative, especially through involvement in other activities (in the areas of education, health care, etc.). Generally, preference is accorded to families. Families tend to better integrate into the local context. Women are more likely to maintain the apartments carefully, and the presence of children can facilitate positive neighborhood relations.

The cooperative does not place a limit on the length of time the immigrant is allowed to remain in the house, but it upholds the provisional character of the offer and helps the immigrant to find a more autonomous solution, in order to guarantee turnover.

Social counseling and ongoing education are side benefits of the program. Tenants are in many cases already involved in the work of housing restoration and are selected by the cooperative from foreigners in need. They receive a variety of information about the rules of living in the apartment. All utility bills are registered under the name of the tenant (and no longer of the cooperative), in order to make the tenant more responsible for expenses. In this way, the immigrants become better acquainted with and are more easily accepted by their host society.

Assistance with living in the new accommodations is the weakest aspect of the program. The volunteer personnel of the cooperative, being closer to the problems and the people, are in the best position to identify specific needs. However, the cooperative can count on very few stable personnel. For budgetary reasons, the cooperative is unable to hire the kind of staff it really needs. Intervention is therefore limited by the short-term engagement of young volunteers—even though staff turnover has been very low so far—and the impossibility of making plans for the long term.

In addition to providing direct services to immigrants, the Nuovo Villaggio Cooperative seeks to network with other organizations to share program experiences in the areas of reception and housing of foreign workers and people in need, in order to promote housing policies, diffuse best practices, exchange know-how, and even start new projects already being financed as part of other European programs. Another general goal of the cooperative's activities is to develop a new culture and new policies relating to housing problems, in order to increase opportunities available to people without housing and promote the reevaluation of the existing private and public estates.

In conclusion, the initiatives in Padua clearly increase socioeconomic and cultural integration, not only by providing housing solutions (a precondition for any successful integration measure), but also by fostering mutual understanding between immigrants and the native population and by improving neighborhood relations. The networking of different actors, each pursuing its own solution to the problem while, collectively, contributing to a common effort, represents a model that can be applied elsewhere. The active involvement of immigrants in the cooperative—restoring houses, living in the houses, respecting new rules and different habits and cultures— is also an important part of the program.

Endnotes

1 Prior to 2003, a fund for immigrant integration policies managed by the Ministry of Social Policies provided 80% of the funds used by projects at the regional, provincial, and municipal levels. In 2003, a general fund for social policies was established, which left the decision concerning the allocation of resources entirely up to the respective regions.

2 In general, Italy attracts illegal immigration more than other countries due to the difficulty of controlling the country's extensive borders and to the strength of its informal economy. Before 1998, immigration laws aimed to normalize the status of those illegally residing in Italy, rather than to regulate new legal entries. Between 1986 and 1998, the Italian government introduced four amnesties covering a total of almost 790,000 people. According to Ministry of the Interior data, 565,596 of these people were still present in Italy on 1 January 2000. To this figure should be added at least 130,000 persons who came to Italy through family reunion with legalized immigrants. Legal residents in Italy from emigration countries numbered 1,112,173 (as of 1 January 2000), which means that the large majority of legal immigrants in Italy (at least 60%) was made up of people who had undergone a legalization process or who had joined relatives who immigrated illegally or irregularly. Even the present center-right government proposed legalizing one housekeeper per family and an unlimited number of care-workers for people who are not self-sufficient and extended this proposal to other employees hired before 10 June 2002 in its reform of 30 July 2002 (Law 189). As of February 2004, there were over 703,647 applications and 634,000 permits granted; 25,400 requests were rejected.

3 The Single Act 286 of 25 July 1998, which was essentially based on Law 40 of 6 March 1998 (called the Turco-Napolitano Law after the names of the then center-left government ministers of social affairs and interior, respectively), addressed for the first time immigrant integration policies and the finances, measures, and administrative structures needed for their implementation. These proposals were continued by Reform Law 189 of 30 July 2002 (called the Bossi-Fini Law after the names of the two vice prime ministers, the leaders of the Northern League and the National Alliance, respectively).

4 More than half of the immigrants present in Italy live in the northern part of the country. In 2002, the Northeast, where the region of Veneto is located, was home to 25.9% of the immigrant population then residing in Italy.

The Netherlands

Ingrid Sijlbing

This chapter begins with a description of the project Towards an Independent Future for Somali Youngsters. It goes on to look in detail at the four principal elements of the project-work and training, coaching, meaningful leisure activities, and skills enhancement-and concludes with an overview of useful experience gained from the project.

Introduction

In the early 1990s Somali citizens fled their country en masse following the outbreak of civil war. The Hague is home to more than 1,700 Somalis, among them 350 young people between the ages of twelve and twenty-five. In 2000, the committee of the Somali Association (SBSS) requested that attention be paid to the position of Somali youngsters in The Hague. This resulted in a survey of the social environment of young Somalis in the city. One of the general conclusions of the survey was that more specific attention and support was needed for these Somali youngsters.

The Hague made a substantial contribution towards this in 2002 and 2003 through the project Towards an Independent Future for Somali Youngsters. The project focused on reinforcing the position of Somali youngsters in The Hague and included activities in four spheres:

- Work and training: assisting young Somalis in finding work and/or training
- Coaching: helping Somali youngsters with problems at school
- Meaningful leisure activities: providing a range of activities for Somali youngsters
- Skills enhancement: training employees of organizations that have dealings with Somali youngsters

The project's target group was Somali youngsters from The Hague aged twelve to twenty-five with residential status. Participants were mainly youth who had problems with school, work, or leisure time. The activities were set up in the neighborhoods where most of the Somali youngsters lived: the Schilderswijk and Escamp.

Towards an Independent Future for Somali Youngsters was financed by the municipality of The Hague and the European Refugee Fund. The municipality of The Hague managed the project, working closely with the Somali Association. The expertise of various organizations was used for different parts of the project.

The project commenced with a meeting held on 6 April 2002 and officially concluded with a conference on 11 March 2003. To continue the most successful parts of the project until 1 January 2004, the municipality of The Hague granted an additional subsidy. Based on the results of the survey of Somalis aged twenty-five and older and the positive results achieved with the project, The Hague decided to begin a project in 2004 that entails visiting all Somalis in The Hague at home. Among the matters discussed during these house visits is what the refugees need in order to further integrate in the Netherlands.

WORK AND TRAINING

The work and training portion of the project was set up to encourage Somali youngsters who do not participate, or who do not fully participate, in mainstream work or education programs to go back to school or work. Via individual case management, a number of youths were guided into employment programs, regular jobs, or mainstream education. This approach has helped these youngsters to take a step on the road to an independent future.

The work and training part of the project is conducted by De Gids Escamp and De Gids Centrum. These organizations have extensive experience in guiding and counseling Turkish and Moroccan youngsters. Somali coaches were appointed to guide and counsel the Somali youngsters. The coaches looked for young Somalis who were not at school or in employment. Centrum adopted an outreach policy: the coaches sought out the young Somalis on the

street, in community centers, and in other places. Escamp opted for a different method: organizing activities aimed at reaching out to the youngsters.

The coaches provided intensive supervision for the youngsters who qualified for a program in order to help get them back in school or into suitable employment. This required removing existing obstacles and solving problems, such as truancy, addiction, or housing problems. A very important part of the approach was aftercare. Supervision did not stop once the youngster was at school or in employment. Supervision continued until the youngster was firmly established in their program of education or work and had a prospect of an independent future.

The project's original goal was to place fifty Somali youngsters in educational and/or training programs. This figure was reduced in the interim to thirty-five due to a delay in appointing the coaches. By March 2003, forty-eight youngsters had been placed in programs.

COACHING

The aim of the coaching aspect of the project was to stimulate and give guidance to Somali youngsters facing difficulties with the educational program in which they were participating. Because Somalis have strong community ties, it was decided to use coaches from the Somali community.

Through contacts with schools and through questionnaires, it was possible to reach young people who could benefit from having a coach. In addition, a recruitment campaign was held to recruit potential coaches. Thirteen candidates were found, and in January 2003 they attended a training course at Centrum 16/22. This organization has prior experience in setting up a mentoring system for Moroccan youngsters. During the training course, the suitability of the candidates inter alia was assessed. Of the thirteen candidates, six were chosen to participate.

In March 2003, six youngsters were paired with six coaches. The goal was for the coaches to supervise the youngsters for a period of one year, meeting with them roughly once a week. This meeting might consist of a conversation, assistance with homework, or an activity. The coaches were given support and guidance by the Somali case manager at De Gids Centrum.

The original objective of the coaching part of the project was to appoint ten coaches. The training course for coaches commenced with thirteen participants. Of these, six were ultimately paired with Somali youngsters.

Meaningful Leisure Activities

Providing meaningful leisure activities is a good way of offering young people structure and care and hence avoiding problems. The activities were organized in the Schilderswijk and Escamp neighborhoods of The Hague and included drop-in evenings, sports events, computer courses, celebrations of Somali holidays, and informative gatherings. The range of activities was based in part on a survey of the interests of the young people. Besides providing opportunities

for spending leisure time, the activities also made it possible to establish contact with youngsters for the work and training part of the project.

The activities were organized by Clubhuizen de Mussen, the Somali Association, and De Gids Escamp. Special youth workers were appointed at Clubhuizen de Mussen for the target group, and a separate room was equipped for the Somali youngsters. This room is available to the youngsters for a maximum of two years; during that period they will work towards transferring to the mainstream activities program (cross over).

In order to reach the youngsters, it was decided mainly to pay house visits. In the course of these visits, it emerged that Somali parents and younger children were also in need of activities and support.

The objective of the meaningful leisure activities part of the project was to increase participation in activities. This objective was most definitely achieved. It started with providing a safe place of their own for the Somali youngsters. Involvement in mainstream leisure activities is the next step.

Skills Enhancement

The skills-enhancement portion of the project targeted employees of organizations that work with Somali youngsters. Via a training program, these employees were able to acquire specific knowledge about the social and cultural backgrounds of Somali youngsters. This knowledge helped them to communicate with the youngsters and to build up and maintain a relationship of trust.

The training was provided by The Hague branch of the Dutch Refugee Council; this organization has a wealth of experience with the target group. Subjects covered at the meetings included the history and culture of Somalia, the background and position of refugees in general, and the position of refugees with a Somali background. The input of Somali guest teachers was of great importance at the meetings.

In 2002, seven skills-enhancement meetings were provided, attended by a total of seventy-three people. The objective was ten meetings and one hundred attendees. Organizations that attended were institutions in the area of case management, education and educational guidance, sociocultural training, and the police.

LESSONS FROM THE HAGUE EXPERIENCE

The experience acquired in the project can be used to set up similar projects in other places or for other target groups. Lessons include

- For, by, and with the target group: The project was initiated at the request of the Somali community, and Somali workers and coaches were employed in the project. This lowered the barriers to contact and allowed the method used to be better geared to the young people.

- Knowledge of the target group: A thorough knowledge of the target group is needed to be able to reach the target group, to be able to gain and maintain trust, and to be able to coordinate activities.

- Reaching some or all youngsters: Young people, Somali or other, can best be reached through personal contact. This can be achieved by using networks and by visiting places where young people congregate. Much use was made of outreach work in the project.

- Step by step: Before young people can integrate, it is first important to unite their own group. Then, the step towards participation in mainstream activities and further integration can be taken. This process of change takes time. This step-by-step approach also applies to case management.

- Demarcating the target group: Somalis below the age of twelve and above the age of twenty-five also need additional attention in the form of coaching, information, and activities. The survey questions make it clear that additional measures are needed, and more still can be done both with and by the Somali target group. Also, at the start of the project, the importance of organizing separate activities for the youngsters' parents and involving parents in the project was not sufficiently acknowledged.

- Domino effect: The activities have had a domino effect on the youngsters' immediate environment. The project has also had a positive impact on the Somali community and can be an example to other migrant groups.

- Central management and timescale: Similar projects should allow more time for a separate preparatory and coordination phase.

- Enthusiasm: The enthusiasm of the participating organizations and of the participants in the project brought the project to life.

POLAND

KRYSTYNA IGLICKA AND MAREK OKÓLSKI

Foreigners residing legally in Poland usually face serious problems satisfying their basic needs. Although the law does not prevent them from pursuing their goals, there are legal and economic obstacles to their full integration. The situation of immigrants, refugees, and repatriates in Poland varies substantially. There is a gradation of their integration into society not dependant on the letter of the law nor on adopted standards but on the commitment of the government and legitimization of the norms the elites want to pursue. In this light the repatriates are in the best position to fully adapt to their new surroundings.

Polish immigration policy has many facets, but its integration component is among the least significant. Although in theory the Polish state pursues a policy of integration based on European standards, the implementation of this policy lags far behind. The central problem concerns the government clerks who work with foreigners, as well as border guards and the police. These officials often are not aware of their own racist attitudes and need training to better handle the situations they face. The standards that exist have been adopted by a narrow political elite and incorporated into the legal system without any grassroots action that would legitimize them and sensitize society. As a consequence, integration programs generally

tend to fail for lack of social support (such as support from the nongovernmental sector). The financial difficulties of the Polish state only serve to make the limited integration efforts less effective. Foreigners who manage to integrate do so mainly because of their own determination and a helpful hand offered by friends or family.

Pre-1989 Poland was not familiar with the phenomenon of mass immigration. The problems associated with integration and discrimination of outsiders were largely ignored in a society believed to be culturally and ethnically homogeneous. It was not until the collapse of the communist regime that the consequences of this position were revealed. In the social sphere, the hypocrisy of the communist authorities and thus the lack of appropriate provisions had allowed the proliferation of discriminatory attitudes and practices that had never been openly discussed. In this state of mind the Poles discovered suddenly that there are people of other nationalities or ethnicities living next door. The shock would have been less if these "others" spoke Polish, were Polish citizens, and had lived in Poland for generations. However, in the last decade Poland became a host to more than fifty thousand newly arriving foreign citizens, including refugees, several types of immigrants, and Polish coethnics repatriated from the former Soviet Union.

The need to cope with otherness on an everyday basis has become imperative. The manner in which the integration of these three groups of people proceeds lays the basis for future coexistence with the receiving society. Facing the international human rights system and the subsequent diffusion of norms associated with liberal democracy has brought about substantial changes in this field.

REFUGEES

The inflow of asylum seekers to Poland has been caused mainly by unilateral decisions taken by European Union Member States, signatories of the Schengen Convention. The application of the safe third country rule has put Poland at the gates of Western Europe. Additionally, as early as 1991 Poland signed bilateral readmission agreements with several Schengen states. The agreement with Germany is the most significant, since it assumes that Poland will subsidize the asylum seekers' stays in Polish territory.[1] The largest number of readmission cases happens to be on the German border. Persons applying for asylum in Poland generally did not intend to begin the procedure in Poland.

Asylum seekers in Poland come from different regions of the world, although primarily from the Caucasus region, Africa, and East Asia. In 2001 the most numerous group was refugees from Chechnya (1,317). Other applications were received from nationals of Armenia (636), Afghanistan (414),

Romania (266), and Bulgaria (178). Most cross the border illegally, as do the majority of the world's asylum seekers. The most common technique of illegal crossing is to walk into the country through the land border with Ukraine in southeastern Poland, Bieszczady. This is the customary route for asylum seekers from the Caucasus region, but those traveling from more distant countries, such as Sri Lanka or Liberia, also use it.

The first months after arrival are spent in one of several refugee centers. There are nine such centers in Poland, currently housing 1,390 asylum seekers. The government spends 1,600 zloty (about 400 euro) monthly on each asylum seeker. The sum, equivalent to the average monthly salary in Warsaw, apparently does not improve the standard of living.

While in the refugee centers, the asylum seekers are free to move in and out within a given timetable. They are not offered organized activities, apart from Polish language courses for children. Thus, many of them try to find illegal odd jobs. They also try to get in touch with other refugees and immigrants in order to build a network of acquaintances for the future. A serious problem with the Polish asylum system is the lengthy procedure involved. People must live in uncertainty for periods from six months to three years while awaiting a final decision. This definitely exceeds the three-month procedure called for in the Alien Act. What makes this especially alarming is the fact that this happens now, when Poland is still receiving only a relatively small share of all asylum seekers coming to Europe.

Asylum seekers in Poland have the right to state protection. While awaiting the decision in the refugee centers they are entitled to accommodation, full board, health care, a monetary allowance, material help, and assistance if they want to leave Polish territory. In the case of status refusal, the asylum seeker can appeal the decision. While awaiting the second decision, refugees still receive aid from their refugee center. The second decision usually comes within one to two months.

The stay at the refugee center must not exceed three months after refugee status has been granted. The refugees granted legal status leave for the outside world and begin the difficult path to integration. For many, their stay in Poland ends in this very moment. Their decision on whether to stay or go depends on the network of contacts available to them in other countries. Those with limited possibilities choose to stay and hope for better times.

The only government program available to refugees for the period immediately following the approval of their claims lasts for only one year. The provincial authorities run the program. The refugees receive a monthly payment, and they are helped with finding an apartment. They are also registered at the Labor Offices. Participation is not automatic—it is only offered on the condition that the refugee takes part in Polish language courses offered as an element of the program. After a year, the integration aid ends, and refugees can then turn to support offered by social assistance centers. It is obvious that a mere twelve months cannot guarantee successful integration.

The most significant problem is housing. Refugees cannot easily find accommodations. There are fewer apartments than there are refugees participating in the program. Some of them have to find a place to live on their own, and they face many obstacles. Refugees consider housing a starting point for further insertion into society. Rent, especially in the capital city of Warsaw, is very high, and many eventually find themselves caught in a situation where the money they earn goes primarily toward rent. They are often forced to change houses, creating the feeling of a constant lack of stability.

The other important factor in the integration process is employment. Refugees can be employed on the same terms as Polish citizens. The difficult economic situation in Poland forces refugees to look for alternative solutions, such as employment in gray market activities. The majority are aware that Poland cannot afford the kind of integration program available in Western European countries. Poland has suffered an economic slowdown during the last two years. The refugees see the growing problem of unemployment, and they understand that their chances of finding work are questionable. They feel like guests who have overstayed their welcome. In a situation in which their basic needs (housing and employment) cannot be satisfied, refugees seek some other way of maintaining their human dignity. Trips to Germany are common among Chechens. Through establishing and maintaining contacts with their extended families on the other side of the border, many of these refugees engage in shuttle migration. This type of migration, popular also among the

Poles, allows them to support their families in Warsaw. Some of them decide to stay in the new country. This second step of migration becomes more common with the growing recession in Poland.

LEGAL IMMIGRANTS

Currently there are 40,500 foreigners working legally in Poland. This number is based on all work permits issued for this year and comprises all types of employees, from low-skilled construction workers to highly qualified managers of international companies. Only part of this group intends to become permanent immigrants and settle permanently in Poland. Workers' motives for coming to Poland vary substantially, and the labor factor is not the main rationale for most. Their economic purpose might be connected with self-development, pursuing temporary immigration to Poland to enhance future profits.

In contrast to some other European countries, legal immigrants currently cannot vote in local Polish elections. As for their social rights, there have been few problems reported with regard to health care or other social services. Many immigrants use the private medical system, because they believe it to be better organized. Not all of them have health insurance.

REPATRIATES

According to Polish law, repatriates are not foreigners. Their status is defined in the Repatriation Act of 9 November 2000. Although the Repatriation Act has been in force since January 2001, repatriation actually started many years earlier, initiated by a national campaign organized by the Catholic Church and right-wing parties. The repatriates are people who know Poland, who are connected to a network in the country (local authorities, extended family, friends), and in almost all cases enjoy the support of the integration program at some stage of their repatriation process. Nevertheless, the experience of this group is very diverse. This complexity derives from different means of arrival.

The Repatriation Act was modeled after regulations in other European countries, first and foremost Germany. The act is based on the ideological concept of national bonds, and thus the obligation of the Polish nation towards the descendants of Poles forcibly displaced to the East. Interestingly, the act only provides for repatriation from the territories of the Asian republics of the former Soviet Union. Nevertheless, repatriation from other areas could be allowed through special government decree, provided persecution of the Polish minority was established.

According to the act, a repatriate is an individual of Polish nationality entitled to enter the Republic of Poland on the basis of a repatriation visa, who arrives with the purpose of seeking permanent settlement. The repatriates, and their minor children, are automatically granted Polish citizenship. The definition of Polish origin has two dimensions: nationality and culture. The repatriation visa can be issued to an applicant who claims Polish nationality and used to have Polish citizenship. The Polish origin rule is also applicable if one of the applicant's parents or grandparents or both great-grandparents were of Polish nationality or were Polish citizens. Such a person should demonstrate a devotion to Polishness, meaning the cultivation of Polish traditions, customs, and language. Owing to their affinity for Polishness, repatriates in this category treat Poland as their final destination, for both sentimental and historical reasons. These repatriates usually come from traditional families with strong Polish national identity. They speak Polish, and thus they have little problem with integration.

However, idealism is not a driving force in all cases. Another category of repatriates consists of people who came to Poland for nonpatriotic motives. This group shares many characteristics with economic migrants. Apart from their declared readiness to leave Poland, they already live as if they were outside of Poland, primarily due to communication difficulties. These are the people whose arrival in Poland is feared most by the European Union. During the EU enlargement negotiations, the flexible procedures of issuing the repatriation visa were perceived as endangering the balance of the EU labor market. Weak links to Poland and a lack of sentimental ties increase the likelihood that this group will seek its fortunes further to the west—especially since the Polish state is unable to provide employment for all repatriates.

The provisions of the Repatriation Act are probably the best operational antidiscrimination measures in Poland. However, they apply only to individuals accepted in the program. All those who did not come to Poland with a repatria-

tion visa or who did not enter the program in 2001 (there was such a possibility for those who arrived earlier) cannot claim repatriation rights. A crucial aspect of the act is that repatriation can take place only if the basic needs of the newcomers are met, and thus they need a special invitation from a local community or a private person. The repatriates from the analyzed group used these means, although their motives for coming varied.

This spontaneous repatriation occurred outside the supervision of the central authorities. Some of those involved were young people of Polish origin from other parts of Eastern Europe. In the early 1990s over 650 students from Ukraine, Belarus, and Kazakhstan received scholarships to study at Polish universities. This program was cofinanced by the Polish diaspora in the West. The students' intentions to stay were not clearly defined at the beginning of their studies. However, many of them eventually stayed in Poland and then pursued family reunification. The immigration process was initiated individually, sometimes as early as 1995. Therefore, many of the repatriates from this group arrived as foreigners and were not granted Polish citizenship on arrival. This category of repatriates was very active and entrepreneurial—their repatriation depended entirely on their luck and determination.

The invitation that began the repatriation process was usually issued by the local administration, motivated by sheer patriotic feeling following the pro-repatriation political and media campaign of the mid-1990s. Political will was one of the decisive elements in this process. The repatriates were invited to settle down in a local community, which also bore the responsibility for providing them with accommodations and employment possibilities. Thus, the whole burden of the early arrivals was borne by the goodwill of the local community.

Repatriation sometimes requires additional financial capital, since housing is not always provided, especially if a person comes to a larger town. In such cases, the repatriates are left to their own resources: either they can be helped out by individual Polish families, or they have to arrange for accommodations themselves.

For a person who arrives as part of the program, the state might cover the one-way trip by train from Kazakhstan to Poland (the cost of transportation of any property is also covered). Two months after the repatriate receives citizenship, the program provides a money transfer amounting to double the average salary for each family member, to cover the expenses of establishing a new household; an allowance for the education of minors; and reimbursement for any needed renovation or adaptation of the offered accommodations (this money is transferred over the course of a two-year period).

Help in finding employment for the repatriates occurs on a discretionary basis. The local administration can refund a portion of the following expenses to employers hiring repatriates: salary, social security tax, bonuses, workplace equipment, or training expenses. The right to this funding is valid for five years from entry into the country, and it can be effective after two years, provided employment is guaranteed for four years. If the repatriate cannot find employment in his or her profession, the local authority can contact a potential employer and offer reimbursement for the cost of training, provided employment is guaranteed for two years. Another important provision is the creation of a national registry of housing and employment possibilities for repatriates.

In practice, the problem of employment, and of achieving economic independence, can be solved for some of the newcomers. The outcome is dependent on the local community in which the repatriates live. Many repatriates, however, are misinformed about the precise nature of their circumstances and are thus unable to reduce obstacles to finding employment. Misinterpretation of the facts leads to disappointment and superficial criticisms. The lack of solid and transparent procedures causes confusion and leads to feelings of insecurity on the part of repatriates.

For those who arrived before January 2001, circumstances were generally not entirely hospitable. Their status as foreigners, not repatriates, caused the newcomers to have many problems in satisfying their basic needs. They could not expect preferential treatment. Their experience was thus especially difficult, since they could not take advantage of a support network. Many people in this group were unemployed for significant periods of time; however, the longer they stay in Poland, the greater the chance their situation might change. People over the age of fifty find themselves in the most difficult situation, especially if they came to Poland without access to the repatriation program (for example, if they come from a country other than Kazakhstan) or if their skills are not needed in Poland. But even young individuals, who are covered by the program, can encounter many obstacles. One of the forms of hidden discrimination lies in the extreme job requirements imposed by some employers.

Persons with repatriate status receive Polish citizenship and therefore have the right to social security on the same terms as Poles. They can collect welfare if unemployed, and some may even get a pension. Some, however, can only find employment illegally, as do many Poles in the poorer regions of the country. As previously stated, the most successful repatriates live in settlements where the local government took advantage of a complex repatriation service and engaged the local community. Adequate housing and employment not only may protect repatriates from entering the welfare chain, but also can provide the basis for further integration.

Another aspect of integration is cultural adaptation. Persons of Polish origin who have proven their affinity to Polish culture seldom have had serious problems in adapting to day-to-day life in Poland. Polish language courses are offered without charge in the country of origin prior to departure and in Poland after arrival. Apart from a few individual exceptions, most repatriates speak Polish. Although most do not require basic language training, many have had to take some additional language courses in order to learn the vocabulary indispensable to understanding advanced media messages or legal documents.

For persons with Polish passports issued at the time they entered the country, language fluency is one of the factors eliminating any possible discrimination that might derive from misunderstandings and misconceptions in everyday life. Insufficient language skills are also a key discriminative factor in the life of repatriates.

THE PILOT INTEGRATION PROGRAMME FOR REFUGEES IN THE MAZOVIA REGION

Over the last three years, Poland has granted refugee status to nearly one thousand foreigners. The number of new applications is growing, and in 2003 applications were in excess of six thousand. In 2002, the regional government of the Mazovia region (wojewodztwo Mazowieckie)[2] launched a concerted refugee integration program composed of ninety-three individual projects that included a total of 241 foreigners. Experience gathered through the implementation of that program has given rise to wider and even more complex activities under the Pilot Integration Programme initiated in early 2003.

Two other regions, Lublin and Podlasie (both located in eastern Poland), have now joined the Pilot Integration Programme. Apart from the continuation of earlier activities focused on small, individual, target-oriented projects,[3] the program is directed at building a more viable and efficient system of refugee integration. Another vital objective of the program is the dissemination of basic facts about refugees and the stimulation of pro-refugee attitudes among local populations. County family assistance centers and social aid centers, overseen by local governments, are responsible for carrying out all of these programs. Two nongovernmental organizations, Caritas Poland and Polish Humanitarian Action, are also deeply involved in these programs. It has been suggested that each refugee participate initially, for approximately one year, in projects run by the local government, after which the nongovernmental organizations take on a greater role.

The program benefits from technical assistance offered by the government of the Netherlands—specifically by the Dutch organization Radar, designated to carry out the task. Radar's experts organize training courses for social workers, and they pass along to Polish professionals the know-how they have gathered in the area of immigrant integration based on the Dutch experience. Other important areas of this collaboration include the design of relevant institutions; the promotion of joint efforts between regional governments and interested nongovernmental organiza-

tions; and the fostering of international cooperation and monitoring of program development. An innovative and fruitful idea introduced by Dutch experts and implemented in the Mazovia region was the creation of dual learning courses for refugees, which assume parallel participation by an immigrant in a Polish language course and vocational (or on-the-job) training, while at the same time encouraging the person to participate in volunteer social work.[4]

The Pilot Integration Programme consists of a number of far-reaching ideas whose full implementation should lead to the fast integration of refugees into a community. Three of these activities are particularly worth noting: First, a special fund is being raised with the support of the government of Poland, which offers highly preferential mortgages for refugees to help them acquire their own flats. Second, a network of drop-in integration centers is being established, which would facilitate direct contact between refugees and the local population. Third, a family volunteer system is being created, through which participating families take care of refugees and gradually introduce them into the Polish reality.

ENDNOTES

1   By 2000 Poland had received 28 billion euro from PHARE, and in the year 2000 an additional 17.5 billion euro was paid to fund projects related to border control and asylum procedures. In the same year Germany paid more than 200 million deutsche marks (about 100 million euro) as part of the framework of the Polish-German agreement.

2   Mazovia, one of sixteen regional administration units in Poland, is centrally located, and its principal city is Poland's capital, Warsaw.

3   For instance, in the Mazovia region, three counties (*powiat*)—Warsaw, Nowy Dwor, and Minsk Mazowiecki—pursued fifty-eight integration projects, which covered some 150 refugees. These projects were supported by 1.3 million zloty from the Mazovia government budget.

4   In addition to rendering expertise, the Dutch counterpart committed itself to financially support the program (in particular, the cost of Dutch personnel and the organization of training courses for Polish social workers).

Scotland

Sally Daghlian

Introduction

Scotland is a part of the United Kingdom with its own distinct culture, traditions, parliament, and institutions. Despite having two culturally diverse cities (Edinburgh and Glasgow), Scotland is not a culturally diverse country.

Before the year 2000, only a few hundred asylum seekers per year arrived in Scotland. However, following the implementation of a UK government-sponsored dispersal program, Glasgow now has some ten thousand refugees and asylum seekers, the largest concentration in any British city.

Glasgow is a city with chronic social problems linked with the poverty that accompanied the decline of the heavy industries that once sustained the city. A declining population and a political will to support refugees prompted Glasgow City Council (the municipal body) to agree to house dispersed asylum seekers. Although the city was enthusiastic in its support for the dispersal program, this enthusiasm was not matched by preparation at a neighborhood level. Refugees were housed in deprived neighborhoods with endemic social problems and few community resources. A lack of community preparation com-bined with an unrelenting hostility to asylum seekers displayed by the tabloid press created a particularly hostile climate for new refugee arrivals.

The Scottish Executive, the devolved government, has responsibility for domestic affairs including refugee integration, while immigration and asylum are matters reserved for the Westminster government. The Scottish Executive, encouraged and supported by the Scottish Refugee Council, has taken active steps to promote integration by developing the Integration Action Plan, recognizing that integration must begin on arrival.

The two projects described here form part of a strategic response to promote refugee integration in this specific context. They reflect the need to build bridges and bonds between the host community and the new refugee communities and to change public and media attitudes through education and advocacy, promoting the real stories of refugees' lives, the human faces behind the stereotypes and myths.

The projects also encompass the need to address and acknowledge host community fears and build on the support and friendship offered by many groups and individuals in the city. Both projects promote the empowerment of refugees and their active involvement in advocacy and integration.

FRAMEWORK FOR DIALOGUE

The Framework for Dialogue Project is a partnership initiative between the Scottish Executive, the Glasgow City Council, and the Scottish Refugee Council that aims to build bridges between the host communities and refugees, enabling refugees to participate actively in civil society. The project also aims to encourage refugees within Glasgow to use their own skills to address their needs and help to solve their own problems.

The project provides a structure to support the development of individual autonomous refugee community organizations and brings together various groups to discuss common concerns and influence policy and services. The purpose of the project is to ensure the active participation of refugees in the planning, delivery, and evaluation of the local services they receive. The project also brings together the host community and refugees to address issues of common concern such as crime and policing. In so doing, the project breaks down barriers, fosters understanding, and provides motivation to both refugees and long-term residents to improve their impoverished communities.

The project is an important tool for bridge building between refugees, the host community, and local organizations. The work of the project is publicized primarily through a local newsletter that provides refugees with information about the activities within their area. The emphasis in the initial phase of the project has been on consultation, agenda setting, and identifying volunteers from host and refugee communities to carry the work forward.

Five major refugee consultative events have been held, which were attended by 380 adults and a similar number of children and involved fourteen different language groups and twenty nationalities. Simultaneous translation was utilized to ensure full participation. These events focused on the experience of refugees in Glasgow and set an agenda for future work towards integration. One hundred thirty-three adult representatives volunteered to remain involved in the work. In addition, four focus groups were held to consult with additionally marginalized groups of women, young people, children, and lone parents. The project also held five consultative meetings with community leaders from host communities focusing on their experiences of dispersal and their views on future priorities for integration.

The measure of success will be the establishment of permanent bridges and bonds within a community, a particularly important feature since the project has only fixed-term funding. Anecdotal evidence so far shows that previously hostile host community members have now become refugee champions.

The project work is led by the Scottish Refugee Council's Community Development Team and is supported by local social and community workers and local refugee support and integration networks. This partnership will increase sustainability. The process of building the framework for dialogue has been monitored by researchers, and a report has been produced as a resource.

REFUGEE MEDIA GROUP

This second project was driven by a recognition that hostility to refugees can be born of ignorance and stereotyping by the host community. There is a recognizable hostility toward refugees in the British tabloid media and, almost certainly as a result, among the public at large.

In addressing this hostile environment, the Scottish Refugee Council was motivated by a belief that empowering refugees to speak out and to tell their own stories would ensure that balance was reintroduced into the debate on asylum. The setting up of the Refugee Media Group ensured that when the media wanted to interview refugees, there was a pool of confident, articulate individuals able to express their views cogently. Participation in any interview was always voluntary, and anonymity was guaranteed if required.

The first stage of the project was to find refugees willing to engage with the media. The Scottish Refugee Council used its various contacts with refugees and refugee organizations to encourage willing participants to come forward. As the project developed, interested refugees also referred friends and colleagues who were willing to engage with the media. Finally, some fifteen individuals, including former politicians, were recruited to the project.

The second stage of the project was to improve the communication skills of the group. Print and broadcast journalists, including those with refugee backgrounds, together with members of the Scottish Refugee Council Communication Team developed a program to improve the confidence levels of the refugees and provide the appropriate tools to deal with (often hostile) media interest. The National Union of Journalists[1] Training Unit was also able to play a leading role in contacting trainers and securing appropriate venues. The final stage of the project was to forge links with the Scottish media and with journalists.

The project continues to evolve with a particular effort currently underway to encourage more women to get involved in the project. As a result, a group of some twenty women has been identified to undergo training. A number of visits to Scottish media offices are planned for the coming months, which will enable members of the group to speak to journalists about their concerns regarding media coverage and help the refugees gain an understanding of the pressures under which the media operates. It is hoped that such encounters will encourage editors to appreciate the impact of some of the more lurid headlines.

The project has been funded by grants from the Scottish Executive and the Community Fund and through in-kind support from other organizations. It will be sustained by developing and supporting a rolling program of participants.

Twenty-five individuals have now undergone media training, with the majority having gone on to engage with the media. Indeed, several have become polished media performers. However, it is important to note that a number of participants were frustrated by the attitude of the media and disengaged from the project, a salutary reminder that the process of reeducating the media is no easy task.

With the Scottish Refugee Council's support, the group has achieved excellent media coverage. Positive case studies, with refugees talking about their experiences both in their home countries and as refugees in Scotland, have been an important way of raising awareness of some of the issues affecting refugees and asylum seekers today. Such outcomes are positive in challenging myths and educating the public. In addition, the project has the effect of empowering refugees, enabling them to develop their confidence and skills and take an active role in challenging the negative media that ultimately impacts on their lives in Scotland.

ENDNOTES

1   The National Union of Journalists is the trade union body for journalists in the United Kingdom.

Spain

Maria Helena Bedoya[1]

"Managing migration is not only a matter of opening doors and joining hands internationally. It also requires each country to do more to integrate new arrivals."
(Kofi A. Annan, speech made to the European Parliament on 29 January 2004)

Immigration Policy and Integration

The debate over what is meant by the social integration of immigrants is very complex. This chapter sketches out some of the measures being taken in diverse situations to avoid division between foreigners and nationals. My focus will be primarily on Catalonia, although I will sketch out the specific ways in which Catalan immigration policy is embedded within the larger governing structure of the Spanish state. Catalonia is worth focusing on because it has the most developed policy toward immigration in Spain.

Spain, like other countries of the European Union, must be capable of offering to those that arrive with a desire to stay and participate in the workforce the possibility of integrating into Spanish society. This opportunity should apply to individual immigrants as well as immigrant communities as a whole. As part of this process of integration, it is possible that some deficits in the social welfare state may be revealed. This, in turn, must lead to the procurement of adequate services for the entire general population, without creating unnecessary tensions between citizens and recent arrivals.

The Importance of Language in Social Integration

Access to benefits and services that the society makes available for its citizens is carried out through interactions in which the capacity to communicate is of primary importance. Persons without command of the language or languages of the welcoming society find themselves in a situation of clear inequality. There are serious repercussions for immigrants and their families who do not have knowledge of the local language. These include lack of knowledge of basic rights, difficulties in searching for employment, the necessity to accept work below their level of professional qualification, the inability to access courses for specialized professional training, lack of knowledge of the norms of hygiene and safety at work, difficulty in accessing public services and public spaces, difficulty participating in the social life of the community (with neighbors, in schools, cinemas, etc.), difficulty in forming friendships, difficulty in helping their children with school work, and distancing between parents and children as children learn the language more rapidly through the educational system.[2]

CONSTRUCTING A SOCIETY THAT CAN RESPOND TO THE CHALLENGE OF IMMIGRATION

Given the need for the government, the business world, social agents, and the third sector to unite their forces and resources throughout the process of integration so that clear lines of action can be drawn, the secretary for immigration in Catalonia organized a series of debates that took place throughout 2003.

These debates were open to contributions from all social agents and focused on the following ten themes:
1. Immigration as a positive contribution
2. Welcoming
3. Administrative coordination of public policy
4. How to promote a policy of coexistence
5. Rights and duties
6. Collaboration with the media
7. Consensus, not confrontation
8. Associations as a guarantee of social participation
9. Cultural pluralism and respect for human rights
10. Immigration and codevelopment

The debates took place within the broader context of the need to confront the challenges of the twenty-first century, including economic globalization, questions of identity, the ordered management of migratory flows, and issues of political power. It was recognized that

the specific challenge is to make immigration a demographic, economic, and cultural asset for the welcoming society.

FACILITATING THE PARTICIPATION OF IMMIGRANTS IN THE HOST SOCIETY

If we accept that the responsibility for the integration of immigrants falls as much on the institutions of the welcoming society as on immigrant communities themselves, we then see that the challenge regarding immigration is how to reinforce and deepen an immigrant's lateral relationships.

Entities to promote the participation of immigrants in the institutions that design immigration policy are necessary. In the case of Catalonia, advisory councils exist on both the regional level and the municipal level that serve this purpose. The Advisory Council on Immigration is dependent on the Generalitat[3] (the secretary for immigration), while the Barcelona Council for Immigration (in existence since 1988) is active at the municipal level. Other examples of direct participation of immigrants in municipal policy and planning regarding immigration in Catalonia are the Mataró Municipal Council for Coexistence, the Immigrants' Roundtable of Manresa, and the Cambrils Consultative Council on Emigration. In all of these councils, immigrants participate actively.

IMPROVING THE RELATIONSHIP BETWEEN IMMIGRANTS AND THE HOST SOCIETY

The Forum for the Social Integration of Immigrants,[4] operating within the Interior Ministry, possesses consultative functions in regard to matters of immigration. The forum consists of eight representatives from government (from the state, Catalonia, and federations that represent local administrations), eight representatives from immigrant and refugee associations, and eight representatives from social organizations (trade unions and neighborhood associations) and business organizations.

The Institute for Migration and Social Services (IMSERSO) is tasked with executing the Ministry of Labor and Social Affairs's plan for integration. The institute is responsible for promoting and fostering activities aimed at providing social protection for asylum seekers, refugees, and displaced persons assigned to both public and private entities (the Red Cross, the Spanish Commission for Refugee Assistance (CEAR), etc.) financed through public subsidies.[5]

With regard to the responsibilities of the autonomous communities, Catalonia stands out. In 1994 the Advisory Council on Immigration was formed. This consultative body of the government of Catalonia is composed of the secretary for immigration, the secretary for religious affairs, a representative of the Ministry of Social Welfare, two representatives of the Interdepartmental Commission on Immigration, two county council members from the areas with the greatest number of immigrants, two representatives from organizational entities that work on the municipal level, six representatives from social organizations whose work in favor of immigrants stands out,[6] ten representatives from the immigrant associations with the widest involvement in

Catalonia, two representatives from the largest labor unions—Comisiones Obreras de Catalunya (CCOO) and Unió General de Treballadors (UGT)—two representatives from umbrella organizations of neighborhood associations, two representatives of professional agricultural organizations, two representatives of federations of parents of students, and two experts, one of them from the association SOS Racism.

THE ACCEPTANCE OF IMMIGRANTS

As immigration increases in Spain, the Spanish citizenry is becoming increasingly aware of the presence and participation of immigrants in the economic life of the country in the production, professional, and sociocultural sectors.[7]

It must be mentioned that the elite among immigrants have never had problems with acceptance within the host country (university students, retirees, elite athletes, residents from other European Union countries, etc.). It is also important to recognize that the question of acceptance and integration does not affect only immigrants. The Gypsy community in Spain also suffers discrimination similar to that of some immigrant groups.

IMMIGRANTS' INVOLVEMENT IN THE HOST SOCIETY

The Generalitat of Catalonia, through its secretary for immigration, has created a series of tools to help immigrants orient themselves through local institutions. One of these tools is the welcoming guide *Get Wired Up to Catalonia*, which, in addition to containing detailed information about Catalonia, also contains practical and useful information about existing public services and how to access them.

The Generalitat also does much to promote the learning of Catalan and Spanish as vehicles for social interaction in the host society by offering free language classes. These classes are available in many of the municipalities throughout Catalonia.

DIVISION OF RESPONSIBILITIES IN SPANISH IMMIGRATION AND INTEGRATION POLICY

As stated in Article 149, section 1, part 2, of the Spanish Constitution, the responsibility for nationality, immigration, emigration, and the right to asylum is the domain of the state.

Nevertheless, the autonomous communities[8] are responsible for matters that directly affect the integration of resident foreigners in their territories, such as town planning, housing, agriculture, handicrafts, promotion of culture, promotion of research, language teaching, social assistance, health, employment policy, abandoned children, the legal framework for associative entities, and prisons.

It is the state, through its ministries, which is directly implicated in the administration and control of flows of migration. Specifically, the Ministry of Foreign Affairs, the Ministry of the Interior, and the Ministry of Labor and Social Affairs have the task of designing policy measures regarding immigration that in turn must be coordinated by transferring or delegating functions and

responsibilities to the autonomous communities. The autonomous communities must then establish an intergovernmental plan to coordinate the work to be done within their own territories.

The final level of administration of immigration policy is the local level. It is at the local level with local institutions that citizens and immigrants have direct contact and through which they access basic services.

Although it is the responsibility of public institutions to design and carry out a plan for the integration of immigrants, as nongovernmental organizations and the labor unions argue,[9] this politics of integration cannot function exclusively as a pyramid moving from the top to the base. It is essential that public institutions first define their objectives and second allocate the means and resources necessary to meet those objectives. But it is crucial that in this overall process public institutions work together with the already existing rich and diverse associative fabric.

There is a contradiction between the enormous degree of centralization of state power in designing the basic outlines of the Global Program to Regulate and Coordinate Foreign Residents' Affairs and Immigration in Spain (GRECO) and the degree of autonomy granted to the autonomous regions in carrying out the bulk of that policy. Despite the centralization, the autonomous communities, within the boundaries of their responsibilities, are designing and carrying out immigration plans with the objective of achieving the integration of immigrants into their local communities.

Immigration Programs and Plans by Level of Responsibility

Level	Program or Plan	Date
State	*Government of Spain* Global Program to Regulate and Coordinate Foreign Residents' Affairs and Immigration in Spain (GRECO) Permanent Immigration Observatory[10]	2000-2004
Autonomous Community[11]	*Catalonia* Interdepartmental Plan for Immigration, Office of the Secretary for Immigration, Generalitat of Catalonia	2001-2004
Autonomous Community	*The Basque Country* Plan for Immigration, Administration for Immigration, Eusko Jaurlaritza	2003-2005
Autonomous Community	*The Community of Madrid* Regional Plan for Immigration	2001-2004
Provincial[12]	Regional Government of Barcelona Consortium of Resources for Integration of Diversity (CRID) Migration and Citizenry, Observatory of Diversity, Accessibility, Training and Administration of Networks	Permanent
Municipal	*Barcelona Municipal Government* Service for Attention to Immigrants and Refugees (SAIER)	Permanent

Immigration policy maintains continuity based on the annual budgets of the different public administrations involved and the personnel and material resources assigned. The following table summarizes various government programs related to immigration at various levels.

Competence

The Role of Volunteers in Immigration Policy

Immigration plans would not be possible without the determined involvement of all of the social actors and agents that work to defend and promote the fundamental rights and social needs of foreigners and ensure equality of conditions with citizens. One such organization is the Service for Attention to Immigrants and Refugees (SAIER) in Barcelona. Created in 1989 based on a proposal by the Council for Social Welfare, SAIER is a municipal service composed of a diverse group of organizations and institutions that coordinate their work to offer services to immigrants, asylum seekers, and refugees in need of specialized attention. The participating entities are the Municipal Government of Barcelona (responsible for reception of users and providing information on services and resources provided by the citizen network), the Catalan Refugee Solidarity and Aid Association (ACSAR, provides legal advice and legal defense for asylum seekers and refugees), the Red Cross (complements Municipal Social Services by attending to urgent needs of immigrants without homes), the Centre for Information for Foreign Workers (CITE, provides legal advice and assistance with applications for permission to work and residency in Spain), the Bar Association of Barcelona (provides specialized legal advice on immigration, research, and filing of appeals before the courts), the Mutual Aid Association of Immigrants to Catalonia (AMIC, provides information and employment orientation), and the Consortium for Linguistic Normalization in Catalonia (provides language classes in Catalan for immigrants). Each of the participating organizations, based on their specific structure, makes available a multidisciplinary and multicultural team through the participation of mediators and interpreters. Each team may also include some volunteers.

The work of the Service for Research and Attention to Mental Health Issues Among Immigrants and Refugees in Barcelona (SAPPIR-GASIR), in particular, stands out in this regard. SAPPIR-GASIR is composed of a team of psychiatrists, psychologists, mediators specializing in intercultural conflicts, interpreters, sociologists, and anthropologists.

EMPLOYING THE RESOURCES AND COMPETENCIES OF IMMIGRANTS

The educational services, mediation, health information, and aid provided to women and children by the Health and Family Association is an example of efficient multidisciplinary work that facilitates the provision of health care to immigrant groups. The association's program, From Compatriot to Compatriot, stands out as a model. Immigrant women are attended to with discretion and respect by volunteers of the same nationality who accompany them and introduce them to the institutions of the city of Barcelona.

THE PARTICIPATION OF EXPERTS

One form of participation by experts in immigration policy in Spain has been the rigorous sociological studies conducted on an annual basis over the last decade. These studies were primarily done under the auspices of the Ministry of the Interior and the Ministry of Labor and Social Affairs.[13] The studies are multidisciplinary and involve the participation of almost all of the Spanish universities. The focus has been on analyzing the situation of immigration in Spain, aiding in government forecasts, and providing recommendations for different levels of public administration. Another example of interaction between experts from different fields can be seen in the work of the Catalan Parliament.[14] The Parliament created a commission of outside experts tasked with collaborating directly with parliamentary representatives on matters of immigration. Twelve experts worked for approximately a year and a half (meeting fourteen times from March 2003 until June 2001) to present recommendations to Parliament, civil society, and immigrant associations.

CITE: A Creative and Innovative Model for Immigration Policy

The labor union Workers' Commission of Catalonia (Comisiones Obreras de Catalunya or CCOO de Catalunya) has been a pioneer in seeking a closer relationship with immigrants and in defending their rights. In 1987 the CCOO created the Centre for Information for Foreign Workers or CITE.[15] CITE specializes in providing information and legal aid to foreign workers and today is the organization that attends to and assists the greatest number of immigrants in Catalonia through its network of thirty-eight offices.[16] CITE was the driving force behind the creation of the Platform for Citizenship and Coexistence, which now includes affiliates from approximately fifty different Catalan associations and immigrant organizations and which has established itself as one of the most important monitoring centers for immigration.[17] CITE together with the CCOO participates in the establishment and maintenance of a system of quotas for foreign workers in Spain, the

process of regularization of undocumented immigrants, and the detection of the emerging hidden economy, as well as demanding that the state and the courts fulfill their legal responsibilities for the violation of the rights of foreign workers. In addition, CITE works through the labor union to guarantee that there will be no discrimination against foreign workers in the labor market; publishes and disseminates information in various languages about labor rights, existing labor agreements, and health and safety norms and codes; and, finally, encourages the participation of immigrants in civil society.

This model is exported to the rest of Spain through the CCOO. Today, throughout Spain, there are over one hundred CITE offices in the different autonomous communities, both on the peninsula and in Ceuta and Melilla.

During a special conference on migration held in 1998, the CCOO decided to extend the work of CITE by establishing new offices throughout Spain. This decision was made because of the success of CITE and the prestige achieved by CITE as a result of its work in representing the interests of immigrants and developing policies to aid in the integration of immigrants.

The institution and characteristics of CITE depend on the autonomous community of which it is a part. The organization has adopted different structures, names, and legal models depending on the organizational, legal, and institutional circumstances of each autonomous region or nationality (Catalan, Basque, Gallego). While other organizations perform valuable work in the area, the work done by CITE regarding immigration and integration is the broadest and most far-reaching within Spain.

The activities of CITE-Catalunya serve as an example of this work. There are thirty-eight CITE offices throughout Catalonia, which are funded by the Generalitat of Catalonia, the provincial governments, and local governments. The offices also receive support from the legal network run by the Ministry of Labor and Social Affairs. CITE is administered under the direction of the department of immigration of the CCOO. Staff include a president, a coordinator of offices and institutional relations, a lawyer responsible for legal services, an accountant, and an administrative secretary. The economic infrastructure is administered through the labor union. There are at this time nineteen legal aides working in the different offices. Currently, the aides are of the following nationalities: Spanish, Moroccan, Saharan, Senegalese, Ukrainian, and Equatorial Guinean. Six are women, and most speak several languages. They are all full-time employees of CITE. CITE regularly provides legal or research training for university students through an internship program. The number of interns varies each year, but usually there are around twenty interns collaborating with CITE during each academic year.

CITE provides information services, advice, and support in the processing of paperwork in the following fields: work and residency permits in Spain; schooling of children; health and housing; welfare; neighborhood associations; creation of new associations; creation of immigrant cooperatives; taxes; driver's licenses; marriages; recognition of professional titles; and nationality.

CITE also offers many services as part of an agreement with the Department of Education of the Generalitat of Catalonia.[18] These include mediation services in schools; language interpretation services;[19] translation of documents; production of didactic material for schools written in different languages and based on the different educational realities of the immigrant communities;[20] organization of meetings and assemblies with parents of immigrant children to provide basic information about the educational system and to promote language classes in Catalan for adults; and a special internship program for secondary students.

In agreement with the Consortium for Linguistic Normalization, CITE offers free courses in Catalan within immigrant organizations. In addition, the labor union provides free Spanish courses through its Adult School.

CITE has agreements to collaborate on a regular basis with almost all of the different immigrant associations currently in existence in Catalonia.[21] These agreements focus on the following tasks: developing joint initiatives between immigrant associations and other host society associations, such as neighborhood associations and merchant associations; promoting integration and intercultural relations; coordinating cultural activities; and providing logistic support to the associations.

CITE works with the different municipal and county administrations in

Catalonia by helping to organize special courses on issues of immigration directed at civil servants. CITE also collaborates in the collection and analysis of statistics.[22]

Collaboration with the academic world and cultural foundations is also part of CITE's work. CITE has signed collaborative agreements for its internship program with the following universities: the University of Barcelona, the Autonomous University of Barcelona, the University of Pompeu Fabra, the Pontificia University of Comillas in Madrid, the Autonomous University of Madrid, the International University of Catalonia, and the Ca' Foscari Venezia University in Italy. CITE also participates in classes, roundtables, and workshops related to immigration at these universities. Social scientists from various prestigious universities have also come and worked with CITE while carrying out their research.[23] CITE works jointly with various cultural foundations in organizing conferences and workshops and edits texts related to themes that affect immigrants in Spain. CITE is a permanent collaborator with the European Institute of the Mediterranean and is a participant in the Dialogue on Human Movements and Immigration, part of the Forum of Cultures 2004 in Barcelona.

ENDNOTES

1   Jed Rosenstein, translator and editor, worked on this text.
2   Bertrán, Carles (2003): Conclusions from the European Seminar on plans for Linguistic Welcoming in the European Union.
3   The Catalan government.
4   Regulated by Royal Decree 367/2001 of 4 April 2001.
5   Includes programs related to welcoming, housing, health, education, training, employment, and legal assistance.
6   Centre for Information for Foreign Workers, Mutual Aid Association of Immigrants to Catalonia, Red Cross, Caritas Barcelona, Grups de Recerca i Actuació amb Minories Culturals i Treballadors Estrangers, and Bay Al Thaqafa.
7   Polls done by the Centre for Sociological Research in 2001 showed that although 92% of those interviewed believed that all persons have a right to live and work in countries other than that of their origin, 42% thought that there were too many immigrants in Spain. For other interesting results from this study, consult http://www.cis.es/ and Juan Diez Nicolás, *Actitudes hacia los inmigrantes*, ASEP Report

(Madrid: Ministry of Labor and Social Affairs, July 1998), http://www.imsersomigracion.upco.es/.
8   The Spanish Constitution of 1978 introduced a political structure of autonomous communities based on the recognition in Spain of a state composed of diverse nationalities and regions with their own specific characteristics, such as language, culture, and history. At the same time, each autonomous community is bound by a statute of an essentially political nature. The so-called historical communities are Catalonia, the Basque Country, and Galicia.
9   As members of the Forum for the Social Integration of Immigrants.
10 The Permanent Immigration Observatory was created by Royal Decree 345/2001 and attached to the Ministry of the Interior. The observatory has the following members: four representatives from departments of the Interministerial Commission for Alien Affairs; one representative of the National Statistics Institute; one representative from the Centre for Sociological Research; four representatives from the autonomous communities (including Catalonia and Madrid) and from the cities of Ceuta and Melilla designated by the High Council on Immigration Policy; two represen-

tatives of local entities; and two representatives from the university system who are experts in immigration. See http://www.dgei.mir.es/.

11 Catalonia elaborated the first immigration plan in Spain in 1993 before any state plan existed, a second plan in 1997, and the current plan in 2001. Catalonia also has its own secretary for immigration. Of the seventeen autonomous communities that make up the Spanish state, five others (Andalucía, Aragón, Baleares, Canarias, Murcia, and Navarra) have elaborated plans or regional programs, but no other autonomous communities have specific organs inside their governmental structures to deal with the issue of immigration.

12 The provincial level is an administrative territorial division based on a grouping of municipalities. Catalonia contains four provinces: Barcelona, Girona, Lleida, and Tarragona.

13 All publications are available at http://www.imsersomigracion.upco.es/ and also at http://www.mir.es/.

14 The Parliament consists of one chamber representing the people of Catalonia and is elected democratically. The Parliament forms part of the system of self-government of Catalonia together with the Generalitat, which is the primary institution through which self-government is organized.

15 In Catalan: Centre d'informació per a treballadors estrangers.

16 CITE assisted more than 20,000 persons during the year 2003.

17 The Platform for Citizenship and Coexistence maintains a database called SIGES, which is integrated into the general system of all the CITE offices throughout Spain. The operation of the system is the responsibility of the May First Foundation, which is part of the network of Spanish research organizations on immigration matters.

18 The equivalent to a ministry but with jurisdiction only in the autonomous community.

19 Interpretation is available in Chinese (Mandarin, Cantonese, and Taiwanese), Urdu (Pakistan), and Tagalog (Philippines). Three professional interpreters in each language are employed in agreement with the Association of Immigrants.

20 This material is produced in collaboration with different immigrant organizations and is designed to assist immigrant families and schools where immigrant children are confronting immersion into a new educational system. The material is often produced in seven different languages: Catalan, Spanish, English, Arabic, Urdu, Tagalog, Russian, Polish, Chinese, French, and Wolof. CITE also produces written material for immigrants on a range of other topics: workers' rights, women's rights, legal questions, etc.

21 Representing more than fourteen nationalities.

22 CITE runs the database SIGES. This database, in turn, provides data to the database of the Permanent Immigration Observatory in Madrid.

23 These social scientists include Bridget Anderson (anthropologist at Oxford University, United Kingdom; member of Servant Thematic Network, University of Liege); Kitty C. Calavita (professor and researcher in criminology, law, and society at the University of California at Irvine, United States); Mette Louise Berg Rundle (doctoral candidate at Oxford University's Institute of Social and Cultural Anthropology); and Luis Eduardo Guarnizo (researcher and associate professor of sociology at the University of California at Davis, United States).

SWEDEN

CECILIA ENGLUND

Sweden is a fairly new immigrant country. Since the 1950s, its population has undergone significant changes due to both major labor force immigration and refugee immigration. In 2002 Sweden had a population of 8,940,788, and more than 8% of the population (1,053,463 people in total) was born abroad.[1] However, a larger proportion of the population holds Swedish citizenship (8,466,689 people in total). In 2002 the five major immigrant groups in Sweden were from Finland, Yugoslavia, Iraq, Bosnia-Herzegovina, and Iran.

Sweden has, like many European countries, difficulty dealing with the new population changes. This expresses itself in inequalities in employment, education, housing, and other socioeconomic factors. In this respect, Sweden could be considered a segregated country. In recent years many activities have been initiated to deal with the inequities between the native and immigrant segments of the population.

The best practices discussed in this chapter provide examples of positive initiatives aimed at promoting integration as well as combating segregation. The first example, the Stockholmsprojektet, relates to the labor market and illuminates how highly educated immigrants can be integrated into Swedish working life. The second example concerns housing and shows how the housing company Gardstensbostäder is combating segregation by taking on greater social responsibility. These two examples have been chosen to illustrate how organizations operating at different levels in society can counteract inequalities between different population groups.

THE STOCKHOLMSPROJEKTET

According to many studies, people with foreign diplomas, in particular from countries outside the European Union, have great difficulty obtaining jobs suitable to their qualifications. One of these groups is doctors with foreign diplomas. Meanwhile, Sweden currently suffers from a shortage of medical professionals.

The major difficulty for doctors with foreign diplomas has been passing the different tests and procedures required by the National Board of Health and Welfare that would allow them to register for work in Sweden. This process is long and demanding. It has also been shown that it is difficult for doctors with foreign diplomas to find their way through the different procedures that are needed for registration in Sweden.

In 1999, in order to meet the increasing demands for qualified doctors in Swedish society and to make the procedures easier (mainly by shortening the procedures for registration), the Stockholmsprojektet (Stockholm Project) for foreign doctors was initiated.[2] Other aims of the project were to increase integration for immigrant doctors and to increase diversity at workplaces within the health-care sector in Stockholm. To achieve these goals the project has focused on helping foreign doctors to increase their knowledge of medicine, better understand the culture of the Swedish medical system, and learn Swedish pronunciation and other necessary vocabulary. In 1999 it was estimated that two hundred doctors with foreign diplomas were unemployed. The project's initial goal was to register at least one hundred of these doctors.

From the very beginning the project has been carried out in cooperation with the Stockholm County Council, the Stockholm County Labor Board, and the Stockholm Doctors' Association and is thus a cooperative effort between state and civil society partners. Other partners include other local authorities and an EU project called Swedish for Academics (Svenska för akademiker). The Stockholmsprojektet has also joined a network of other county councils currently participating in similar projects for foreign medical professionals. Until the end of 2003, it was run as an interim project. However, as of the beginning of 2004, the activities of the project have become permanent, regular activities of the Stockholm County Council.

During the four and a half years of its existence, the Stockholmsprojektet has

been financed by the Swedish government with 7 million kronor. The Stockholm County Council Board and the Stockholm County Labor Board have contributed 20 million and 27 million kronor, respectively, from the start. The project has been of major interest generally and as a model for similar activities aimed at better integrating other highly educated professional groups into the Swedish labor market.

The Stockholmsprojektet has several parts: advisory and consulting activities; introductory, preparatory courses; and vocational training. A project office with full-time staff administers the project and also works as an advisory body for the participating doctors. The only requirement for involvement in the project is that participants have Swedish language skills at the level of medical Swedish—although it has been possible to apply to participate in the project before passing the language course in medical Swedish.

Since the Stockholmsprojektet's initiation, 355 doctors with foreign diplomas have participated in the project, and 145 have passed the knowledge test in medicine. By the end of 2003, 115 had been registered as doctors, exceeding the original goal of 100. One hundred forty-five of the participants are working as assistant physicians before being registered. The participants come from all parts of the world. However, the majority of the participants have been from Eastern Europe, the Middle East, and Russia.

The project's organizers observed that participants had little experience with the Swedish medical system, the supervisory role of the National Board of Health and Welfare, the use of medicines, and the administration. In response to these observations, an introductory course on Swedish medical practices was initiated in 2002.

A positive result of the project has been the establishment of the association Internationella läkare i Sverige (IliS, International Doctors in Sweden), which serves as an interest organization representing the needs of this set of professionals.

In 2003 the Stockholmsprojektet was evaluated by the Swedish research institution TEMO. According to this evaluation, the project was deemed a success, particularly in achieving two crucial goals: First, 70% of project participants fulfilled the conditions for being registered after completing the medical test called TULE. This group was able to find work as assistant physicians, compared to 50% of the doctors outside the project. Second, the time required to pass the language test for registration was shorter for those participating in the project than for doctors not involved in the project.

The project also showed that the recruitment of immigrant doctors is cost-effective; that these doctors are a necessity in multicultural medical care; and that there may be many gains both for the individual doctor as well as for society as a whole through directed support activities. Attitudes towards immigrant doctors have changed in a positive way as a result of the project.

The Stockholmsprojektet for integration of immigrant doctors has been suc-

cessful and can serve as a model for other professionals.[3] In January 2004 the project was granted an integration prize by the Council for Integration in Working Life, a group consisting of civil society partners, such as Swedish Enterprise, the Swedish Trade Union Confederation (LO), the Confederation of Professional Employees (TCO), the Swedish Confederation of Professional Associations (Saco), and the Swedish Association of Local Authorities, to name just a few. The project was recognized for making it easier to register doctors with diplomas obtained outside the European Union, allowing them to work as doctors.

GARDSTENSBOLAGET

Housing is one of the most significant contributors to segregation. Evidence of segregation is particularly pronounced in three metropolitan areas in Sweden: Stockholm, Gothenburg, and Malmö. The problem is especially acute on the outskirts of these cities, in sections called "million program areas," which were part of the government's housing policy during the 1960s to build a million new apartments.

Several measures have been implemented regarding housing segregation, although very few of them have proven successful. In Gardsten and Hjällbo, suburban areas of Gothenburg, the housing companies have assumed greater social responsibility than in other segregated suburban areas in Sweden. The local housing companies in Stockholm have not pursued similar objectives. AB Framtiden, the local housing company in Gothenburg, has been given a central role in promoting integration and combating segregation and serves as a good example for other housing companies to follow.

In 1997 AB Framtiden decided to establish a new housing company: Gardstensbostäder.[4] The main purpose of Gardstensbostäder was to focus on the development of Gardsten. This suburban community, part of the million program area, was built during the 1960s and 1970s on the outskirts of Gothenburg. In 2002 Gardsten had approximately 6,700 residents, with approximately half of the population born abroad and approximately 80% of foreign background-that is, born abroad or having two parents born abroad.[5]

As many similar areas, Gardsten suffered in the 1990s from outward migration. The community also suffered from neglect for many years. One area of neglect was access to social services. For a short period of time, Gardsten did not have a food store, and there was a lack of other kinds of services, services normally found in richer areas. The houses and living conditions were also inferior.

Since its establishment, Gardstensbostäder has worked in various ways and at different levels to create better housing conditions for the residents. The housing company has sought to keep residents from moving out of the area, aiming to instill a sense of community pride among residents while also making the area more attractive to prospective residents.

One of the issues on which Gardstensbostäder has concentrated is the surrounding environment. Since

the company's inception, it has worked at refurbishing the houses and planting green areas. One overriding objective has been to develop sustainable housing solutions. This has been achieved in part by equipping some of the houses with solar energy conservation tools. Gardstensbostäder has built greenhouses and introduced an individual measurement of electricity. The housing company has also arranged social activities.

One major innovation was the establishment of a local employment agency, Gardstensbyran, which is independent from the state-run National Employment Agency. Between 1998 and 2002, 474 jobs were supplied to the residents. In addition, vocational training courses have been organized for the residents in such areas as cleaning, construction, parks management, and retail work. The agency also has supported the establishment of local small-scale businesses in Gardsten. Gardstensbyran assists in job search activities through cooperation with businesses, both large and small. Gardstensbyran's vocational courses have been very successful, with the majority of participants finding employment afterwards.

In addition, the housing company has promoted the expansion of social services. For example, public transportation between Gothenburg and Gardsten has been improved by establishing a direct transportation link. A cash dispenser has been placed in the area, which is an important social service function that many disadvantaged areas lack.

The issue of democracy has also been of great importance. Gardstensbostäder has worked to increase the residents' real influence and to create meeting places. A house manager has been appointed for each neighborhood. The house manager is partly responsible for building maintenance and for following up on residents' demands for improvements and other adjustments. The residents' opinions are of great importance in making decisions about possible solutions for problems facing the suburb, such as planting green areas.

Gardstensbostäder is a housing company that works towards combating segregation at the local level in one suburban area. The most interesting and probably rather remarkable contribution of this housing company is that they have chosen not to use the term "integration." Although the company does act to facilitate greater participation by the residents, of whom the majority are of foreign background—by working with residents on different aspects of living conditions, such as outdoor environment; by supplying residents with jobs and vocational training to make it easier for poorly educated residents to obtain jobs; and by offering a democratic alternative to residents-Gardstensbostäder is not focused on integration in a traditional sense. Neither is the company focused on immigrants. Instead, they focus on the residents themselves. Therefore, the company has not concentrated on ordinary integration activities, such as creating fora where people of different backgrounds can meet. Their focus is instead on breaking down segregation due to both ethnicity and class, since these factors are closely intertwined in most areas of society. In this way, Gardstensbostäder promotes integration. The work of Gardstensbostäder thus provides an interesting and rather new model for other local housing companies that wish to take on greater social responsibility.

ENDNOTES

1   Statistics Sweden, chap. 18 in *Befolkningsåret 2002* (The year of demography 2002) (Stockholm: Statistics Sweden, 2003).
2   Information and evaluation reports of the project were provided by the project leader, Ulrika Gellerstedt.
3   There is a comparable project in Sweden for nurses with foreign diplomas. The objectives are similar to the project for foreign doctors.

4   This section is based on interviews with Stina Fransson, MD for Gardstensbostäder, and Salma Nazzal, project leader at Gardstensbostäder, and also informational material provided by Gardstensbostäder: Gardstensbostäder, *Förvandlingen av Gardsten* (The changes in Gardsten) (Gothenburg: Gardstensbostäder, 2001).
5   Swedish Integration Board, *Utvecklingen i storstadssatsningens 24 bostadsomraden 1997-2000*, Integrationsverket rapportsserie 2001, no. 9 (Norrköping: Swedish Integration Board, 2001).

APPENDIX:

WHO IS WHO IN INTEGRATION IN EUROPE

WHO'S WHO IN INTEGRATION

THE 1990 TRUST Suite 12 Winchester House 9 Cranmer Road London SW9 6EJ United Kingdom Phone: 020 7582 1990 Fax: 020 7793 8269 E-mail: blink1990@blink.org.uk URL: http://www.blink.org.uk/	The 1990 Trust is the first national black organization set up to protect and pioneer the interest of Britain's black communities. Its mission is to establish and influence the practical implementation of the principle that racism is a violation of human rights; to establish an international reputation for excellence and innovation, as an exemplar organization demonstrating the benefits of African, Caribbean, and Asian communities working collectively in tackling racism; to develop self-organization and community leadership to empower black communities in tackling racism and in reaching their full potential.
ACADEMY FOR MIGRATION STUDIES IN DENMARK (AMID) Aalborg University Fibigerstraede 2 DK-9220 Aalborg East Denmark Phone: +45 96359133 Fax: +45 98151126 E-mail: amid@amid.dk URL: http://www.amid.dk/	The primary objectives of the Academy for Migration Studies in Denmark (AMID) are to promote research on migratory issues in order to better understand and cope with social, cultural, and political problems associated with integration, exclusion, and co-citizenship and to provide an informed knowledge base for political decisions, public debates, and popular perceptions on migrants and immigration. The consortium also aims to create high quality

research training in migration issues. Lastly, AMID seeks to build a center of international quality that will interact with other individuals and institutes in Denmark and with centers of excellence internationally.

THE ASSOCIATION OF EUROPEAN MIGRATION INSTITUTIONS (AEMI)

AEMI-Secretariat
Arkivstraede 1, Box 1731
DK-9100Aalborg
Denmark
Phone: +45 99314230
Fax: +45 98102248
E-mail: aemi@aemi.dk
URL: http://www.aemi.dk/

The Association of European Migration Institutions (AEMI) is composed of over thirty institutions and organizations in Europe whose fields of interest concern migration, research, and exhibitions portraying emigration and that seek to promote an understanding of common goals.

CENTER OF MIGRATION RESEARCH (CMR)

Institute for Social Studies
Warsaw University
Stawki 5/7
00-183 Warsaw
Poland
Phone: +48 22 831 51 53
+48 22 554 97 30
Fax: +48 22 831 49 33
E-mail: maciaga@mercury.ci.uw.edu.pl
ewa_kepinska@poczta.onet.pl
URL: http://www.iss.uw.edu.pl

The Center of Migration Research (CMR) is an interdisciplinary group of researchers representing various departments of Warsaw University, the Warsaw School of Economics, and the Institute of Political Studies (Polish Academy of Sciences) with a focus on international population movements, migrants' integration, ethnic relations, and migration policy. CMR's primary activities currently include extensive studies on the causes and consequences of migration from Poland and on perspectives of foreign integration in Poland. CMR serves as a consulting body to various government and nongovernmental agencies in Poland and abroad.

CENTRE FOR INFORMATION FOR
FOREIGN WORKERS (CITE)
Lope de Vega, 38-1ª planta
28014 Madrid
Spain
Phone: +91 536 53 20
Fax: +91 536 52 98
E-mail: cite.madrid@usmr.ccoo.es
URL: http://www.usmr.ccoo.es/Servicios/
Sindicales/Cite/inferior.htm

The Centre for Information for Foreign
Workers (CITE) specializes in providing
information and legal aid to foreign
workers who come to Spain. CITE
organizes socioeconomic integration
activities, Spanish culture and language
classes, intercultural events for migrants
and Spanish natives, and information
meetings for arriving and returning
migrants.

CENTRE FOR RESEARCH IN ETHNIC
RELATIONS (CRER)
University of Warwick
Coventry CV4 7AL
United Kingdom
Phone: +44 24 7652 4869
Fax: +44 24 7652 4324
E-mail: d.s.joly@warwick.ac.uk
URL: http://www.warwick.ac.uk./fac/soc/
CRER_RC/index.html

The Centre for Research in Ethnic
Relations (CRER) based at the
University of Warwick is the major academic body in the United Kingdom for
the research and teaching of aspects of
race, migration, and ethnic relations.
CRER's research agenda includes a
focus on the processes of racial discrimination, issues of citizenship, political
participation, cultural identity, refugees,
ethnic mobilization, and nationalism.
Considerable emphasis is placed on the
dissemination of research findings, both
to the academic community and the
wider world. Through its teaching,
training, conferences, seminars, workshops, and publications, CRER aims to
promote a better knowledge and understanding of the processes that impact
ethnic minorities.

CENTRE FOR RESEARCH IN
INTERNATIONAL MIGRATION AND
ETHNIC RELATIONS (CEIFO)
Stockholm University
SE-106 91 Stockholm
Sweden
Phone: +46 8 16 26 91
Fax: +46 8 15 67 20
E-mail: ceifo.editor@ceifo.su.se
charles.westin@ceifo.su.se
URL: http://www.ceifo.su.se/

The Centre for Research in
International Migration and Ethnic
Relations (CEIFO) at Stockholm
University was the first center of its
kind in the Nordic countries. CEIFO is
an interdisciplinary center. Its main
research concerns are focused on causes,
mechanisms, processes, and consequences of international migration (voluntary and forced) and on interethnic
relations that result from international
migration in terms of processes of
exclusion and inclusion. The research

priorities at CEIFO may be categorized as follows:

1. International migration: processes, interventions, and consequences
2. State, politics, and policies in relation to migration and ethnicity
3. Racism, discrimination, and belief systems
4. Multiculturalism and diversity management
5. Integration and incorporation into the welfare state

CENTRE FOR STUDIES ON ETHNICITY AND MIGRATION (CEDEM)
Université de Liège
Faculté de Droit
Science Politique
Bâtiment 31, Boîte 38
7, Boulevard du Rectorat
4000 Liège
Belgium
Phone: +32 43663040
Fax: +32 43664557
E-mail: M.Martiniello@ulg.ac.be
URL: http://www.ulg.ac.be/cedem/

The Centre for Studies on Ethnicity and Migration (CEDEM) is an academic research center at the Université de Liège whose overall aim is to conduct theoretical and empirical research in the fields of migration, ethnic relations, and racism, with a special focus on the link between migration processes and unequal development. The center conducts its research in an interdisciplinary manner, combining political science, sociology, anthropology, international relations, and law.

CENTRE ON MIGRATION, POLICY AND SOCIETY (COMPAS)
58 Banbury Road
Oxford OX2 6QS
United Kingdom
Phone: +44 (0)1865 274711
Fax: +44 (0)1865 274718
E-mail:
emma.newcombe@anthro.ox.ac.uk
URL: http://www.compas.ox.ac.uk/

The mission of the Centre on Migration, Policy and Society (COMPAS) at the University of Oxford is to provide a strategic, integrated approach to understanding contemporary and future migration dynamics across sending areas and receiving contexts in the United Kingdom and the European Union.

EUROPEAN COORDINATION FOR
FOREIGNERS' RIGHT TO FAMILY LIFE
Brussels Office
avenue du parc 89
1060 Brussels
Belgium
E-mail: coordeurop@coordeurop.org
URL: http://www.coordeurop.org/

Genoa Office
Piazza De Marini 1/24A
16123 Genoa
Italy
Phone: +39 010 2530050
Fax: +39 010 2530050
E-mail Presidency:
coordeurop.presid@coordeurop.org
E-mail Secretariat: coordeurop.secretariat@coordeurop.org

The European Coordination was formed in 1994 on the initiative of several French associations. The mission of this nonprofit association is to set up information campaigns, to undertake initiatives to support the right to family life for third country nationals residing within the European Union, and to take part in constructing a democratic Europe in which members of immigrant families find their place as citizens, without discrimination. The European Coordination acts through its member associations and through national coordinators, where they exist.

THE EUROPEAN COUNCIL ON
REFUGEES AND EXILES (ECRE)
ECRE Secretariat
103 Worship Street
London EC2A 2DF
United Kingdom
Phone: +44 20 7377 7556
Fax: +44 20 7377 7586
E-mail: ecre@ecre.org
URL: http://www.ecre.org/about/secretariat.shtml

ECRE Brussels Office
205 rue Belliard
Box 14
1040 Brussels
Belgium
Phone: +32 2 514 5939
Fax: +32 2 514 5922
E-mail: euecre@ecre.be

The European Council on Refugees and Exiles (ECRE) is the umbrella organization for cooperation among European nongovernmental organizations concerned with refugees. Currently ECRE has seventy-four member agencies in twenty-nine countries. Principal activities include policy development and research, advocacy, legal analysis, information services to members, networking, and capacity building in southeastern, central, and eastern Europe. ECRE's work is coordinated by the secretariat in London and an office in Brussels. Much of ECRE's legal work is carried out through the European Legal Network on Asylum (ELENA), a network of lawyers who promote the highest human rights standards in the treatment of refugees and asylum seekers. ECRE's advocacy work is carried out through member agencies, through the secretariat's London office, and through its office in Brussels, which undertakes advocacy initiatives aimed at influencing the positive development of existing policy and the future EU agenda.

EUROPEAN FORUM FOR MIGRATION STUDIES (EFMS) Katharinenstr. 1 D-96052 Bamberg Germany Phone: +49 951 932020 - 0 Fax: +49 951 932020 - 20 E-mail: efms@sowi.uni-bamberg.de URL: http://www.uni-bamberg.de/~ba6ef3/main_e.htm	The European Forum for Migration Studies (efms) is an academic research center at the University of Bamberg in Germany. Its work in the areas of migration, integration, and migration policies encompasses research, documentation, consultative services, training, and providing information to the public. Since 1994, the efms Migration Report has been published quarterly in a German and an English version, as well as online on the center's home page. The efms Migration Report provides executive abstracts on reports from more than twenty newspapers and journals from Germany and the international sphere on current issues of migration, migration policies, and integration of migrants in Germany. These abstracts are listed chronologically and include source references.
THE EUROPEAN MIGRATION CENTRE (EMZ) Schliemannstr. 23 10437 Berlin Germany Phone: +49 30 4465 1065 Fax: +49 30 444 1085 E-mail: info@emz-berlin.de URL: http://www.emz-berlin.de/start/noAnimation.htm	The European Migration Centre's (EMZ) overall aim is to intensify networking between European institutions working in the wide field of migration and ethnicity. The activities of the EMZ include international research as well as practical guidance for immigrant entrepreneurs in Berlin. With regard to documentation, the EMZ runs an extensive library and provides modern online data banks with statistics and literature on migration topics. The EMZ has always strived to link research, practice, and politics in order to contribute to the implementation of a sustainable European migration policy. By publishing research results and by organizing public discussions on current migration topics, the EMZ is able to

keep in touch with processes in society and in the political realm and present a scientific basis for reasonable integration and immigration policies. In response to the growing political and economic cooperation on the European level, the EMZ tries to intensify networking among European research institutions. Their addresses are published online in the EuroFor handbook.

EUROPEAN MONITORING CENTRE ON RACISM AND XENOPHOBIA (EUMC)
Rahlgasse 3
1060 Vienna
Austria
Phone: +43 1 580 30 - 0
Fax: +43 1 580 30 - 99
E-mail: information@eumc.eu.int
URL: http://eumc.eu.int/

The primary task of the European Monitoring Centre on Racism and Xenophobia (EUMC) is to provide the European Community and its Member States with objective, reliable, and comparable information on racism, xenophobia, islamophobia, and anti-Semitism at the European level in order to help them to establish measures or formulate courses of action against racism and xenophobia. The very core of the EUMC's activities is the European Information Network on Racism and Xenophobia (RAXEN). It is designed to collect data and information at the national as well as at the European level. On the basis of the data collected, the EUMC studies the extent and development of the phenomena and manifestations of racism and xenophobia and analyzes their causes, consequences, and effects. It is also the task of the EUMC to work out strategies to combat racism and xenophobia and to highlight and disseminate examples of good practice regarding the integration of migrants and ethnic and religious minority groups in the EU Member States.

EUROPEAN RESEARCH CENTRE ON MIGRATION AND ETHNIC RELATIONS (ERCOMER)
Faculty of Social Sciences
Utrecht University
Heidelberglaan 2
3584 CS Utrecht
The Netherlands
Phone: + 31 30 253 4166
Fax: + 31 30 253 4733
E-mail: ERCOMERsecr@fss.uu.nl
URL:
http://www.uu.nl/uupublish/onderzoek/o
nderzoekcentra/ercomer/24638main.html

The purpose of the European Research Centre on Migration and Ethnic Relations (ERCOMER) is to actively encourage, support, and promote comparative research in the fields of international migration and ethnic relations within the European context.
The research program includes three themes: migration, immigrants in host societies, and host societies' responses to immigrants, ethnic minorities, and foreign countries and peoples. Research topics include multiculturalism, ethnic exclusionism, ethnic conflict, racism, and nationalism.

EXPO FOUNDATION
Mailbox 349
111 73 Stockholm
Sweden
Phone: + 46 8 652 62 04
Fax: + 46 8 652 60 04
E-mail: info@expo.se
URL: http://www.expo.se/

The Expo Foundation is a nonprofit organization that was established in 1995. The aim of the foundation is to study and map out antidemocratic, extreme-right, and racist tendencies in society. The Expo Foundation's platform is to protect democracy and free speech against racist, extreme-right, anti-Semitic, and totalitarian tendencies in society. The foundation is not aligned with any specific political party or group, but gladly cooperates with any party that supports the platform. The Expo Foundation is an opinion research organization. Since 2001 the Expo Foundation has been the Swedish National Focal Point in the European Monitoring Centre on Racism and Xenophobia's information network RAXEN.

FORUM INSTITUTE OF
MULTICULTURAL DEVELOPMENT
Postbus 201
3500 AE Utrecht
The Netherlands
Phone: +31 30 297 43 21
Fax: +31 30 296 00 50
E-mail: informatie@forum.nl
URL:
http://www.forum.nl/engels/index.html

FORUM Institute of Multicultural Development is a national center of expertise in the field of multicultural development. FORUM stands for a society in which people from various communities live together as fully recognized citizens. To help realize this objective, FORUM receives subsidies from the Ministry of Health, Welfare and Sport. FORUM is active in diverse fields, including upbringing, communication, legislation, housing, employment, education, health care, leisure time, sport, political participation, art, and culture.

GLOBAL COMMISSION ON
INTERNATIONAL MIGRATION (GCIM)
1, Rue Richard Wagner
1202 Geneva
Switzerland
Phone: +41 227484850
Fax: +41 227484851
E-mail: info@gcim.org
URL: http://www.gcim.org/

The Global Commission on International Migration (GCIM) began its activities on 1 January 2004. The mandate of the commission is threefold: placing international migration on the global agenda; analyzing gaps in current approaches to migration and examining interlinkages with other issue areas; and presenting recommendations to the United Nations secretary-general and other stakeholders.

INSTITUTE FOR MIGRATION AND
ETHNIC STUDIES (IMES)
O.Z. Achterburgwal 237
1012 DL Amsterdam
The Netherlands
Phone: +31 20 525 3627
Fax: +31 20 525 3628
E-mail: imes@fmg.uva.nl
URL: http://www2.fmg.uva.nl/imes/

The Institute for Migration and Ethnic Studies (IMES) is an interdisciplinary research institute of the University of Amsterdam established in 1994. The research program promotes the aggregation and, where possible, the integration of different perspectives. The research program of IMES focuses on the Dutch case with specific attention given to the city of Amsterdam, but from an international and comparative perspective. A United Nations Educational, Scientific and Cultural Organization (UNESCO) program of comparison of European cities and a cooperative effort undertaken with Metropolis International are examples of this.

INSTITUTE FOR MIGRATION RESEARCH AND INTERCULTURAL STUDIES (IMIS)
Universität Osnabrück
IMIS / Fachbereich 2
Neuer Graben 19/21
49069 Osnabrück
Germany
Phone: +49 541 969 4384
Fax: +49 541 969 4380
E-mail: imis@uni-osnabrueck.de
URL: http://www.imis.uni-osnabrueck.de/

The Institute for Migration Research and Intercultural Studies (IMIS) examines historical and contemporary demographic, geographic, social, economic, political and legislative, women's and gender, psychological, educational, and language and linguistic issues of migration and integration from an interdisciplinary perspective. The goals of IMIS include developing interdisciplinary migration research and cross-cultural studies, coordinating research projects, cooperating with other national and international research institutes, offering consultations, and organizing lectures, conferences, and publications.

INTERNATIONAL AND EUROPEAN FORUM OF MIGRATION RESEARCH (FIERI)
Via Ponza 4/E
10121 Torino
Italy
Phone: +39 011 5160044
Fax: +39 011 6702612
E-mail: fieri@fieri.it
URL: http://www.fieri.it/

The International and European Forum of Migration Research (FIERI) is an Italian and international interdisciplinary research network, developed in Europe and a member of the International Migration, Integration and Social Cohesion Network of Excellence. FIERI focuses its research on migratory phenomena and the absorption of foreign minorities. The network is made up almost exclusively of university staff, but is open to nonuniversity researchers with proven credentials. FIERI intends to foster the creation of research groups on migratory phenomena and to build a bridge between academic work, public decision making, and public opinion. This bridge is built through both Italian and comparative research aimed at providing support for public decisions. FIERI also works to provide easily accessible information, such as a data bank, a chronology, a forum on the most controversial questions concerning migration, and a listing of the main publications on the issue. Most of the information and documentation is produced initially by the Italian team and aims to inform public decision makers about what is happening abroad and give foreign specialists information on key Italian events and studies.

INTERNATIONAL CENTRE FOR
MIGRATION POLICY DEVELOPMENT
(ICMPD)
Möllwaldplatz 4
A-1040 Vienna
Austria
Phone: +43 1 504 46 77
Fax: +43 1 504 46 77 75
E-mail: icmpd@icmpd.org
URL: http://www.icmpd.org/

The International Centre for Migration Policy Development (ICMPD) is an intergovernmental organization based in Vienna. ICMPD was created in 1993 at the initiative of Switzerland and Austria. A total of twenty-five governments now support the center. It was granted partial diplomatic status in 1997 and full status in 2000. The purpose of the center is to promote comprehensive and sustainable migration policies and to function as a service exchange mechanism for governments and organizations, primarily on European migration issues. ICMPD cooperates closely with the Office of the United Nations High Commissioner for Refugees and the Council of Europe. The European Commission is a major partner and donor. ICMPD acts as secretariat for the Budapest Process, which deals with harmonizing entry control and involves more than forty states and ten international organizations.

INTERNATIONAL ORGANIZATION FOR
MIGRATION (IOM)
17, Route des Morillons
1211 Geneva 19
Switzerland
Phone: +41 22 717 9111
Fax: +41 22 798 6150
E-mail: info@iom.int
URL: http://www.iom.int/

The International Organization for Migration (IOM) was established in 1951 as an intergovernmental organization to resettle European displaced persons, refugees, and migrants. IOM has now grown to encompass a variety of migration management activities throughout the world. While not part of the United Nations system, IOM maintains close working relations with United Nations bodies and operational agencies. IOM has as partners a wide range of international and nongovernmental organizations. With offices and operations on every continent, IOM acts with its partners in the international community to assist in meeting the growing operational challenges of migration management; advance understanding of migration issues; encourage social and economic development through migration; and uphold the human dignity and well-being of migrants.

KING BAUDOUIN FOUNDATION
Rue Brederodestraat 21
1000 Brussels
Belgium
Phone: +32 2 511 18 40
Fax: +32 2 511 52 21
E-mail: info@kbs-frb.be
URL: http://www.kbs-frb.be/

The King Baudouin Foundation came into being in 1976 on the occasion of the twenty-fifth anniversary of the coronation of King Baudouin. In its deed of formation, the foundation was described as an independent structure to encourage original ideas and set up new projects. The mission of the King Baudouin Foundation is to help to improve people's living conditions. With its Social Justice Programme, the King Baudouin Foundation seeks to help improve the condition of vulnerable persons and victims of discrimination so that they can take control of their own destiny. The King Baudouin Foundation's migration projects are aimed at contributing to the debate on migration policy; supporting initiatives that benefit new immigrants; and supporting the victims of human trafficking.

MIGRATION POLICY GROUP (MPG)
205 Rue Belliard, Box 1
1040 Brussels
Belgium
Phone: + 32 2 230 59 30
Fax: + 32 2 280 09 25
E-mail: info@migpolgroup.com
URL: http://www.migpolgroup.com/

The Migration Policy Group (MPG) is an independent organization committed to policy development on migration and mobility, diversity, and antidiscrimination by facilitating exchange between stakeholders from all sectors of society, with the aim of contributing to innovative and effective responses to the challenges posed by migration and diversity.

MIGRATION RESEARCH UNIT (MRU)
Department of Geography
University College London
26 Bedford Way
London WC1H 0AP
United Kingdom
Phone: +44 20 7679 7569
Fax: +44 20 7679 7565
E-mail: mru@geog.ucl.ac.uk
URL: http://www.geog.ucl.ac.uk/mru/

The Migration Research Unit (MRU) is based in the Department of Geography at University College London. Its purpose is to carry out high quality research, independently or in collaboration with others, designed to increase knowledge and understanding of international population migration issues. The following are the MRU's overarching research aims: to contribute to knowledge on patterns and trends in migration at the national, European, and global levels; to increase understanding of the interrelationships between public policy and patterns of migration at each level; and to develop new conceptual approaches to the study of migration. In fulfilling these aims, the MRU seeks to consolidate a national and international reputation for research excellence and to disseminate research findings in a way that ensures maximum benefit. The MRU was established in 1988. Extensive links have been developed with governmental organizations, academic institutions, and other agencies both in the United Kingdom and overseas. Those commissioning research from the MRU have included the European Commission, the Organisation for Economic Co-operation and Development, the Council of Europe, the UK Department for Education and Employment, and the Home Office. In recent years research has focused particularly on European migration.

MIGRINTER, INTERNATIONAL
MIGRATIONS, SPACES AND SOCIETIES
MSHS—99 avenue du Recteur-Pineau
86000 Poitiers
France
Phone: +33 (0) 5 49454640
Fax: +33 (0) 5 49454645
E-mail: migrinter@mshs.univ-poitiers.fr
URL: http://www.mshs.univ-poitiers.fr/migrinter/

MIGRINTER, International Migrations, Spaces and Societies, is a research team specializing in the study of international migration and interethnic relations. It is part of a research laboratory (UMR 6588 MIGRINTER-TIDE) that links the Centre national de la recherche scientifique to the universities of Poitiers and Bordeaux 3. MIGRINTER is situated in the Faculty of Social Sciences of the University of Poitiers. Although research may be considered the main activity, teaching, publishing, and facilitating access to information are also very important for MIGRINTER.

NETWORK MIGRATION IN EUROPE
Limonenstr. 24
12203 Berlin
Germany
Phone: +49 30 84109266
Fax: +49 30 8324947
E-mail: info@network-migration.org
URL: http://www.network-migration.org/

The Network Migration in Europe is a cooperative effort between people and institutions aimed at promoting knowledge and understanding of migration in Europe and intensifying the exchange between research and practice. The organization seeks to serve as a forum for questions on migration and to establish and expand an international, mostly European, network in this area of study. The network is engaged in promoting a stronger representation of migration in society, the public arena, and culture, particularly through network building within existing organizations; research in the area of migration and migration history; conferences and seminars on the subject of migration in Europe; publications in related academic circles and in the media; exhibitions on the subject of immigration and immigrants in Europe; documentation and presentation of historical and social-scientific knowledge for multipliers (schools, nonschool educational institutions, authorities, media); and political education.

SUSSEX CENTRE FOR MIGRATION
RESEARCH
School of Social Sciences and Cultural
Studies
University of Sussex
Falmer, Brighton BN1 9SJ
United Kingdom
Phone: +44 1273 678722
Fax: +44 1273 620662
E-mail: R.Black@sussex.ac.uk
URL: http://www.sussex.ac.uk/migration/

Through its Development Research
Centre on Migration, Globalisation and
Poverty, funded by the Department for
International Development, and other
externally funded research projects, the
Sussex Centre for Migration Research
seeks to influence both understanding
of migration and the policies that affect
migrants. It provides doctoral and mas-
ter's-level training in migration studies
and also publishes the internationally
recognized *Journal of Ethnic and
Migration Studies*.

SWISS FORUM FOR MIGRATION
STUDIES (SFM)
Rue St-Honoré 2
2000 Neuchâtel
Switzerland
Phone: +41 32 718 39 20
Fax: +41 32 718 39 21
E-mail: secretariat.fsm@unine.ch
URL: http://www.migration-
population.ch/

The Swiss Forum for Migration Studies
(SFM) is an independent research institute affiliated with the University of
Neuchâtel. It conducts scientific
research in the fields of migration and
demographic issues with the aim of contributing towards a pragmatic discussion
on topics associated with migration.
Since it is positioned at the national
level, the SFM plays a key role in the
coordination and networking of
research in Switzerland. This also makes
it a preferred partner for numerous foreign
bodies. The SFM comprises a multilingual and interdisciplinary team.

LINKS TO RELEVANT EUROPEAN UNION DOCUMENTS

Presidency Conclusions, European Council, (Tampere), October 1999
http://europa.eu.int/council/off/conclu/oct99/oct99_en.htm

Communication on a Community Immigration Policy, November 2000
COM(2000) 757 final
http://europa.eu.int/eur-lex/en/com/cnc/2000/com2000_0757en01.pdf

Communication on Immigration, Integration and Employment, June 2003
COM(2003) 336 final
http://europa.eu.int/eur-lex/en/com/cnc/2003/com2003_0336en01.pdf

Presidency Conclusions, European Council, (Thessaloniki), June 2003
http://ue.eu.int/ueDocs/cms_Data/docs/pressData/en/ec/76279.pdf

CONTRIBUTORS

AUTHORS' AFFILIATIONS TO THE ORGANIZATIONS LISTED REFLECT THOSE AT THE TIME OF WRITING.

AUDREY ADAMS, The 1990 Trust, London.

RAINER BAUBÖCK, Austrian Academy of Sciences, Research Unit for Institutional Change and European Integration, Vienna.

MARIA HELENA BEDOYA, Centro de Información para Trabajadores Migrantes (CITE), Barcelona.

RENSKE BIEZEVELD, European Research Centre on Migration and Ethnic Relations (ERCOMER), Rotterdam University, Rotterdam.

MICHAEL BOMMES, Sociology and Methodology of Interdisciplinary and Intercultural Migration Research, Institute for Migration Research and Intercultural Studies, University of Osnabrück, Osnabrück.

SALLY DAGHLIAN, Scottish Refugee Council, Glasgow.

CATHERINE DE WENDEN, Centre national de la recherche scientifique (CNRS), Paris; Institut d'Etudes Politiques de Paris, Paris.

CECILIA ENGLUND, Expo Foundation, Stockholm.

HAN ENTZINGER, European Research Centre on Migration and Ethnic Relations (ERCOMER), Rotterdam University, Rotterdam.

BIMAL GHOSH, New International Regime for Orderly Movements of People (NIROMP), Geneva.

ULF HEDETOFT, Department of History, International and Social Studies, Aalborg University, Aalborg; Academy of Migration Studies in Denmark (AMID), Aalborg.

GIULIA HENRY, Ministry of Welfare, Rome.

KRYSTYNA IGLICKA, Centre of International Relations, Warsaw.

HOLGER KOLB, Sociology and Methodology of Interdisciplinary and Intercultural Migration Research, Institute for Migration Research and Intercultural Studies, University of Osnabrück, Osnabrück.

HAVEN LUTAAYA, The 1990 Trust, London.

DIETER OBERNDÖRFER, German Council of Migration; Arnold-Bergstraesser-Institute, University of Freiburg, Freiburg.

MAREK OKÓLSKI, Centre of Migration Research and Department of Demography, Warsaw University, Warsaw.

RINUS PENNINX, Department of Sociology and Anthropology and Institute for Migration and Ethnic Studies (IMES), Amsterdam University, Amsterdam.

ANJA RUDIGER, UK Secretariat, European Monitoring Centre on Racism and Xenophobia, London.

BERND SCHULTE, Max-Planck-Institut für ausländisches öffentliches Recht und Völkerrecht, Munich.

INGRID SIJLBING, Kenniscentrum Grote Steden (Dutch Urban Expert Centre), Den Haag.

RITA SÜSSMUTH, Independent German Council of Experts on Immigration and Integration; Bertelsmann Foundation, Berlin.

ANNA TERRÓN I CUSI, General Secretary of Patronat Català, Barcelona.

DIETRICH THRÄNHARDT, Department of Political Sciences, University of Münster, Münster; Netherlands Institute of Advanced Study (NIAS), Wassenaar.

THIERRY TIMMERMANS, King Baudouin Foundation, Brussels.

KATRIN UHL, Federal Office for the Recognition of Foreign Refugees, Nuernberg.

HELENE URTH, Directorate-General for Justice and Home Affairs, European Commission, Brussels.

ANTÓNIO VITORINO, Commissioner for Justice and Home Affairs, European Commission, Brussels.

WERNER WEIDENFELD, Bertelsmann Foundation, Guetersloh; Center for Applied Policy Research, Ludwig-Maximilians-University, Munich.